WHAT THE BIBLE REALLY SAYS

WHAT THE BIBLE REALLY SAYS

Edited by

Morton Smith
and R. Joseph Hoffmann

HarperSanFrancisco
A Division of HarperCollins*Publishers*

FIRST HARPERCOLLINS PAPERBACK EDITION PUBLISHED IN 1993

Library of Congress Cataloging-in-Publication Data

What the Bible really says / edited by Morton Smith and R. Joseph Hoffmann. — 1st HarperCollins pbk. ed.
    p. cm.
Originally published: Buffalo : Prometheus Books, © 1989.
Includes bibliographical references.
ISBN 0–06–067443–1 (alk. paper)
    1. Bible—Criticism, interpretation, etc. 2. Ethics in the Bible. I. Smith, Morton, 1915– . II. Hoffmann, R. Joseph.
[BS540.W535   1993]
220.3—dc20   92–56742

93   94   95   96   97   RRD(H)   10   9   8   7   6   5   4   3   2

This edition is printed on acid-free paper that meets the American National Standards Institute Z39.48 Standard.

TABLE OF CONTENTS

PREFACE

So much has been made of the Bible recently that it seems worthwhile to call attention to what the Bible *really* says about a number of topics now often discussed.

This attention is all the more needed because professional discussion of the Bible has become more and more concerned with other subjects. The "exegetic" schools of this century—liberal, eschatological, neo-ortho-dox, existentialist, liberationist, feminist (to name only the better publi-cized)—have gone by like a procession of bandwagons. Each has attracted a crowd of hangers-on, who cheer for it and themselves and chant the proof texts of their own party. At the same time they have tried to obscure or explain away whatever evidence has contradicted them. Mean-while, the professional study of the Bible has been more and more dis-placed by related disciplines (archaeology, ancient Near Eastern studies, comparative religion, etc.), all valuable in themselves, but from the view-point of *biblical* study, mainly distractions. Between interested propa-ganda and disinterested scholarship, the study of what the Bible itself really says has been too much neglected.

Yet what the Bible says is far more important than what its interpreters say. Most interpretations are soon forgotten, and even in Judaism, where some interpretations have become classics, they are not nearly so well known or so widely influential as the biblical text.

Every culture is constituted by the sets of forms it has either developed or appropriated and regularly uses for its needs. These range from forms of utensils and building to styles of painting and sculpture (whence the models of men and gods), forms of private and social behavior, and forms of speech—especially languages, literary forms, and forms of thought. The Bible is one of the most important sets of literary forms in Western civilization. It goes on, relatively unchanged, from generation to generation, saying what it obviously says. It is taught daily to millions of children, who understand its plain statements, learn its stories, and cast themselves (more or less) in one or more of the forms it provides. In times of stress Western culture is apt to revert to the Bible for further guidance—hence the present rise of fundamentalism in Christianity and Judaism. (There is also much biblical material in the Koran.) The first purpose of biblical study, therefore, should be to look carefully at the Bible and see just what it really says. This book tries to do just that for a group of topics that have especially great importance today.

Question: Which Bible? There are a dozen different models on the market: Jewish, Orthodox Christian, Roman Catholic, Protestant, and so forth.

Fortunately, the books collected in the Jewish Bible are the core of almost all the others and are constantly echoed (though sometimes with radical variations) in the books the others add. "The Bible" can therefore be used as a short term for "the biblical tradition." As a representative of that tradition this book will use the Orthodox Christian Bible, the largest of the collections used by major religious bodies. For the books that this particular version of the Bible contains, see our *List of Abbreviations* on p. 245.

The attempt here is to present "what the Bible really says." But does this not suggest that the Bible is a single book, bearing one teaching? On the contrary, no matter what version you choose, the Bible is a collection of books. These books took their present shape at different times over the course of a thousand years. Sometimes their teachings contradict each other. So the misleading suggestion of the title cannot be denied, but will be corrected by the book's content. Any reader will find that "what the Bible really says" is taken quite literally: The concern is for what it says, not what it "means." What it "means" is usually a matter of *interpretation* (the pretentious word for "guess work"), but what it *says* is a matter of observable facts. In telling what the Bible says, contradictions among and within its books must be accurately described.

"But you cannot just begin with the text!" I hear some say. "To understand a text you must first understand its background."

This is not true. We often understand texts without knowing their backgrounds. In fact, texts of which we know the backgrounds are exceptions. How many readers of our newspapers and journals know the backgrounds of the articles?

"But knowledge of the background is necessary for precise understanding."

Precise understanding, however, is impossible. We can never fully and accurately know the mind of any writer, ancient or modern. Moreover, we necessarily misunderstand everything we read by relating it to our own experiences and ideas, not to the writer's. The consequent misunderstanding we normally and sensibly overlook, except when it causes trouble. When it does not, we often describe statements or documents as "clear" and "readily understandable." Such are our everyday standards.

By these standards the bulk of the Bible is clear and readily understandable. The geographic and historical references need explanation, but we can usually get on without it. Was the story of Abraham substantially changed by the discovery of the location of Ur? I don't think so. Admittedly, one can pick out exceptional sections that are self-contradictory, linguistically uncertain, muddled, incoherent, or allegorical—the prophets, Job, Daniel, part of the Epistles, and Revelation all provide examples. But even in these sections, the plain sense of the sentences is often apparent. The difficulties arise when one goes on to "interpretation," and this book will not.

The contributors have been asked to treat topics briefly, clearly, and for readers of high-school education or better. What was requested were "bare statements of the bare facts, presented so far as possible by quotations of the essential texts, with . . . neither exegesis nor moral judgments. The texts should speak for themselves." It was also specified that footnotes and bibliographies should be minimal: A parade of scholarship distracts from the quiet march of the evidence. For translations, the contributors were left free to use standard versions or make their own. Many have done both.

Few found these requests easy to comply with. Scholarly training produces neurotic compulsions to annotate the obvious and to explain what one does not understand—probably lingering symptoms of adolescent anxiety. Hence came wastebaskets full of notes and bibliographies that would have doubled the size, trebled the price, and obscured the point of this book. As might be expected, the drive to interpret was strongest when the biblical statements were least palatable. A prime example were the God-given commands to exterminate all the people of Palestine (Deut. 7:1-5; 20:10-18; cf. Josh. 6-11; and, for evidence of disobedience and divine anger, Judg. 1-2). But even matters less serious than God's call to genocide elicited elaborate explanations. Whenever

God fell foul of someone's favorite convictions the result was apt to be, if not blatant "interpretation," at least a string of references to cover the improprieties of divine revelation with a wreath of learned fig leaves. Some of these decorations remain in the present text; it is hoped that they will inform some readers and amuse others.

It is hoped, too, that the whole book will do the same. I conclude it with this expression of sincere gratitude to all contributors for their fine work, and to the publishers and staffs at Prometheus Books and Harper and Row for their interest, assistance, and willingness to gamble, which have enabled this project to be carried through.

Morton Smith

CAPITAL PUNISHMENT
Baruch A. Levine

Normally defined, capital punishment is the imposition of a penalty of death on one convicted of a crime deemed sufficiently grave to warrant depriving the criminal of life. As a legal act, capital punishment is pursuant to a sentence of a court, though in some societies it may be imposed by executive decree.

In biblical terminology, the concept of capital punishment is conveyed by a Hebrew term meaning "a sentence of death" (Deut. 19:6, 21:22; Jer. 25:11, 16). We also find reference to "a capital offense" in Deuteronomy 22:26. Interestingly, the Hebrew word for "blood" connotes both the crime itself—the shedding of human blood—and the guilt and punishment incurred by that act. One finds such usage in Leviticus 17:4, Numbers 35:27, and Deuteronomy 17:8. Since the plural form of words can have an abstract connotation in biblical Hebrew, we also find plural forms of the word for "blood" referring to capital crimes in Exodus 22:1-2 and Deuteronomy 19:10, 22:8, and 2 Samuel 16:8.

We would not regularly include in the category of capital punishment legitimate retaliation against the perpetrator of a homicide. In the biblical system, however, avenging the blood of a murdered clan relative figures prominently in legislation governing the death penalty, and we will discuss it on that basis.

The purpose of this study is to describe the way the Bible views capital punishment. Primarily this consists of legal provisions, but we also encounter normative statements referring to crimes that *should* be punished by death. Certain persons, so we read, deserve to die for their crimes. Such references, often couched in narrative, prophecy, and wisdom, reveal the postulates of biblical criminal law and do a lot to characterize the ethos of biblical society.

I.

Given the nature of the biblical evidence, it is easiest to begin with its legal sources and then continue our discussion with nonlegal materials in an effort to understand what underlies the provisions of biblical law. The Torah preserves several collections of laws, *all* of which demonstrate that capital punishment was integral to biblical justice. The first of these collections to be encountered by the reader, and the earliest historically, is the Book of the Covenant (Exodus, chapters 21–23). It is true that the Decalogue of Exodus, chapter 20, actually precedes the Book of the Covenant; though its categorical pronouncements clearly bear on the subject of capital punishment, they refrain from stipulating specific penalties, which is characteristic of commandments, as distinct from laws. The provisions of the Decalogue will be discussed in due course.

Exodus 21:12–14 mandates the death penalty for one who premeditatively deals a death blow to another. If the homicide was *not* premeditated—that is, if the killer did not "stalk" his victim, or was not intent on doing him evil—that killer was allowed to seek refuge at a designated place of asylum. We read further that the deliberate murderer was emphatically denied asylum, and he would be seized even from the altar of a sanctuary and sentenced to death. The Hebrew Bible actually records two instances of persons who feared retaliation and clung to the horns of the altar in the sanctuary of Jerusalem, seeking asylum. Both incidents relate to the Davidic succession. In the former, Adonijah, David's own son, clung to the altar after rebelling against his brother, the king. Solomon had him forcibly removed from the sanctuary, but spared his life after the renegade swore fealty to his king (1 Kings 1:50–53). In the second instance, Joab, David's longtime general, clung to the same altar after having supported Adonijah in his sedition. When Joab refused to withdraw, Solomon ordered him slain on the spot. We note, however, that in the ensuing verses the biblical writer justifies denying Joab asylum. He had often committed murder and actually deserved to die for shedding innocent blood (as recounted in 1 Kings 2:28–34).

In fact, the right of asylum presupposes the right of retaliation. One who has killed another should fear retaliation, which was customary, and seek asylum, at least until he could establish that his killing was either unintentional or justified.

The precise formulation of the opening statement of law on the subject of murder is significant. The Canaanite petty king Abimelekh tells his people, "Anyone who harms this man [Isaac] or his wife [Rebecca] shall be put to death" (Gen. 26:11). The conjugated form of the Hebrew verb "to die" used here consistently connotes execution by human agency, never simply that someone deserves to die. Nor does it merely predict someone's death, as do other forms of the same verb. There is no question that Abimelekh would have had any such person executed. Similarly, in Exodus 19:12–13 we read the admonition delivered to the Israelite people just prior to the theophany at Mount Sinai: "Anyone who has contact with the mountain shall be put to death. . . . For such a one will be stoned or shot (with an arrow)," etc. So much for legal formulation.

Chapter 21 of Exodus describes additional circumstances in which capital punishment is demanded. In most cases, when the death penalty is prescribed it is mandatory, not optional. Only rarely do we find allowance for discretionary sentencing. Let us review the specific contents of this chapter.

One who "strikes" either of his parents will be put to death. Although the Hebrew verb employed here is ambiguous, we can assume that the present law does *not* refer to one who kills a parent, only to one who intentionally injures a parent. The death penalty is mandated because of the special relationship between the perpetrator and the victim. (This is one of several laws that emphasize the seriousness of all forms of disrespect toward parents.)

A kidnaper receives the death penalty whether the victim is in his custody when he is apprehended or has been sold by him. One who shows extreme disrespect for his parents shall be put to death. The precise sense of the Hebrew verb used in this case is difficult to establish. At times it means "to curse, blaspheme," as in Exodus 22:27, and in Leviticus 24:14, 23; 1 Kings 2:8, and elsewhere. But it can also mean "to degrade, shame," reflecting its primary sense of treating *lightly*. This appears to be the sense in the present law, but because this statement is less than legally precise, one assumes that the courts were obliged to define certain acts as being sufficiently grave to warrant the death penalty, while excluding others.

If one beats his slave to death, the slave "shall be avenged" (Exod.

21:20f.); the verb "to avenge" here denoting the death penalty, in retaliation, against the life of the master. Such is the force of this verb in similar contexts. If the slave does not die instantly but lingers on for a day or two, however, the master "is not to be punished, for the slave is his property." Some compensation was sometimes allowable in such cases, though.

This law delivers a double message. By allowing mitigation of punishment, it reflects extreme social stratification. In other words, slaves did not have the same rights their owners did. And yet, the law does insist on the death penalty when death is instantaneous, notwithstanding the inferior status of the slave.

Exodus 21:22-25 addresses a situation in which a pregnant woman in killed by men fighting close by. The loss of the embryo could be compensated for by an appropriate payment, but the loss of the woman's own life could not. The principle of retaliation is explicitly invoked: "a life for a life." In fact, it is in this very passage that we first encounter the classic formulation of the law of retaliation: "an eye for an eye, tooth for a tooth, hand for a hand, foot for a foot, burn for a burn, wound for a wound, stripe for a stripe. . . ." No allowance is made for the likelihood that the woman's death was accidental; the death penalty is mandated unequivocally, probably because of the gross negligence and indifference to human life exhibited by the fighting men.

Capital punishment figures, at least indirectly, in the well-known law of the goring ox in Exodus 21:28-32. One who leaves his ox unrestrained, after there is clear evidence that the ox in question had gored a person to death previously, is liable to the death penalty if the ox kills someone else. If "its owner has been warned but has not kept [his ox] in, and it kills a man or woman, the ox shall be stoned, and its owner shall also be put to death." There could be a way out for the owner, though, if the deceased's family lays "a ransom on him": "He shall give for the redemption of his life whatever is laid upon him." This emphasized the crucial distinction between a human act that directly caused the death of another person, and death brought about indirectly through the agency of one's property. (Again, slaves are a special case. If an ox gores a slave, "The owner shall give the master thirty shekels of silver, and the ox shall be stoned.")

Capital punishment also figured in the laws governing theft, at least theoretically. Exodus 22:1 states that one who kills a man caught in the act of breaking into his house would not be charged with a capital crime. We should understand that this applies only if the intruder was caught by night, since 22:2 says that if he was caught after sunrise, the killer would be charged with a capital crime (this is indicated by the words, "A blood claim applies to him"). It is doubtful whether this law actually mandates the death penalty. More likely, the case could be disposed of in less severe ways.

Such latitude hardly applied, however, to other dicta forthcoming in the Book of the Covenant. A sorceress is not to be allowed to live (Exod. 22:18), nor are those caught having sexual relations with a beast (22:19). One who worships or offers sacrifice to a god other than Yahweh, the God of Israel, "shall be condemned to destruction." Though somewhat ambiguous, the Hebrew verb used in this context denotes capital punishment, as it does in the Books of Leviticus and Deuteronomy.

To summarize the provisions of the Book of the Covenant, we list the death penalty as mandatory in the following cases: premeditated murder; striking a parent with resultant bodily injury; kidnapping; beating a slave to instant death; killing a pregnant woman in the course of a physical struggle between men; sorcery; having sexual relations with a beast; and offering sacrifice to any god other than the God of Israel.

In the following cases, one could be charged with a capital offense, but allowances would sometimes be made and substitute penalties given: certain forms of disrespect toward parents; the goring to death of a person by one's ox, in cases where the ox had done so previously and the owner had been warned to take proper precautions; killing an intruder caught by daylight.

II.

In addition to the Book of the Covenant, the Torah contains two other major collections of laws: the Deuteronomic legislation (contained in Deuteronomy, roughly chapters 12-26), and the priestly codes of law, concentrated in the Book of Leviticus and in parts of Exodus and Numbers. These collections add several new categories of capital crimes and further extend the provisions of the Book of the Covenant. Let's discuss the Deuteronomic laws first. For the most part, their promulgation seems to have been more ancient than that of the priestly laws, which, indeed, often synthesize the Deuteronomic laws with the Book of the Covenant.

According to Deuteronomy 17:6 and 19:15f., the death penalty may only be imposed pursuant to the valid testimony of at least two corroborating witnesses. "A person shall not be put to death on the evidence of one witness" (Deut. 17:6). Also, Deuteronomy 10:15–21 deals with the question of adequate—or false—testimony. In a case where a witness, by testifying falsely, would have brought about the execution of an innocent person, the law mandates retaliation against the life of the conspiring witness; no quarter would be shown: The conspirator should suffer the very penalty of death he sought to have imposed on another. "You shall do to him as he meant to do to his brother; so you shall purge the evil from the midst of you" (Deut. 20:19).

Deuteronomy 22:20-29 incorporates a series of laws governing a variety of serious sexual crimes. Some background is required to understand what underlies these regulations. In biblical society marriage, as a legal relationship, took effect in two stages: Initially, a woman was pledged to a particular man who "sought" her as his wife and entered into a contract to marry her. At that point, sexual access to the woman in question was prohibited to other men on penalty of death, just as if she were fully married. Custom may have varied as to whether the intended husband was himself allowed to consummate the marriage in advance, but the prohibition was absolute as regards all other men. Now, if a man who had pledged to marry a woman, represented to him at the time as a virgin, subsequently claimed at the final marriage that she had lost her virginity to another man, he was required to substantiate that claim conclusively. If he was able to do so, the woman was guilty of adultery and was to be stoned to death at the gate of her father's house. If, however, the man's allegations proved to be unfounded, he was penalized for shaming a daughter of Israel.

Chapter 22 continues with further legislation governing adultery. Sexual relations between consenting partners, in a case where the participating woman was pledged or married to another, condemned both partners to the death penalty. In cases of rape, where the female victim was pledged or married to another, only the rapist was condemned to death; the woman was regarded as an innocent victim. It should be clarified that rape, as such, was not a capital offense. When a man raped an unattached woman, he was obliged to "give the father of the woman fifty shekels of silver, and she shall be his wife, because he has violated her; he may not put her away all his days" (Deut. 22:29).

In several cases, Deuteronomy elaborates on already-stated cases of capital crime:

Worship of other gods

Deuteronomy, chapter 13, is devoted to the subject of pagan worship. The false prophet who advocates worshiping other gods is to be put to death. A relative or an associate of an Israelite who urges him to worship other gods is to be executed by stoning. In fact, the principle of collective punishment is invoked: The entire population of an Israelite town that had taken to worshiping other gods in response to the incitement of evil men was to be wiped out. In a more brief statement, Deuteromony 17:2-7 mandates the death penalty by stoning for any Israelite who worships other gods. Deuteronomy 18:20 reiterates the death sentence for the false prophet who advocates pagan worship: "But the prophet who presumes to speak a word in my name which I have not commanded him to speak, or who speaks in the name of other gods, that same prophet shall die." A priestly narrative, preserved in Numbers 25:1-15, records that those Israelites who worshipped Baal-Peor were put to death at God's specific command.

Retaliation and the right of asylum

Deuteronomy 19:1-13 presents a major statement on capital punishment and its relation to the ancient institution of "blood restoration." We are provided with hypothetical examples of both accidental and premeditated homicide as a way of clarifying exactly when the right of asylum was in force. It is here that we find reference to "the restorer of blood," a designation applied to a clan relative of a victim of homicide, who bore the responsibility to avenge his death. Three towns were to be set aside as cities of asylum, with three more to be added when the settlement of the land would extend to broader areas. The law is emphatic in denying the right of asylum to actual murderers. The elders of the town from which a murderer came were required to extradite him from any place of asylum and deliver him for execution. The determination of guilt was made by the court, but the customary prerogative of the clan relative to take the life of his relative's murderer was respected. The "restorer of blood" actually participated in the execution of the murderer.

Disrespect for parents

Deuteronomy 21:18-21 mandates the death penalty for a son who is defiantly disobedient toward his parents, who is gluttonous, or who is habitually drunk. If all efforts at disciplining him fail, the elders are to condemn such a son to death: "All the men of the city shall stone him to death with stones" (Deut. 21:21). This statement of law has been recognized as elusive, and the terms of reference it employs are either unique to it or rare in biblical usage; so it is very possible that the death penalty was not mandatory.

Extreme negligence

Deuteronomy 22:8 orders Israelites to install protective fences around the roofs of their houses to prevent loss of life. As in Exodus 22:1-3, the word "blood" here connotes the claim against the life of the negligent homeowner from whose roof someone had fallen to his death. Once again, we sense that the case could be disposed of without imposing the death penalty.

Kidnapping

Deuteronomy 24:7 mandates that a kidnapper be put to death, in much the same terms as were used in Exodus 21:16.

Before leaving the Deuteronomic laws, we should take note of a general principle of law that has far-reaching implications for our understanding of capital punishment in biblical Israel. Deuteronomy 24:16 states that parents are not to be put to death for the crimes of their children, nor children for those of their parents. This principle disallows "substitution," the penalization of someone other than the guilty party. Undoubtedly, this statement means to exclude retaliation against members of a murderer's family—a practice well known in antiquity, not to mention recently. At times, substitution has been a function of social stratification, whereby a slave or subordinate would be punished in place of the actual offender.

We may now proceed to discuss those *priestly* laws that cover capital punishment. The first new category introduced is Sabbath violation. Exodus 31:12-17 and 35:2 mandate the death penalty for an Israelite convicted of intentionally violating the Sabbath. The tasks forbidden on the Sabbath are not fully specified, subsumed as they are under the category "assigned tasks," and the act of violation is conveyed by a Hebrew verb that means "to desecrate."

In Numbers 15:30-36, we find a priestly "story" of sorts. While the Israelites were in the desert they apprehended one of their group gathering firewood on the Sabbath. They placed him under guard and awaited instructions as to his punishment. "And the Lord said to Moses: 'The man shall be put to death; all the congregation shall stone him with stones outside the camp.' And all the congregation brought him outside the camp, and stoned him to death with stones, as the Lord commanded Moses" (Num. 15:35-36).

Priestly law also introduces the crime of blasphemy as a capital offense. In the Book of the Covenant (Exod. 22:27), cursing God is prohibited, but no specific penalty is stated there. A brief priestly narrative in Leviticus 24:10-13 relates that an Israelite of mixed parentage (his mother was an Israelite and his father an Egyptian) committed public blasphemy and was placed in detention. As was true in the account of Numbers, chapter 15, this incident also served as background for a statement of law mandating the death penalty, by stoning, for blasphemers. This applied not only to Israelites, but also to aliens living in Israelite communities. The act of blasphemy is expressed in a specific formula: "uttering the [divine] name explictly, in the act of cursing [God]."

An understandable concern of priestly law, in particular, was preserving the purity of the sacred precincts of Israelite sanctuaries, especially of the Temple of Jerusalem. In Numbers, we find repeated a key formula: "Any alien who intrudes shall be put to death" (Num. 1:51, 3:10, 17:38, and 18:7). It was the duty of certain of the Levitical clans to guard the Tabernacle against intruders, in the traditions of Numbers.

Priestly law also elaborates on some of the capital crimes already mentioned. A major priestly source is Leviticus, chapter 20, whose principal subject is incest and other sexual crimes. Example: "The man who lies with his father's wife has uncovered his father's nakedness; both of them shall be put to death, their blood is upon them" (Lev. 20:11).

On penalty of death, Israelites as well as aliens are admonished against sacrificing their children to Molech. Verse 9 of chapter 20 restates the provisions of Exodus 21:17 regarding any person who treats his parents with extreme disrespect. That person shall be put to death. Verses 10-16 of Leviticus list a series of sexual crimes for which the penalty is death. As stipulated in Deuteronomy 22: 20-29, both partners to adultery are to be put to death. Ezekiel dramatized the penalty when prophesying the destruction of Jerusalem for infant sacrifice and the worship of alien gods:

> O harlot, hear the word of the Lord. Thus says the Lord God, Because your shame was laid bare and your nakedness uncovered in your harlotries with your lovers, and because of all your idols, and because of the blood of your children that you gave to them, therefore, behold, I will gather all your lovers, with whom you took pleasure, and all you loved and all you loathed; I will gather them against you from every side, and will uncover your nakedness to them, that they may see all your nakedness. . . . And I will give you into the hand of your lovers, and they shall throw down your vaulted chamber and break down your lofty places; they shall strip you of your clothes and take your fair jewels, and leave you naked and bare. They shall bring up a host against you, and they shall stone you and cut you to pieces with their swords (Ezek. 16:35-37, 39-40).

Male homosexuality and intercourse with a beast, by man or woman, were punishable by death. (Even the participating beast was to be executed!) We may add here the law of Leviticus 21:9, which condemns to death by stoning a priest's daughter who became a harlot.

Numbers 35:9-34 contains major statements of priestly law on the subject of murder and the right of asylum. Examples of both premeditated murder and unintentional homicide are enumerated. Amnesty is introduced as a factor mitigating the administration of criminal justice. When the incumbent High Priest died, those who had been confined to the cities of refuge were to be released in safety.

We conclude the summary of priestly law with a cryptic statement disallowing commutation of the death penalty: "Any condemned human being, who is marked for elimination, may not be ransomed; he shall be put to death!" (Lev. 27:29). This statement immediately follows another, which, in contrast, allows compensation in the case of condemned property. The language of condemnation used here suggests that reference is to an Israelite who had been condemned to death for worshiping other gods (compare Exod. 20:19 and Deut. 13-19).

The above review more or less exhausts the explicit legal provisions of the Torah on the subject of capital punishment. We may now look beyond legal evidence to other biblical sources that clarify, in their own ways, the postulates of biblical criminal law.

III.

In both of its versions, the Decalogue categorically prohibits certain acts that elsewhere are classified as capital crimes. There are also positive pronouncements in the Decalogue relevant to capital offenses, including commands to honor one's parents and keep the Sabbath. Worship of other gods is emphatically forbidden, as are false testimony, murder, adultery, and perhaps kidnapping, if it is correct to subsume that crime under the commandment prohibiting theft, in line with traditional Jewish interpretation.

Leviticus, chapter 19, echoes the Decalogue and rephrases six, or possibly seven, of the Ten Commandments. Even in the Book of the Covenant we find, alongside laws formulated casuistically, categorical prohibitions of acts elsewhere classified as capital crimes. An example already noted is the crime of blasphemy (Exod. 22:27). These statements reinforce the role of the death penalty.

Biblical literature, as a whole, tells us little about the operation of the criminal justice system in ancient Israel. We know that stoning, burning to death, and impalement were standard methods of execution. (We refer the reader to the following sources: Deut. 13:11, 22:21, 24; Lev. 20:9, 24:14; Num. 15:35; Lev. 21:9; and Deut. 21:22f.). We read of executions conducted outside the encampment or town (Num. 15:35; 1 Kings 21:13, etc.). In some ways, this practice reflects magical attitudes and concepts of purity. Witnesses whose testimony had been instrumental in convicting criminals at times participated personally in their execution (Deut. 17:7).

Some students of biblical law have suggested that the mode of execution prescribed for particular offenses is significant. Certain methods of execution are normal for particular crimes, but precise correlations are difficult to determine. So, we remain with unanswered questions about both the operative details of criminal justice and more basic matters, such as the source of judicial authority. Who, for example, were these judges, and how were they chosen? How great was the authority of heads of families and clans? Upon hearing that his daughter-in-law, Tamar, was pregnant at a time when her status made sexual relations tantamount to adultery, Judah summarily condemned her to death by fire (Gen. 38:24-25). One assumes that Judah possessed traditional authority, as head of the family, to decide such matters and impose sentence.

Still another set of questions pertains to the realism of the canonical laws of the Torah. Are they a reliable index of actual practice? Did kings, for instance, honor these laws? Are the laws of the Torah rooted in commonly held notions of crime and punishment? It is hard to know for sure, but we do possess windows that look in on the life of biblical society and afford us a glimpse of its reality. One biblical narrative with this function is the account of Naboth, the Jezreelite, and his confrontation with Ahab, king of northern Israel, and his queen, Jezebel. As recounted in 1 Kings, chapter 21, the story is set in Samaria of the ninth century B.C.E. Naboth possessed a vineyard located near Ahab's palace. Ahab approached Naboth with an offer to purchase the vineyard or trade for it another parcel of land, even a better one, located somewhere else.

Naboth emphatically refused to part with his property, invoking his inalienable right to it as a family homestead. Ahab's initial response was resignation to failure in his bid to acquire the vineyard. This suggests that there was no legal recourse left to the king. But Jezebel, Ahab's wife, subverted the law. She arranged with the leaders of Samaria to proclaim a public fast, and seated Naboth at the head of the people so that evil men could later accuse him of blasphemy against the king. The charge leveled against Naboth was precisely that he had cursed both God and king. This charge combines, in effect, the two crimes of Exodus 22:27: "You shall not curse God, nor damn a chieftain among your people." As a result of the perjured testimony of bought witnesses, Naboth was condemned to death and stoned outside the city. Ahab promptly expropriated his vineyard, but the prophet Elijah denounced Ahab's crime as murder. As it turned out, God commuted Ahab's sentence because the king had shown contrition. The death sentence was deferred to Ahab's son, Jehoram, who would later be put to death in a dramatic manner for his father's crime (2 Kings 9:22-26).

Of particular interest are the legal predications of this narrative. Naboth could be condemned only on the testimony of witnesses; the king could not simply issue a decree ordering his execution. The story adds yet another insight: God may establish the guilt of a criminal without recourse to testimony, whereas human agencies may not.

The cycle of stories about David and Bathsheba (1 Samuel, chapters 11-12) similarly suggests that kings were bound by the rule of law, at least with respect to certain heinous crimes like adultery and murder. This conclusion emerges logically from the lengths to which David went to conceal his liaison with the wife of another man, going so far as to conspire to have Uriah, Bathsheba's husband, killed in battle in order to keep his crime from becoming known. Ultimately, God spared David's life—sentencing his son, the product of his adultery, to death in his stead.

Both of these narratives endorse the principle of substitution in deferring the death penalty from father to son. This principle contradicts what we have seen established in Deuteronomy 24:16 and reinforced in Ezekiel, chapter 18, for instance, that only the guilty may be punished. "But if this man begets a son who sees all the sins which his father has done, and fears, and does not do likewise . . . he shall not die for his father's iniquity; he shall surely live" (Ezek. 18:14, 17). Yet it also calls to mind this well-known pronouncement of the Decalogue: "I the Lord your God am a jealous God, visiting the iniquity of the fathers upon the children to the third and fourth generation of those who hate me" (Exod. 20:5).

Leaving aside this apparent paradox, let's look more deeply into the concept of deferral of punishment. Is it regarded as merciful, or unjust? In biblical literature, we find the interaction of two tendencies. Notions of justice disallow substitution through deferral. Other attitudes do affect justice, however: mercy and forgiveness, on the one hand, and vengeance and wrath, on the other.

Two aspects of the incident concerning Naboth (the unlucky landowner), require further comment: the crime of sedition and the subject of loyalty to king and country. This issue dominates the trial of the prophet Jeremiah, recorded in Jeremiah, chapter 26, which speaks of "a sentence of death," the very language used in the legislation of Deuteronomy.

As the chapter opens, Jeremiah is speaking in the Temple courtyard in Jerusalem. This was at the beginning of the reign of Jehoiakim, king of Judah, soon before the destruction of Jerusalem by the Babylonians in 586 B.C.E. Jeremiah's message is blunt: Obey God, who communicates his will through his true prophets, or the Temple will be destroyed. Jeremiah was seized by the priests and court prophets, and the "people" threatened him with death: "You shall die! Why have you prophesied in the name of Yahweh saying: 'This Temple shall be as Shiloh, and this city shall be in ruin and uninhabited?' " (compare Jer. 7).

Jeremiah's trial began. The "princes" of Judah took their seats at the entrance of the New Gate of the Temple. They acted as judges by virtue of their position of leadership among the people. The court prophets and priests demanded the death penalty for Jeremiah. The prophet appealed on the grounds that he was merely delivering God's message and that condemning him to death would be shedding innocent blood.

The elders, who were also representing the people of Judah, cited the precedent of an earlier prophet who, in the days of Hezekiah a century or more earlier, had similarly warned the people of impending destruction. At that time, Hezekiah had heeded the prophet's warning and entreated God sincerely, and Jerusalem was spared. To put Jeremiah to death would therefore constitute a great evil.

The account of Jermiah's trial includes reference to a contemporary of his, Uriah, a prophet who said pretty much what Jeremiah was saying. His words were cited as corroboration of the truth of Jeremiah's prophecy. Uriah had fled to Egypt, but Jehoiakim, the king, had him extradited and returned to Jerusalem, where he was put to death at the king's command. The chapter concludes by reporting that Jeremiah, who was also sought by the king, was rescued by an official of the well-known scribal family of Shaphan.

In addition to yielding information on the administration of justice in biblical Israel, the account of Jeremiah's trial clearly indicates that sedition was a capital offense under the monarchic system. The issue in Jeremiah's case was whether or not words of prophecy, uttered publicly by a prophet, constituted sedition when they were subversive of royal authority. In the narratives about David, we also find statements indicating that Saul, when accusing David of sedition, marked him for death (1 Sam. 20:31), condemning those who gave him aid and comfort as well (1 Sam. 26:16).

There are other biblical statements on the judicial process that are harder to place in an historical setting. For instance, Deuteronomy 16:18-21 ordains the establishment of local courts "in all your gates," with appointed justices. These courts were to adjudicate all cases brought before them without prejudice or favoritism. Judges were not to be bribed! In Deuteronomy 17:8-13, we read of the establishment of a central court, located in the temple complex of the religious capital. There, Levitical priests and a judge would together decide cases brought before them by local courts, on capital as well as civil matters. The decisions of this superior court were final and binding, and any who blatantly disobeyed them faced the death penalty themselves.

Based on recent studies, there is reason to trace such provisions as we read in Deuteronomy to the northern Israelite kingdom of the eighth century B.C.E. Subsequently, these doctrines were transmitted to Judah as well. What we read in Exodus, chapter 18, as advice given to Moses on the adminstration of justice may reflect a similar background.

References to judges lead us to other indications of how the judicial process operated in biblical Israel, especially as regards the judicial role of the king. Royal authority is fully taken for granted in the accounts about Naboth and Ahab, David, and Jeremiah that have been discussed above. Deuteronomy 17:14-20 insists that the king of Israel is bound by the laws of Deuteronomy. There are, however, other more realistic indications of a customary role for kings, one which gave them greater sanction, even in capital cases. One theory of the kingship in ancient Israel places considerable emphasis on the judicial role of leaders, especially military leaders. Perhaps the main basis of the authority that accrued to such leaders as David, in his early years, was their ability to secure for the defenseless redress for grievances. It is on this basis that the charismatic leaders who governed Israel prior to the rise of the monarchy were known as "judges." It is also on this basis that in Hebrew a king is called *melek,* which derives from a verb meaning "to counsel, deliberate." So, there is a real framework for the judicial role of the king, and any Israelite could appeal to him for justice, as in 2 Kings 6:26.

Kings probably had the right to impose the death penalty for crimes traditionally regarded as of a capital nature. One could only hope that kings would be wise and just. "Give the king thy justice, O God," begins Psalm 72, "and thy righteousness to the royal son." And one proverb warns, "By justice a king gives stability to the land, but one who exacts gifts ruins it" (Prov. 29:4; Ps. 72:1).

IV.

The right of duly constituted authorities to impose the death penalty reflects certain perceptions of life and death, family and community. These perceptions go beyond legality, bringing us face to face with myth and magic, ritual and drama.

In Genesis 9:1-7, we find a significant statement on the ritual meaning of blood. God has blessed Noah and his family after the flood: "Be fruitful and multiply, and fill the earth. . . . Every moving thing that lives shall be food for you; and as I gave you the green plants, I give you everything" (Gen. 9:1,3). But this permission is immediately qualified: "Only you shall not eat flesh while it is alive—its blood" (Gen. 9:4). The unusual formulation of this statement has been a problem in biblical interpretation since late antiquity. Inevitably, it must be understood as combining two thoughts. Humans must slaughter creatures before eating their meat, and, in any event, they may not eat the blood (compare Deut. 12:23; Lev. 17:10–13). The text then shifts attention away from considerations of diet to the subject of murder, as if to anticipate the inference that once humans have been permitted to slaughter animals they might assume license to kill other humans too. The text reads: "Moreover, your blood, to the extent of your lives, shall I requite; from every beast shall I requite it, and from human beings, each from the other, shall I requite human life. Whoever sheds human blood, from among mankind, his blood shall be shed; for He [God] fashioned human beings in God's form."

I have given a stilted translation on purpose, as a way of bringing out the underlying concepts of this singular statement. Humans enjoy a special status in God's creation because they resemble God in form. Beasts who kill humans must be put to death, as is the law for humans who kill one another. But, humans may kill beasts with impunity.

Deuteronomy 21:1-9 prescribes a communal ritual relevant to the subject of capital punishment. When a murdered corpse was discovered in the open field, outside the jurisdictional limits of any town, and the murderer could not be found, it became necessary to deal with the unsolved crime in special ways. The matter could not simply be neglected or ignored. The Levitical priests were to slaughter a female calf near a perennial stream and pour its blood into the stream. The elders of the nearest town were summoned, and they would wash their hands, literally, of responsibility for the homicide, reciting a formula of clearance: "Our hands have not shed this blood nor have our eyes seen [the act]. Grant expiation to your people, Israel, whom you have ransomed, Yahweh, and do not allow innocent blood to remain [unrequited] in the midst of your people, Israel. Let the blood be expiated on their behalf!" This ritual, with its accompanying formula, projects the return of blood to the earth. An animal's blood is substituted for the blood of the murderer.

"Innocent blood" is a complex concept. Most simply, it characterizes victims of homicide as being innocent. It is used most often, perhaps, in speaking of the death of the innocent resulting from the miscarriage of justice. (See Deut. 19:10). Thus, the passengers and sailors on the ship heading for Tarshish prayed that in casting Jonah overboard they would not be guilty of shedding innocent blood (Jonah 1:14). Whenever the Hebrew Bible speaks of innocent blood in this sense, it expresses the unquestioned consensus that taking a human life unjustly would bring down God's wrath. Deuteronomy 27:25 pronounces a curse on those who take bribes to shed the blood of the innocent. Jonathan was once able to persuade his father, Saul, not to attempt killing David, for to do so would be to shed innocent blood (1 Sam. 19:5). "Innocent blood" must be requited; someone must pay for it!

We recall the words God addressed to Cain, recorded in Genesis 4:10: "Hark! The blood of your brother cries out to me from the earth!" So long as Cain, the fratricide, remained alive, the lost blood of his brother Abel had not been requited. Although God commuted Cain's sentence, the story attests to the anathema of unrequited blood. Another example is that of the murders of the family of Ahab. Someone would have to pay for "the blood of Jezreel" (Hos. 1:4; 2 Kings 9:26).

There is a clear difference, however, between condemning a murderer to death and executing an adulterer, for example, just as there is between executing a false witness who has threatened the life of an innocent person and condemning an idolator to death. What is the underlying principle that allows the death penalty to be imposed when no one's life has been either lost or threatened?

In these cases, we are dealing with *tabu,* with fear of punishment when norms of behavior held sacred by the group are flagrantly violated. In the monotheistic context of biblical Israel, the operative principle is disobedience to the God of Israel. When we consider that the biblical theory of law attributes all law to God, directly, not to kings or intermediaries, we understand how all violations of law constitute actual disobedience to God. Biblical traditions about the God of Israel place considerable emphasis on death as a divine punishment and as a feature of his relationship to humankind, and to Israel in particular.

One need not read very far into Genesis to encounter this theme. God forbade Adam to eat of the Tree of Knowledge on penalty of death (Gen. 2:16f.). Adam and Eve's sentences were eventually commuted, or perhaps suspended, but the Eden narrative established the principle that disobedience to God is punishable by death.

Ten generations later, God brought a flood upon the earth, sparing of all humankind only one man and his family (see Genesis, chapter 6, and following). In the story of Moses, God drowns Pharaoh's army, after having slain the firstborn of Egypt as punishment for disobedience (see Exodus, chapters 1–15). When the God of Israel becomes angry at a disobedient Israel (or at its enemies), he strikes out at them with plagues, pestilence, and other forms of deadly punishments. The sanctions of God's admonitions sound like ancient Near Eastern execrations, calling down death on covenant breakers. Capital punishment, as a legal sentence, correlates with ancient Israelite conceptions of God. God mandated capital punishment in his revealed law, and he also demonstrated this commitment, one might say, by punishing wrongdoers with death, acting as the divine judge.

The validity of our conclusion about death as a punishment may be tested by asking whether biblical literature ever voices an objection to capital punishment. Does any biblical spokesman ever protest that it is wrong for a duly constituted jurisdiction to impose the death penalty for prescribed crimes, under proper judicial procedures? We often read of mercy and forgiveness, but legally speaking, is there an objection to taking the life of a convicted criminal?

Perhaps the closest we come to this is in the notion of *repentance*. In Ezekiel, chapter 18, we read that God, the divine judge, does not really desire the death of the sinner. God would prefer that a guilty person "turn back" from evil ways and go on living. The theme of repentance is epitomized in the parable of Jonah.

As important as the idea of repentance became in biblical teaching, there is no indication that it enjoyed legal status. Moreover, there is no suggestion that a convicted premeditated murderer could have his sentence commuted by the court through repentance. Some argue that there is a message in the fact that God is said to have commuted the sentences of certain murderers and otherwise guilty persons when they showed remorse and submission to his will. Some note that repentance figured meaningfully in projections of Israel's destiny as a people. This message actually relates to ideals more than legality, however, and does not mean that the biblical criminal system ever renounced capital punishment, or that in practice biblical spokesmen ever advocated its suspension.

V.

The New Testament contains no codes of law of the kind found in the Torah of the Hebrew Bible. Yet the subject of capital punishment nonetheless figures in the career of Jesus and his disciples. Jesus was accused of blasphemy, a capital crime, by certain Jewish authorities in Jerusalem; and Stephen, one of Jesus' disciples, was stoned to death in Jerusalem for the same crime. Jesus acted on behalf of an adulteress who would have been stoned for her crime. Generally, the tone of narrative and discussion in both the Gospels and Epistles indicates that the categories of capital crimes defined in the Hebrew Bible were normative within the Jewish communities of Palestine during the time of

Jesus and his followers.

The account of Jesus' action in the case of an adulteress is a good starting point for our discussion. This passage, in John 7:53-8:11, has often been cited as evidence that Jesus questioned the death penalty for adultery. This is certainly an unwarranted inference.

Jesus had been teaching in the Temple of Jerusalem to a large audience. Some scribes and Pharisees sought to entrap him by requesting him to rule on a case of law. Were he to rule in contradiction to the accepted law, they would be able to accuse him of deviation from authoritative teaching, which was a capital offense according to Deuteronomy 17:8-13. So they brought before him an adulteress caught in the act; there was no doubt concerning her actual guilt. After evading the question of her proper punishment, Jesus challenged the scribes and Pharisees by questioning their right to execute judgment: "He that is without sin among you, let him first cast a stone at her!"

Not one of the scribes and Pharisees could, in good conscience, state that he had the moral right to execute the woman, and one by one they departed. Jesus dismissed the woman, adjuring her to sin no more, and thereby suggesting the efficacy of repentance.

There are, of course, questions about the realism of this account, and this passage is not present in the oldest manuscripts of John. For our purposes, its legal predications are of primary interest. The penalty for adultery was stoning, as ordained in Deuteronomy 22:20-21. What happened here? Those who were about to bring the woman to trial thought better of the matter after their attempt to entrap Jesus had failed.

The most dramatic references to the death penalty in the New Testament pertain to the accusation of blasphemy leveled against Jesus by a Jewish council. In the version of this encounter preserved in John there is no explicit references to blasphemy, but in the other three versions the charge of blasphemy is explicit (Matt. 26:59-68; Mark 14:55-66; Luke 22:66-77). The interrogation of Jesus by the Jewish authorities proceeded in two stages: Jesus was first asked to confirm that he said he could destroy the Temple of Jerusalem (or would, in fact, destroy it) and rebuild it in three days. This accusation, which is more explicit in Matthew and Mark, misconstrues what Jesus had really said. According to Matthew 24:2, Mark 13:2, and Luke 20:43f., Jesus had predicted (or prophesied, if you will) the destruction of the Temple of Jerusalem on account of the historic sins of Israel, in much the same manner as Jeremiah prophesied in an earlier age. This misconstruction is significant, because it changed a prediction into an arrogation of more-than-human power on the part of Jesus. In turn, this set the stage for the charge that Jesus had identified himself as the Christ, the son of God, an arrogation interpreted as blasphemy.

On the first charge, Jesus stood mute. When pressed with the second accusation, he responded. In Matthew and Luke, he tacitly concedes what his accusers had charged, whereas in Mark (14:62) he actually replies in the affirmative. Jesus follows up by predicting that he would take his place at the right hand of God. Hearing these things, the council members determined that Jesus had confessed his own crime, and there was no further need for testimony. He was guilty of blasphemy, and he should be put to death. In the course of the legal process we find, in some of the versions, references to false witnesses and the lack of corroboration of testimony. All of these references correlate with the Deuteronmic laws and recall the perfidy of Jezebel.

What transpired after Jesus responded to the Jewish authorities need not concern us, except to point out that Gospel accounts indicate that Jewish courts at the time could not actually execute convicted criminals; they could only deliver them to Roman jurisdiction.

In Acts 6:8–8:2, we read the account of Stephen, a disciple of Jesus, who preached his master's teachings and performed wonders in Jerusalem. Stephen was likewise accused of blasphemy and brought before a Jewish court. We find reference to what Jesus had said about the destruction of the Temple, as well as criticism of what Stephen himself was preaching in Jesus' name. These teachings were said to demonstrate a lack of respect for the law. Jesus is accused of having advocated altering the law of Moses.

After a lengthy jeremiad on the sins of Israel throughout its history, Stephen reports his vision of Jesus at the right hand of God. This persuades the council that Stephen is indeed guilty of blasphemy, and he is taken outside the walled city and stoned to death. Here the Jewish authorities carry out the actual execution of Stephen themselves, an action some have found puzzling. In any event, this account was surely modeled after those of the Gospels pertaining to Jesus himself.

Reference to altering the law of Moses again recalls the Deuteronomic statements on the crime of the false prophet (Deut. 13). Execution of the criminal outside the city recalls the provisions of Leviticus 24:10–13. What we observe in Acts, and throughout the New Testament, is a composite of various charges, and attempts at incrimination, involving such capital crimes as violation of the Sabbath (or its advocacy), promoting disobedience to law and authority, blasphemy, and so forth. Superimposed on the legalities of these charges is the unique identity of Jesus as the Christ, the son of God. Jesus' identification as "a divine man" takes us beyond law, so that the charge of blasphemy leveled against Jesus had no legal precedent, strictly speaking.

The right of earthly rulers to impose the death penalty is upheld by Paul in Romans, chapter 13, in the well-known passage that speaks of rendering to civil authorities the obedience due them. The principle that earthly, temporal power is valid later became the dominant policy of the Christian church. As for the definition of capital crime, little had changed since the time of the Hebrew Bible. One senses from reading the New Testament that contemporary Jewish interpretation of criminal law was severe in first century Palestine. It has been debated as to whether this impression is accurate, since Jewish sources like the *Qumran* documents and later Rabbinic literature have been cited to prove that the imposition of capital punishment was infrequent in the last phase of the period of the Second Temple.

In our discussion of capital punishment in the Hebrew Bible, we made the point that pronouncements about divine behavior correlated in the judicial context to attitudes toward death as a proper punishment. Quite clearly, the New Testament carries on the earlier mentality. Obedience will be rewarded with life; disobedience will be punished with destruction. As Jesus says in the Sermon on the Mount:

> Everyone, then, who hears these words of mine and does them will be like a wise man who built his house upon a rock; and the rain fell, and the floods came, and the winds blew and beat upon the house, but it did not fall, because it was founded on the rock. And every one who hears these words of mine and does not do them will be like a foolish man who built his house upon the sand; and the rain fell, and the floods came, and the winds blew and beat against the house, and it fell; and great was the fall of it" (Matt. 7:24-27).

This polarity is reiterated throughout the New Testament.

A God who rewards with life and punishes by death is one whose laws provide for death as a judicial punishment.

FOR FURTHER READING

Albrecht Alt. "The Origins of Israelite Law." In *Old Testament History and Religion*. Translated by R. Wilson. Oxford: Blackwell, 1966. 79-132.

David Daube. *Studies in Biblical Law*. New York: Ktav, 1969.

Moshe Greenberg. "Some Postulates of Biblical Criminal Law." In *Jubilee Volume, Yehezkiel Kaufmann*. Edited by Menahem Haran. Jerusalem: Magnes Press, 1960. 5-28.

Jacob J. Finkelstein. *The Ox that Gored*. Transactions, American Philosophical Society. Vol. 71, part 2, 1981.

Anthony Phillips. *Ancient Israel's Criminal Law*. Oxford: Blackwell, 1970.

Mayer Sulzberger. *The Ancient Hebrew Law of Homicide*. Philadelphia: Julius Greenstone, 1915.

A. Sherwin White. *Roman Society and Roman Law in the New Testament*. Oxford, 1963.

THE FUTURE
James D. Tabor

There is no simple and single response to the question of what the Bible really says about the future. What one finds is just what one would expect in any book composed of documents from many times, places, circumstances, and authors—variety and development. There is a lot of both, although by "development" I mean here simply change. My treatment presupposes no particular valuation of the various dreams and schemes regarding the future. My approach in this chapter will be mainly chronological, tracing the topic through various periods of history, from ancient Israelite down to the Roman period, when the final parts of the New Testament were written. I have also roughly divided the topic into two subtopics: what the Bible says about the future of the world; and what it says about the future of the individual, that is, the *afterlife*. The two are always interrelated, and they often overlap.

THE EARLY HEBREW BIBLE

In the earlier parts of the Old Testament, or Hebrew Bible, one finds fairly uniform views of both the future of the individual human person and that of the world or society. I have in mind here texts and traditions dating from the second millennium B.C.E. down through the time of the Exile of the kingdoms of Israel and Judah by the Assyrians and the Babylonians (8th-6th B.C.E.).

To understand this somewhat singular view of the future one needs to get a general grasp of ancient *cosmology*. Cosmology is the theory and lore of how the world or universe is structured. A kind of map or picture of the cosmos, cosmology is a way of naming things and putting them in their proper places.

The ancient Hebrews pictured the universe divided into three parts or realms, as did other civilizations of the period. First, there was the upper realm of the Firmament (Sky) or Heavens, the dwelling place of God and his divine angelic court, as well as the place of the sun, moon, planets, and stars. Here no mortal belonged.[1] Then there was the realm of earth below, what the first chapter of Genesis calls "the dry land." It is the proper human place, shared with all the other forms of plant and animal life—a thoroughly mortal realm. The earth was seen as a flat disk; at the edges were the threatening waters of chaos, held back by the command of God (Gen. 1:9-10; Ps. 104:5-9). Finally, below the earth was the dark realm of the dead, which was called Sheol by the Hebrews and Hades by the Greeks. Psalms 115:16-18 puts it succinctly: "The heavens are Yahweh's heavens, but the earth he has given to the sons of men. The dead do not praise Yahweh, nor do any that go down into silence. But we [the living] will bless Yahweh from this time forth and for evermore."[2]

There is a particular set of perceptions, tied closely to this cosmic structure, that has great bearing on the ancient Israelite view of the future. The emphasis on order and proper place is of central importance. Yahweh and the divine beings of his court, whether gods (*elohim*) of the nations or angels, inhabit the upper heavenly realm and are not subject to death. Such heavenly beings, including Yahweh or his "Angel," can "come down" to earth and appear to human mortals (see Gen. 11:5-7; 18:20-21; Exod. 3:1-6).[3] Jacob sees in a dream the very "ladder of heaven" with such beings moving up and down between the two realms (Gen. 28:10-17). Yahweh comes down upon Mount Sinai and speaks to the whole vast assembly of Israelites following the Exodus from Egypt (Exod. 19:11, 18; 34:5). Moses and the elders of the nation go up the mountain, meeting him halfway as it were, and encounter him there (Exod. 24:9-11, 15-18). Moses speaks with Yahweh face to face in personal conversation and actually sees his "form" (Exod. 33:11; Num. 12:8). But clearly the immortal beings, or "gods," *belong* in heaven—it is their proper sphere, while they only *visit* the earth below. Conversely, humans are mere mortals, placed on the good earth below, with no idea whatsoever of any "future" in heaven. Their only permanent movement is down, to the lower world of the dead.

The Individual and the Future

First I will consider the notion of the future of the individual human person. The ancient Hebrews had no idea of an immortal soul living a full and vital life beyond death, nor of any resurrection or return from death. Human beings, like the beasts of the field, are made of "dust of the earth," and at death they return to that dust (Gen. 2:7; 3:19). The Hebrew word *nephesh,* traditionally translated "living soul" but more properly understood as "living creature," is the same word used for all breathing creatures and refers to nothing immortal. The same holds true for the expression translated as "the breath of life" (see Gen. 1:24; 7:21-22). It is physical, "animal life." For all practical purposes, death was the *end.* As Psalms 115:17 says, the dead go down into "silence"; they do not participate, as do the living, in praising God (seen here as the most vital human activity). Psalms 146:4 is like an exact reverse replay of Genesis 2:7: "When his breath departs he returns to his earth; on that very day his thoughts [plans] perish." Death is a one-way street; there is no return. As Job laments:

> But man dies, and is laid low;
> man breathes his last, and where is he?
> As water fail from a lake,
> and a river wastes away and dries up,
> so man lies down and rises not again;
> till the heavens are no more *he will not awake,*
> or be aroused out of his sleep. (Job 14:10-12)[4]

All the dead go down to Sheol, and there they lie in sleep together— whether good or evil, rich or poor, slave or free (Job 3:11-19). It is described as a region "dark and deep," "the Pit," "the land of forgetfulness," cut off from both God and human life above (Pss. 6:5; 88:3-12). Though in some texts Yahweh's power can reach down to Sheol (Ps. 139:8), the dominant idea is that the dead are abandoned forever. This idea of Sheol is negative in contrast to the world of life and light above, but there is no idea of judgment, or of reward and punishment. If one faces extreme circumstances of suffering in the realm of the living above, as did Job, it can even be seen as a welcome relief from pain—see the third chapter of Job. But basically it is a kind of "nothingness," an existence that is barely existence at all, in which a "shadow" or "shade" of the former self survives (Ps. 88:10).

This rather bleak (or comforting, depending on your point of view) understanding of the future (or nonfuture) of the individual at death is one that prevails throughout most of the Hebrew Bible. It is found throughout the Pentateuch (the Books of Genesis, Exodus, Leviticus, Numbers, and Deuteronomy), and it runs through the books of history, poetry, and prophecy (from Joshua through Malachi) with few exceptions.

Those exceptions, however, are noteworthy. The most obvious is the infamous account of the seance in which King Saul has the "witch" (or medium) of Endor conjure up the spirit of the dead prophet Samuel. The narrative is fascinatingly realistic. The medium asks Saul, "Whom shall I *bring up* for you?" Saul replies, "Bring up Samuel for me" (1 Sam. 28:11). What follows is worth quoting in full:

> The king said to her, "Have no fear; what do you see?" And the woman said to Saul, "I see a *god (elohim) coming up out of the earth.*" He said to her, "What is his appearance?" And she said, "An old man wrapped in a robe." And Saul knew that it was Samuel, and he bowed with his face to the ground, and did obeisance. Then Samuel said to Saul, "Why have you *disturbed me by bringing me up?*" (1 Sam. 28:13-15) (my emphasis)

Saul's intent in trying to contact Samuel was to consult him regarding the wisdom of going into battle against the Philistines. Samuel appears to him in bodily form and gives him a clear prediction of what would befall him, just as he would have done in his prophetic ministry while still alive. He clearly *knows the future,* even though he has departed below, to Sheol.

Here the dead (at least Samuel) are viewed as "gods" of sorts, resting below in Sheol, but potentially capable of "coming back"—after being "disturbed"—and participating in the life of the living to the extent of even knowing the future. The practice of consulting the spirits of the dead was strictly forbidden in both the Torah and Prophets, but it obviously went on persistently (see Deut. 18:11; Isa. 8:19, 29:4). Throughout this period Israelites apparently thought that the dead could be consulted on behalf of the living. This indicates that their view of the state of the dead in Sheol below was not entirely static. Although generally pictured "at rest," such spirits could assume special power and still have verbal intercourse with the living world above.

Some have also noted as exceptions texts such as Psalms 73:18-26 and 49:13-15, which contrast the fate of the wicked as perishing in

Sheol with that of the righteous, who will somehow be "ransomed" from its power. These texts are impossible to date with any certainty, and they might reflect some beginning "hints" of an idea of a resurrection hope for the departed righteous. If so, they probably come from the late Persian period. But even these texts lack a clear affirmation of resurrection of the dead. They might reflect the mere notion of God saving one *from* Sheol, i.e., rescuing from danger, sickness, and pro-longing life. This is clearly the sense of passages like Psalms 22:19-24 and 103:1-5, Isaiah 38:10-20, and Jonah 2:1-9. It is only in certain late portions of the Hebrew Bible, and in sections of the Apocrypha, that we find the beginning expressions of any kind of an actual "future" for the individual beyond death. These will be discussed later in this chapter.

Surprisingly, this view of the future holds true for even the greatest of Israel's heroes. Genesis 25:7-8 records the death of the greatest of all, Abraham: "These are the days of the years of Abraham's life, a hundred and seventy-five years. Abraham breathed his last and died in a good old age, an old man and full of years, and was gathered to his people." The same is said for Moses, David, and all the others (Deut. 32:48-50; 34; 1 Kings 2:10; cf. 2 Sam. 12:22-23). Death is the great equalizer. So, one might accurately say, in ancient Hebrew there is *no view of the future* for the individual human person, certainly not when contrasted with the later ideas that arose—such as resurrection of the dead or eternal life in heaven. And yet the "religion" of Israel functioned very well without these ideas for more than a thousand years.

The Future of the World

Scholars use the term "eschatology" to refer to what they call the "last things," i.e., the events and realities at the end of history or, more popularly speaking, "the end of the world." However, this idea of the "end of the world" does not necessarily mean the destruction of the planet. More often it refers to the end of an "age," following which history takes a dramatic turn for the better. Eschatology addresses these questions: Where is history headed? And what will be its final determination and meaning? Obviously, one is presupposing here that there *is* some meaning to history and that the end will make it all clear.

We find little or no eschatology of this sort in the Pentateuch or in the historical books. This is not strictly a matter of chronological development, since before and after the time of the Exile (8th-6th B.C.E.)

we do find plenty of material in the Prophets that is clearly "eschato-logical." And yet it is around this same time that both the Pentateuch and many of the historical books receive their final edited forms. What we encounter here is fascinating: two very different ways of looking at the future, existing side by side, but in some tension and competition with one another.

The first, which is earlier and predominates in the bulk of the Hebrew Bible material, I shall call the "historical." In this view of things, there is obviously a "future," since history proceeds on its linear path and generations come and go. But there is no expectation of any dramatic change ahead, i.e., the massive intervention of God through which everything gets set right. The book of Ecclesiastes contains the most systematic and poignant expression of this "noneschatological" view of the future. I quote here its opening lines:

> Vanity of vanities, says the Preacher,
> vanity of vanities! All is vanity.
> What does a man gain by all the toil
> at which he toils under the sun?
> A generation goes, and a generation comes,
> but the earth remains for ever. . . .
> What has been is what will be
> and *what has been done is what will be done;*
> *and there is nothing new under the sun.* (1:2-4, 9)

Obviously, such a view of things, in which there is "nothing new under the sun," can fill one with a deep sense of despair. After all, the human realm below is full of injustice, suffering, and tragedy, which is what the book of Ecclesiastes is all about. Is there to be no change, ever? The author of Ecclesiastes, like all ancient Hebrews, shares the view that death is the end of all human aspiration and experience, as I described above. He writes:

> For the fate of the sons of men and the fate of beasts is the same; as one dies, so dies the other. They all have the same breath, and *man has no advantage over the beasts;* for all is vanity. All go to *one place;* all are from the dust, and all turn to dust, again. (3:19-20)[5]

Surprisingly, this mood of fatalistic resignation and despair, which is expressed so powerfully in Ecclesiastes, does not dominate the Pentateuch and the historical books. By and large, these materials, though sharing at root the same bleak view of the future, reflect another element that tends to make them guardedly, or at least provisionally, optimistic. They are concerned primarily with the future fortunes of the people or nation of Israel, and such a future is seen, potentially at least, as full of abundant good and blessings.

This idea of a good future for the nation of Israel begins with texts in Genesis, which promise such to Abraham and his descendants. God tells Abraham, "I will make of you a great nation, and I will bless you, and make your name great, so that you will be a blessing" (Gen. 12:2). Later he is told, "I will make my covenant between me and you, and will multiply you exceedingly . . . you will be the father of a multitude of nations" (17:2,4), and "to your descendants I will give this land [i.e., Palestine]" (Gen. 15:18). These elements of "chosen people," covenant, land, and blessings form the foundation of this view of the future. The twenty-eighth chapter of Deuteronomy best sums up this whole idea. Israel is to be "set high above all the nations of the earth" (Deut. 28:1) and experience incredible material blessings—peace, power, wealth, and health (Deut. 28:3-14), if only she will obey the commandments of Yahweh. However, the bulk of the chapter catalogs in lengthy detail the very *reverse* of that potential future. If Israel turns from Yahweh, serves other gods, and disregards his commandments, she will experience terrible curses, plagues, and disasters, and finally, near complete destruction, captivity, and exile. This is the basic story line of much of the Hebrew Bible. Yahweh offers Israel all these potential blessings, she consistently rejects him and his laws and suffers various curses, and all the while there is a constant call for her to repent and come back.

I have called this view of the future "historical" rather than properly "eschatological," because it still sees the cosmos (world, universe, history) as a whole, as running along normally with its repeated tale of death, war, disease, suffering, and tragedy. In other words, the lower human realms of earth (history) and Sheol (individual fate) remain fundamentally the same. There is the *potential* for the chosen *people* of Israel to experience the blessings of Yahweh, and thus some respite from the brunt of this common human experience. But by and large, for most individual Israelites at most times, the stark view of Ecclesiastes remains the same. Death is the end. There is nothing new under the sun. I should point out that in some few texts there is the notion that the blessings to be poured out upon Israel will "spill over" to other nations (Gen. 12:3). But a more common idea is that such non-Israelite nations will partake of these blessings at a much lower level, as the proverbial "hewers of wood and drawers of water," that is, as Israel's *slaves* (Deut. 20:10-15; Josh. 9:21-27).

THE TIME OF THE EXILE AND BEYOND

Beginning in the eighth century, and well down into the sixth century B.C.E., the nation of Israel suffered through political, social, and military catastrophes. First under the Assyrians, then successively under the Babylonians and Persians, large parts of the population were exiled and their land was occupied. This is the time of the Hebrew Prophets—whose books comprise Isaiah through Malachi. It is primarily in these texts—written before, during, and after this period of exile—that we find the beginnings of a new view of the future. It is this new view, in contrast to what I called the "historical" view above, that can properly be called "eschatological." It seems to develop over time from a rather simple hope for the ultimate restoration of the national fortunes of the tribes of Israel to a fantastic vision of total cosmic renewal and transformation. This development is somewhat, though not strictly, chronological. The type and range of "eschatological" solutions proposed seem to correspond directly to the perception of the scope of the historical problem.

The Restoration of National Israel

One of the dominant and ubiquitous refrains of the Hebrew Prophets is that all twelve tribes of Israel will someday be gathered back to the land and, once fully restored, experience in an unprecedented measure all the blessings of their special relationship with Yahweh (Deut. 28 again). This picture of a "golden age" is sketched out over and over again in similar terms: All the tribes return to the land; they repent of their idolatry and sinful ways; the Davidic kingship is restored; peace and prosperity abound; and all the nations either submit to them or they are converted to Israel's God.[6] This state of affairs apparently lasts indefinitely. To illustrate, I cite three quotations from Jeremiah:

> At that time Jerusalem shall be called the throne of Yahweh, and all nations shall gather to it, to the presence of Yahweh in Jerusalem, and they shall no more stubbornly follow their own evil heart. In those days the house of Judah shall join the house of Israel [i.e., the

twelve tribes reunited], and together they shall come from the land of the north [i.e., exile] to the land that I gave your fathers for a heritage. . . .

Behold the days are coming, says Yahweh, when I will raise up for David a righteous Branch, and he shall reign as king and deal wisely, and shall execute justice and righteousness in the land. In his days Judah will be saved, and Israel will dwell securely. . . .

Behold the days are coming, says Yahweh, when I will make a new covenant with the house of Israel and the house of Judah. . . . I will put my laws within them, and I will write it upon their hearts; and I will be their God, and they shall be my people . . . and I will remember their sin no more. (Jer. 3:17-18, 23:5-6, 31:31-34)

This final state of things, however "golden" and ideal, is still described in most of these texts in thoroughly "historical" terms. In other words, all the promises of national grandeur made anciently to Israel, which became utterly hopeless during the Exile, are grandly projected into the future. But the cosmos is still basically the same. Humans stay on earth. The normal cycles of nature continue. Generations still come and go, and the dead of past ages remain in Sheol, thoroughly "dead."

A Transformed Cosmos

However, in a few texts, scattered here and there in the Hebrew Prophets, a dramatically different vision of the future begins to emerge. It is built around the view of a restored Israel, as described above, but it also sets forth the hope of an utterly transformed cosmos, extending from the heights of heaven to the depths of Sheol, and including all normal cycles of nature and human history. In other words, all that led the author of Ecclesiastes to cry out, "vanity of vanities, all is vanity," will be reversed. Isaiah describes a time when even the violence of nature, "red in tooth and claw," will end:

> The wolf shall dwell with the lamb,
> and the leopard shall lie down with the kid,
> and the calf and the lion and the fatling together,
> and a little child shall lead them.
> The cow and the bear shall feed;
> their young shall lie down together;
> and the lion shall eat straw like the ox.
> The sucking child shall play over the hole of the asp,

and the weaned child shall put his hand
on the adder's den.
They shall not hurt or destroy in all my holy mountain;
for the earth shall be full of the knowledge of Yahweh
as the waters cover the sea. (Isa. 11:6-9)

This transformed state of things is so dramatic, it is like a new or second creation. A "new heavens and new earth," Isaiah terms it (Isa. 65:17-25, 66:22-24). It is inaugurated by a highly idealized Davidic King (Isa. 11:1-5; Mic. 5:2-4).[7] Total peace reigns among all nations (Isa. 2:4; Mic. 4:3). The suffering and toils of life are eliminated as "Yahweh wipes away tears from all faces," and death itself is "swallowed up forever" (Isa. 25:8). This apparently includes the "resurrection" of the righteous dead of the past (Isa. 26:19).[8] This era of complete justice and righteousness is ushered in by the terrible Day of Yahweh's wrath in which all wicked sinners are utterly destroyed.[9] The topography of the land of Israel and the city of Jerusalem is drastically altered: The deserts bloom like a rose; fresh water flows into the Dead Sea; and the whole Jerusalem area is elevated (Isa. 35; Zech. 14:8-11; Ezek. 47-48). Some few texts seem to imply that wicked angelic powers are also disposed of in this overthrow of all evil by Yahweh (Isa. 24:21-22, 27:1).[10]

Still, even in this thoroughly idealized transformation of the cosmos, it is interesting and important to note that in one sense the vision is still rather "earthly." Humans remain on the earth, however "renewed." And indeed, Yahweh himself descends from heaven with his angels. His "feet stand on the Mt. of Olives," and he becomes "king over all the earth," dwelling in his perfect Temple forever (Zech. 14:4-9; Ezek. 43:6-7). The view that these texts begin to develop represents a kind of "compression" of the cosmos. In other words, the immortal heavenly realm above "comes down" to earth, and the world of death below is eliminated or "moved up" through resurrection. There is a certain sense in which this can still be seen, typologically at least, as linear or "historical." Salvation here is eschatological. It comes *at the end* of history, through God's dramatic intervention in the affairs of this world, as the new transformed age is inaugurated.

This is in contrast to views of the future that pictured salvation as taking place "away from the earth," without any required end of history. I have in mind here the notion, particularly widespread during Greek and Roman times, of the immortal soul, leaving the body and the earthly realm at death, and obtaining immortal life in heaven above.

OLD TESTAMENT MATERIALS
FROM GREEK AND ROMAN TIMES

As we move to the period of first Greek and then Roman domination of the eastern Mediterranean world (the fourth century B.C.E. to the first century C.E.), the biblical materials reflect drastic development with regard to the view of the future. All the ideas I have discussed so far— the older Hebrew view of the cosmos, the restoration of national Israel, and the transformed cosmos of the new age—continue, but they are fundamentally transformed and merged in rather complicated ways. Two views dominate: the hope of an eschatological transformation of the cosmos and the notion that an immortal soul escapes the body at death to enter the heavenly world. Both are closely tied to a deep despair regarding the course of history and the possibility of things ever changing. How and when might the many dreamlike promises of salvation for God's faithful people, which I have just surveyed, ever be realized?

The Rise and Development of Apocalyptic Scenarios

One can find, as we have seen, the general outline of the major themes of Jewish eschatology in the Hebrew Prophets. However, such a general hope for change was apparently not enough to satisfy some of the minority parties of the period that were disenfranchised from the social, political, and religious establishment, groups that experienced real or imagined persecution. Increasingly we find evidence of a turn to some very definite apocalyptic schemes and scenarios. Apocalypticism focuses on the "signs of the end," which have been revealed by God to his special "elect," or "chosen" ones. They alone understand the secrets of the cosmos, particularly the "times and the seasons" that will lead to God's dramatic intervention.

The most important and influential apocalyptic work in the Bible is the Book of Daniel. Scholars date this text to near the time of the Maccabean revolt, c. 165 B.C.E. Chapters 2, 7, 8, 9, 11, and 12 contain visions that claim to show the sequence of events, in some detail, that will lead up to the time of the end, when God sets up his Kingdom over all the earth. The basic scenario is this: Following a succession of world kingdoms (Babylon, Persia, Greece, and Rome—as they were subsequently interpreted), a terribly evil ruler would come, march into Palestine, defile the Temple at Jerusalem, persecute God's people for a limited time (about three and a half years), but be utterly and decisively crushed by the sudden intervention of God (Dan. 7:19-25; 8:23-26; 11:31-45). The resurrection of the dead and final judgment would follow, with the Kingdom passed to God's elect and persecuted "saints" (see especially Dan 2:44; 7:13-18, 26-27). This basic scheme of events became enormously influential among Jewish and Christian groups of the period and is the backbone of all the major apocalyptic schemes in the New Testament. Each time a likely candidate showed up in Palestine—whether Antiochus Epiphanes (the original subject of the visions), the Roman general Pompey (63 B.C.E.), the threat of the emperor Caligula to have his statue placed in the Jewish temple (41 C.E.), or the actual destruction of the Temple in August of 70 C.E. by the Roman general Titus—the specific expectations of Daniel's scheme came into play. Various groups of Jews and Christians would be whipped up into a kind of apocalyptic frenzy, utterly convinced that the time of God's Kingdom was at hand.

2 Esdras is another thoroughly apocalyptic work, which builds on the book of Daniel and is concerned with the "delay" of the end.[11] In a crucial section, 12:10-30, the author recasts Daniel's basic vision and brings it down to his own time, with detailed predictions of what lies just ahead leading up to the arrival of the Messiah and the Kingdom of God.

Immortality of the Soul and Resurrection of the Dead

Side by side with the expanded speculation about when and how the end of the age would arrive are two important developments regarding the future of individuals beyond death. First, there is a vastly increased concern with the state and fortunes of the dead, both wicked and righteous, *before* the end of the age. Second, we see the full-blown development of the notion that some (or all) of the dead will rise to face a final judgment. As we have seen, in the Hebrew Bible the dead are in Sheol, barely existing, and never to return. The "state" of these dead is hardly any state at all.

Daniel 12:2-3 is the earliest text in the Bible to speak clearly and absolutely about a resurrection of the dead, both wicked and righteous.[12] His reference to the dead as "those who sleep in the earth" shows that he does not yet know, or share an interest in, their so called "interim" state (i.e., before the resurrection at the end). 2 Maccabees (written sometime between the first century B.C.E. and the first century C.E.) reflects an interesting state of development in this regard. Not only does the author believe in the resurrection (at least of the righteous martyrs), but he advocates prayer and sacrifice for the dead and believes that they can intercede for those on earth and vice versa (2 Macc. 12:43-45, 15:11-16). Likewise, in 2 Esdras the dead are fully conscious, already suffering either punishment or comfort in various levels and compartments of the heavenly realms, awaiting the final day of judgment (2 Esd. 7). Here the view of the immortal soul that departs the body at death is combined with a view of final and future resurrection of the dead. We know from texts outside the Old Testament canon, like the Ethiopic Enoch (third century B.C.E. to first century C.E.), that such views were common among various Jewish and Christian groups during this period.

The Wisdom of Solomon is most interesting in this regard. In chapter 2, we have a powerfully poetic description of the ancient Hebrew view of death:

> Short and sorrowful is our life,
> and there is no remedy when a man comes to his end,
> and no one has been known to return from Hades.
> Because we were born by mere chance,
> and hereafter we shall be as though we had never been;
> because the breath in our nostrils is smoke,
> and reason is a spark
> kindled by the beating of our hearts.
> When it is extinguished, the body will turn to ashes,
> and the spirit will dissolve like empty air.
> Our name will be forgotten in time,
> and no one will remember our works. (2:1-4)

This is precisely the view of Ecclesiastes, as we have seen. But here the author of The Wisdom of Solomon attributes this view to the grossly wicked (Wisd. of Sol. 2:21-24)! He strongly supports a view that is the very opposite of Ecclesiastes, that of the immortality of the soul and resurrection of the dead. He declares:

> But the souls of the righteous are in the hand of God,
> and no torment will ever touch them.
> In the eyes of the foolish *they seemed to have died,*
> and their departure was thought to be an affliction,
> and their going from us to be their destruction;
> but they are at peace.

> For though in the sight of men they were punished,
> their hope is full of immortality. (3:1-4)

He goes on to declare that in the time of their visitation they will "shine forth" (be resurrected?) and will end up governing and ruling nations in the Kingdom of God (3:7-8).

THE NEW TESTAMENT'S VIEW OF THE FUTURE

The New Testament's view of the future of the individual human person (at death or beyond), and of the world, incorporates and builds upon most of these developments and changes. The ancient Hebrew views, which are so dominant in the bulk of the Hebrew Bible, are simply ignored, or they are read and interpreted in the light of the newer views.

The Resurrection of the Dead

Perhaps it is only too obvious that the idea of resurrection of the dead has a central place in the New Testament documents. Nowhere in the New Testament do we find reflected or upheld the old Hebrew idea of death as the final end. In fact, in several places this idea is directly opposed. In the Synoptic tradition, the Sadducees, who held such a view of death, challenge Jesus, and he sharply refutes them, arguing for some kind of continued existence after death as well as a future resurrection (Mark 12:18-27). In the Book of Acts, Paul too makes a point of distinguishing his faith in resurrection of the dead from the view of the Sadducees (Acts 23:6-10).

Still, what these early Christians meant by the idea of "resurrection" is not always so clear. Take the case of Jesus. In Luke 24, he appears after his resurrection to have a normal physical body; he eats and drinks and presumably exercises all bodily functions, just as before his death. So we seem to have here the notion of the resuscitation of a corpse, i.e., the same physical body of Jesus, wounds and all, that was laid in the tomb (see John 20:24-27, 21:9-14). Yet this body comes through locked doors (John 20:19), and Paul defends the idea of some kind of a "spiritual body," definitely *not* "flesh and blood," but immortal and glorified. What connection this "spiritual body" is supposed to have with the body put in the tomb is not clear (1 Cor. 15:42-54). Resurrection, however, throughout the New Testament, is at the end, when Jesus returns with the clouds of heaven to gather his elect people together (Luke 20:34-36; Matt. 11:20-24; John 5:28-29; Acts 24:15; 1 Thess. 4:15-17; 1 Cor. 15:51-52; 2 Tim. 4:1; Rev. 11:18). (There are exceptions: Jesus and the Saints of Matthew 27:52f., as well as the dead raised by Jesus and Paul.)

As for the "state of the dead" before the end, Paul prefers the image of "sleep" (1 Cor. 15:6, 18, 20, 51; 1 Thess. 4:13-18; 5:9-10). But he also believed that the "spirit" of a departed Christian went to "be with Christ" (Phil. 1:19-26; 2 Cor. 5:6-10; 1 Thess. 4:14). Several places in the New Testament we clearly find the notion that the dead are conscious, dwelling somewhere in the heavenly realms beyond, and awaiting, either in torment or comfort, the final judgment (Luke 16:19-31, 23:43; 1 Pet. 3:18-20; 4:6; Rev. 6:9-11; 7:9-12).

The Close of the Age

The early Christians believed in the "close of the age"—and also what might properly be called the "end of the world." They looked to a future, following the return *(parousia)* of Jesus in the clouds of heaven, in which the physical world would "pass away," replaced by a new creation (Rom. 8:21; 2 Pet. 3:10-13; Rev. 21-22). Here, is it difficult to lay out a single eschatological scheme for all the New Testament documents. Revelation, chapter 20, speaks of a thousand-year reign of Christ on earth before the "new creation" (see Rev. 1:6; 2:25-26; 3:21; 5:10; 11:15-18). Paul seems to anticipate such a time, between the coming of Christ and the final "end" *(telos),* when the elect group will "judge the world . . . and angels" and reign as kings in the kingdom of God (1 Cor. 15:23-28; 4:8; 6:2-3). The author of Luke through Acts speaks of Christ coming back to "restore" all the things spoken by the prophets (Acts 3:20-21), and Jesus chooses twelve disciples to rule over the regathered twelve tribes of Israel in the Kingdom of God (Luke 22:28-30). This rather "literal" or concrete view of the Kingdom of God on earth, drawn from the Hebrew Prophets, appears often in the Synoptic tradition. Jesus will return to earth and sit on his glorious throne, surrounded by his twelve apostles ruling over the twelve tribes (Matt. 19:28-30). All the Old Testament patriarchs will be resurrected and participate in this Messianic kingdom (Matt. 8:11-12). The nations will be gathered before this throne of Christ and judged (Matt. 25:31-46). Whether all this can be fully systematized or not, Revelation, chapters 19-22, does contain the key elements of the overall vision of the future in some kind of rough order:

the return of Christ, the utter defeat of Satan and his agents, the resurrection of the dead and the reign with the saints on earth, a return of Satan to lead the nations against Jerusalem, their defeat and the immersion of the Devil and the false prophet in a lake of burning sulphur for eternal torment, a final resurrection and judgment, and the new creation and final perfection. Most New Testament passages on the future will fit somewhere into this general scheme. And most of the themes cited earlier from the Hebrew Prophets anticipate one part or another of this final New Testament eschatological outline.

Signs of the End

Any actual apocalyptic scenario, when reflected here and there in the New Testament, seems to be remarkably consistent with the visions of Daniel. In the Synoptic tradition (Mark 13; Matt. 24; Luke 21), Jesus connects the destruction of the Jerusalem Temple to the more general "signs of the end of the age": false prophets, wars and disruptions, earthquakes, famines, pestilence, persecution, and a world-wide proclamation of his message. These then lead up to "the sign," spoken of by Daniel the prophet as the desolating sacrilege ("abomination of desolation"), apparently some kind of profanation of the Jewish Temple rites (Dan. 8:13-14, 9:271; 11:31). This is followed immediately by the greatest time of tribulation in history (Dan. 12:1-2), which in turn ushers in the disruption of the cosmos ("heavenly signs") and the return of Christ. The scheme is very tightly connected, and Jesus declares at the end that "this generation will not pass away until all these things are fulfilled" (Mark 13:30). Those words alone must have had a tremendous impact on the expectations of the Christian communities that lived through the Jewish-Roman war (unless they were made up during it). Remarkably, the same scenario occurs in Revelation, chapter 6, with the opening of the "seven seals" of the apocalyptic book, and the further details in Revelation, chapter 11, regarding the three and a half years during which the Temple is defiled by the Gentile "beast" power.[13] We get more of this kind of interpretation in the second chapter of 2 Thessalonians, where Paul (or one of his followers) says the Day of the Lord cannot come *until* this wicked ruler, who profanes the Temple, arrives on the scene. This is a remarkable example of just how literally Daniel 11:31ff. was taken by Christian groups.

This means that besides the more general schemes of Hebrew Bible eschatology, and along with the specifics about resurrection of the dead, early Christians were actually watching world events, including political figures and troop movements in the Palestine area, with an eye on Daniel 11:35-12:1.

After the scare of 41 C.E., when it appeared that Caligula would literally fulfill Daniel's predictions by putting his own statue in the Jewish Temple, and the terrible war of 66-70, which resulted in the utter destruction of the Temple—but no return of Christ—it is likely that this kind of apocalyptic fervor began to wane. We see a very general scheme, complete with an exhortation not to scoff or give up on the end-of-the-world hope, in the third chapter of 2 Peter, one of the latest documents of the New Testament. Here, we have a view of the future that can take one ahead several millennia—and it would serve the Christians well. The writer declares that "one day with the Lord is as a thousand years" (2 Pet. 3:8).

Earliest Christianity is often described as a Jewish apocalyptic sect ("end-of-the-world movement"), which, drawing upon Daniel and the Hebrew Prophets, pinned its hopes and dreams of the future on the catastrophic events before, during, and after the Jewish War. What they most expected to happen never came—the return of Jesus on the clouds of heaven to usher in the Kingdom of God. What they least expected to happen was what in fact *did* happen: the utter demise of the Jewish state and the increased power and stability of Rome for the next several centuries. The fact that Christianity survived these disappointments suggests that its center was not solely apocalyptic expectation, but there is no denying that such expectation was active in it.

What is most remarkable about all these images and views of the future, taken from all parts of the Bible, is their amazing flexibility. They were, and continue to be, applied to all kinds of situations and circumstances, always shaping the way readers ask and answer some of their most profound questions.

NOTES

1. Enoch and Elijah are possible exceptions here. Rather than recording the death of Enoch, the geneology of Genesis 5:24 simply says, "He was not, for God took him." Elijah is taken to heaven in a chariot of fire (2 Kings 2).

2. See also Psalms 104 for a celebration of the proper place and created order of Genesis 1. I have generally used the Revised Standard Version translation

of the Bible. However, I have rendered the divine personal name of God as "Yahweh" rather than "the LORD." All emphases within quotations of biblical texts, as well as explanations in brackets, are my own.

3. The "Angel of Yahweh" sometimes appears to be an epiphany of Yahweh himself (Gen. 16:7; 13; 21:17; 19; and Exod. 3:2; 6; 14:19, 21), sometimes his chief representative (Exod. 23:20-21; 33:2-3, 12).

4. The verses that follow (14-15) are sometimes *misunderstood* as offering some hope of life after death or resurrection from the dead. The context makes clear that the answer to Job's question, "If a man die, shall he live again?" is *no*. That is precisely Job's point.

5. In the next verse he asks, "Who knows *whether* the spirit of man goes upward and the spirit of the beast goes down to the earth?"—expressing skepticism about such an idea. See 9:3-10; his view is clearly that death is the end.

6. The main passages are Isaiah 2:2-4, 11-12; 27:12-13, 35, and 66:18-24; Jeremiah 3:15-25; 16:14-21; 23:1-8; and 30-31; Ezekiel 11:14-21, 34:11-31, 36:8-38, 37, and 40-48; Hosea 1:10-11; 2:16-23, and 3:1-5; Joel 3; Amos 9:9-15; Micah 5; Zephaniah 3; Haggai 2; Zecharaiah 10:6-12 and 12-14.

7. This idea of a royal agent of Yahweh, an ideal descendent of David, is linked to various passages in the Psalms (mainly Psalms 2 and 110) that speak of divine priesthood and sonship. All these (King, Priest, and Son) later go into the idea of a heavenly Messiah arriving and bringing about the Kingdom of God.

8. This important section of Isaiah (24-27) is often called the "Isaiah Apocalypse," and it was apparently written much later than Isaiah's time (eighth century B.C.E.). It is one of the earliest examples of apocalyptic material in the Hebrew Bible.

9. There are dozens of passages describing this "great and terrible Day of Yahweh." Some are: Isaiah 2:12-22; 13:9-13; 24; 59:15-19; 63:3-6; and 66:15-16; Jeremiah 25:30-33; Ezekiel 38-39; Joel 2:1-11 and 3:9-15; Zephaniah 1:2-18 and 3:8-13; and Zechariah 14.

10. Unlike the New Testament, the Hebrew Bible does not contain the developed view of a powerful Satan with wicked rebellious angels set in opposition to God. These ideas apparently began to develop in the late Persian period. A hint of the beginning may appear in this late text of Isaiah. The only other book in the Hebrew Bible that contains anything like this is Daniel (written in the second century B.C.E.). In later times, texts such as Isaiah 14:12-14 and Ezekiel 28:11-17 were understood to refer to Satan and his original rebellion against God.

11. The composition and textual transmission of 2 Edras is extremely complicated. The central portion (chapters 3-14) were probably Jewish, written in the first century, but it now contains Christian interpolations, which were composed at a later date.

12. It is not entirely clear whether Isaiah 26:19 and Ezekiel 37 should be

taken as literal references to resurrection of the dead. The latter might be a kind of parable for the regathering of the twelve tribes of Israel.

13. For this reason I think it is likely that the Book of Revelation, at least in these sections, was composed under Nero, as the Jewish-Roman war was breaking out.

FOR FURTHER READING

S. G. F. Brandon. *The Judgement of the Dead.* New York, 1967.

O. Cullman. "Immortality of the Soul and Resurrection of the Dead: the Witness of the New Testament." In *Immortality and Resurrection: Death in the Western World: Two Conflicting Currents of Thought.* Edited by K. Stendahl. New York, 1965. 9-53.

A. Heidel. *The Gilgamesh Epic and Old Testament Parallels.* Chicago, 1963.

John Hick. *Death and Eternal Life.* New York, 1976.

G. Nickelsburg. *Resurrection, Immortality and Eternal Life in Intertestamental Judaism* (HTS 26). Cambridge, 1972.

GOVERNMENT
John Priest

A full account of what the Bible says about government would include a description of the structures of government and a history of their development in Israelite society. Since, however, convenient summaries of these are available in R. de Vaux's *Ancient Israel* and relevant articles in the *Interpreter's Dictionary of the Bible,* let me focus on biblical theories of government, making comments here and there on the function of government.

THE WILDERNESS PERIOD

It is important to remember that most of the written evidence we have concerning the Israelites' "forty year" period of wandering in the wilderness comes from texts inscribed almost a thousand years after the fact. Nonetheless, much of what these texts say about government is clear. Moses is represented as the supreme leader in the wilderness period, but he was not above seeking advice. His father-in-law, Jethro, for example, counsels him to select "able men from all the people, such as fear God, men who are trustworthy and who hate a bribe; and place such men over all the people as rulers of thousands, of hundreds, of fifties, and of tens. And let them judge the people at all times; every great matter they will bring to you, but every small matter they shall decide themselves; so it will be easier for you, and they will bear the burden with you" (Exod. 18:21-22). While divided and delegated authority is assumed, the exact nature of that division and delegation is not explained.

There are three specific instances in Exodus (21:6 and 22:7-8) in which men are ordered to be brought "to the *elohim*" for depositions or judgment. *Elohim* commonly meant "gods" or "God." Although the King James Version renders "elohim" in all three passages as "judges," most modern English translations (including the Revised Standard Version) render the first and third as "God." Judgment between these translations is moot. If one accepts the Revised Standard Version's translation, the conclusion could be that, somehow, judicial decisions came from God, even if they were *implemented* by human instruments (judges, priests, etc.). A theocratic theory is therefore implied by *both* translations.

Exodus 22:28 states, "You shall not revile God, nor curse a ruler of your people." This seems to show that a sacral aura is associated with the ruler, but this text in isolation does not demand such an inference.

The Book of Numbers presents an elaborate picture of the wilderness community. A bewildering number of terms are used to designate the leaders, but neither the distinctions among them nor their precise functions are explicated. (Numbers 31:48-52 is a good example of the confusion.) Numbers lays special emphasis on the congregation/assembly, probably of all free Israelites. This has been thought a "primitive democracy," but this interpretation may be a later idealization. Numbers also has interesting references to shared leadership, especially between Moses and Aaron/Eleazar. A good example is Numbers 27:2: "And they [the daughters of Zelophehad who were seeking their father's inheritance] stood before Moses, and before Eleazar the priest, and before the leaders and all the congregation." (The role of the priesthood in government will be examined in later sections of this article.)

PREMONARCHICAL ISRAEL IN CANAAN

Evidence here is drawn from the Books of Deuteronomy, Joshua, Judges, and the early chapters of 1 Samuel. Deuteronomy purports to be the farewell address of Moses, given just prior to his death and the entrance of the people into the land of Canaan, but it gives a prophetic picture of life as it will be when the Israelites have settled in the Promised Land. Various officials are mentioned, but how they were selected and related is not clear. Sometimes priests and judges share authority (as in Deut. 17:9 and 19:17). In other instances (Deut. 21:5), the priests are the sole arbiters, in others only the judges are mentioned (Deut. 25:2), and in still others the elders stand alone (Deut. 22:13-21).

Deuteronomy 17:14-20, however, is of particular significance:

> When you come to the land that the Lord your God gives you, and you possess it and dwell in it, and then say "I will set a king over me, like all the nations that are round about me"; you may indeed set as king over you him whom the Lord your God will choose. One from among your brethren you shall set as king over you; you may not put a foreigner over you, who is not your brother. Only he must not multiply horses for himself, or cause the people to return to Egypt in order to multiply horses, since the Lord has said to you, "You shall never return that way again." And he shall not multiply wives for himself, lest his heart turn away; nor shall he greatly multiply for himself silver and gold.
>
> And when he sits on the throne of his kingdom, he shall write for himself in a book a copy of this law, from that which is in charge of the Levitical priests; and it shall be with him, and he shall read in it all the days of his life, that he may learn to fear the Lord his God, by keeping all the words of his law and these statutes, and doing them; that his heart may not be lifted up above his brethren, and that he may not turn aside from the commandment, either to the right hand or the left; so that he may continue long in his kingdom, he and his children, in Israel.

It is difficult to miss the allusion to Solomon's horse-trading enterprises, his multiplicity of wives, and his reputed amassing of great wealth. The second section of the passage, however, is more important for our purposes. Although provision is made for monarchy, the king is to govern strictly according to the statutes in the Deuteronomic code (chapters 12-26). The Israelite monarchy is to be a limited one, limited not by any sort of assembly but by the Law of God.

Joshua, chapters 23-24, is often cited as evidence that a twelve-tribe league (an "amphictyony") was the basic structure of premonarchical Israel. This once highly popular view is increasingly under attack.[1] Our concern, however, is not the historical fact but the biblical report, which is supplemented in the Book of Judges. The evidence in Judges is complex, and space limits us to the different reports about "judges" and the divergent attitudes toward monarchy. Some of the so-called "major judges" (charismatic military leaders) are said to continue leadership after their military exploits (10:1-2; 12:7). The stories about "minor judges" (not charismatic leaders in war but those with some undefined governmental function) may indicate that already in this period there was some leadership beyond the local level. This contradictory evidence and the question of the historical reliability of the sources permit no certain understanding of how this government was put together.

Two divergent attitudes toward monarchy are found in Judges. After Gideon had delivered Israel (or a portion thereof) from Midianite oppression, "the men of Israel said to Gideon, 'Rule over us, you, and your son and your grandson also; for you delivered us out of the hand of Midian.' Gideon said to them, 'I will not rule over you, and my son will not rule over you; the Lord will rule over you' " (Judg. 8:22-23). Nevertheless, Abimelech, a half-Canaanite son of Gideon, *did* become king over Shechem and its environs. (The comment in Judges 9:22 that Abimelech ruled over Israel for three years is surely a stylized exaggeration.) This abortive attempt at monarchy, whether limited to a local area or applicable more broadly, came to a disastrous conclusion (Judg. 9:50-57). One part of the narrative recounting Abimelech's career is the most famous fable in the Old Testament. Jotham, the youngest son of Gideon, tells a story of the time when the trees sought to find a king to rule over them. Useful trees, the olive, the fig, and the vine, declined. The bramble (Abimelech) accepted (Judg. 9:7-21).

These passages preserved in Judges take an unfavorable view of kingship. On the other hand, four passages comment that there was then no king in Israel (17:6, 18:1, 19:1, 21:25). The middle two are noncommittal about the consequences of this fact, but the first and the last add, "every man did what was right in his own eyes." The implication is that the chaotic conditions of the time, reflected particularly in chapters 17-21, required a remedy only a king could provide. This chaos formed a prelude to the establishment of the monarchy in 1 Samuel.

THE BEGINNING OF THE MONARCHY

The Books of Samuel are invaluable for understanding biblical views of government. A brief historical setting is in order: The Israelites, having captured most of central and eastern Palestine, were threatened by the Philistines, newly settled in cities along the southwest coast. The Philistines had iron weapons and could raise forces that the local Israelite militia could not hope to match. According to the text of 1 Samuel, the Israelites were saved by Samuel, their last judge, who made his judgeship permanent and tried to make it hereditary. 1 Samuel 7:15-8:3 is instructive.

> Samuel judged Israel all the days of his life. And he went on a circuit year by year to Bethel, Gilgal and Mizpah; and he judged Israel in all these places. Then he would come back to Ramah, for his home was there, and there also he administered justice to Israel. And he built there an altar to the Lord.
>
> When Samuel became old, he made his sons judges over Israel. The name of his first-born son was Joel, and the name of his second, Abijah; they were judges in Beersheba. Yet his sons did not walk in his ways, but turned aside after gain; they took bribes and perverted justice.
>
> Then all the elders of Israel gathered together and came to Samuel at Ramah, and said to him, "Behold you are old and your sons do not walk in your ways; now appoint for us a king to govern us like all the nations." But the thing displeased Samuel when they said, "Give us a king to govern us." And Samuel prayed to the Lord. And the Lord said to Samuel, "Hearken to the voice of the people in all that they say to you, for they have not rejected you, but they have rejected me from being king over them." (8:4-7)

God instructed Samuel to tell the people of all the evils a monarchy would bring, but the people were adamant: "No! but we will have a king over us, that we also may be like all the nations, and that our king may govern us and go out before us and fight our battles" (1 Sam. 8:19b-20). The monarchy came into being because of the people's self-will and had the sanction neither of Samuel, God's spokesman, nor of God himself.

A quite different picture emerges as the story unfolds in 1 Samuel 9:1-10:16. Saul, a young Benjaminite, sought Samuel's help in finding some lost animals. Prior to Saul's arrival, the Lord had already instructed Samuel:

> Tomorrow about this time I will send to you a man from Benjamin, and you shall anoint him to be prince over my people in Israel. He shall save my people from the hand of the Philistines; for I have seen the afflictions of my people, because their cry has come to me. When Samuel saw Saul, the Lord told him, "Here is the man of whom I spoke to you! He it is who shall rule over my people." (1 Sam. 9:16-17)

Here, God takes the initiative in establishing the monarchy. This initiative is ratified by Saul's charismatic defeat of the Ammonites and the public proclamation of his kingship by Samuel, which is accepted with joy by the men of Israel (1 Sam. 11:1-15).

In chapter 12, Samuel renews his criticism of the monarchy. The people are castigated for saying, "No, but a king shall reign over us" when "the Lord your God was King" (1 Sam. 12:12). Indeed, the people are made to admit that "we have added to all our sins this evil, to ask for ourselves a king" (1 Sam. 12:19). Discussion of the causes of this descrepancy lies beyond the scope of this volume.[2] What is relevant here and immediately clear is that in 1 Samuel 8-12 the Bible expresses diametrically diverse attitudes toward monarchical government. On the one hand, the monarchy is a divine gift. This picks up God's assurance that kings should come forth from Abraham (1 Gen. 17:6), Sarah (1 Gen. 17:16), and Jacob (1 Gen. 35:11). Kings are the consequence of the divine promise. On the other hand, the monarch is presented as a *repudiation* of God and his judges.

One additional item requires comment. On three occasions David refrains from slaying Saul because the latter is "the Lord's anointed" (1 Sam. 24:6, 26:9, 23), and in 2 Samuel 1:11-16 David wreaks vengeance upon the Amalekites, who have falsely claimed that they had slain Saul, the Lord's anointed (see 1 Sam. 13:1-6). The sacral nature of the king leads directly to our next section, the Davidic convenant set forth in 2 Samuel 7:1-17.

In this passage David proposes to build a temple for the Lord. The prophet Nathan, however, receives a vision from God prohibiting this action but telling him to make David the following promise:

> The Lord declares to you that the Lord will make you a house. [He says,] "When your days are fulfilled and you lie down with your fathers, I will raise up your son after you, who shall come forth from your body, and I will establish his kingdom. He shall build a house for my name, and I will establish the throne of his kingdom for ever. I will be his father, and he shall be my son. When he commits iniquity, I will chasten him with the rod of men, with the stripes of the sons of men; but I will not take my steadfast love from him, as I took it from Saul, whom I put away from before you. And your house and your kingdom shall be made sure for ever before me; your throne shall be established for ever." In accordance with all these words, and in accordance with all this vision, Nathan spoke to David.

Put in the simplest form, the promise is that there will always be a Davidic king on the throne in Jerusalem. Allusions to this eternal convenant are found clearly in the following passages: 2 Samuel 23:5; 1 Kings 11:36; 2 Kings 8:19; 1 Chronicles 17:3-14, 22:10; Psalms 18:50, 89:3-4, 28-37; and probably Isaiah 31:5, 37:33-35, and 38:8. This list is not exhaustive, but it proves the existence of a tradition that proclaimed not only divine legitimation for the Davidic dynasty but also a divine guarantee of its perpetuity.

Biblical scholars have long proposed that a number of the Psalms that refer to the king form a special category, the Royal Psalms. Two of these, in addition to the ones listed in the previous paragraph, require attention. Psalm 2:7 states, "I will tell of the decree of the Lord: He said to me, 'you are my son, today I have begotten you.' " And Psalm 45:6 says of the king, "Your divine throne endures for ever and ever. Your royal scepter is a scepter of equity."

The first line of 45:6 has been interpreted in a wide variety of ways.[3] No interpretation of this or of Psalms 2:7, however, can support an inference that the Judean king was considered to be divine. (The evidence against this, elsewhere in the Bible, is overwhelming.) They do, however, indicate the extreme boundaries that belief in divine legitimation of an eternal dynasty could reach.[4]

The same biblical books that contain traditions of an eternal unconditional covenant between God and the Davidic dynasty also contain traditions representing that covenant as *conditional.* One somewhat lengthy passage illustrates this:

When Solomon had finished building the house of the Lord . . . the Lord said to him, "I have heard your prayer and your supplication, which you have made before me; I have consecrated this house which you have built, and put my name there for ever; my eyes and my heart will be there for all time. And as for you, if you will walk before me, as David your father walked, with integrity of heart and uprightness, doing according to all I have commanded you, and keeping my statutes and my ordinances, then I will establish your royal throne over Israel forever, as I promised your father David, saying, 'There shall not fail you a man upon the throne of Israel.' But if you turn aside from following me, you and your children, and do not keep my commandments and my statutes which I have set before you, but go and serve other gods and worship them, then I will cut off Israel from the land which I have given them; and the house which I have consecrated for my name I will cast out of my sight; and Israel will

become a proverb and a byword among all peoples. And this house
will become a heap of ruins; every one passing it will be astonished,
and will hiss; and they will say, 'Why has the Lord done thus to this
land and to this house?' Then they will say, 'Because they forsook the
Lord their God who brought their fathers out of the land of Egypt,
and laid hold on other gods, and worshiped them and served them;
therefore the Lord has brought all this evil upon them.' " (1 Kings 9:1-9)

Similar comments are found in 1 Chronicles 28:6-8 and 2 Chronicles
6:16 and 7:19-22.

A curious mixture of the unconditional and conditional appears
again in Psalms 132:11-12:

> The Lord swore to David a sure oath
> from which he will not turn back:
> One of the sons of your body
> I will set on your throne.
> If your sons keep my covenant
> and my testimonies which I shall teach them,
> their sons also forever
> shall sit upon your throne.

Further, Psalm 89—cited above as supporting the unconditional eternal
covenant with the Davidic dynasty—concludes with a passage clearly
written *after the fall* of that dynasty. The author of the conclusion painfully
wrestles with the contradiction between the theological promise and the
historical reality. "But now thou has cast off and rejected, thou art full
of wrath against thy anointed. Thou has renounced the covenant with
thy servant; thou hast defiled his crown in the dust. . . . Lord, where
is thy steadfast love of old, which by thy faithfulness thou didst swear
to David?" (Ps. 89:38-39, 49).

As there are diverse opinions about the establishment of the monarchy
and about its unconditional or conditional nature, so there are
contradictory attitudes in the Bible toward the essential purpose and
function of government. Military protection and social stability have
been mentioned above—see, for example, 1 Samuel 8:20 and Judges
17:6 and 21:25. Above all, however, the ideal was that the king would
administer justice: "So David reigned over all Israel; and David
administered justice and equity to all his people" (2 Sam. 8:15). This
view is stated most eloquently in Psalm 72:

Give the king thy justice, O God,
  and thy righteousness to the royal son!
May he judge thy people with righteousness,
  and thy poor with justice! . . .
May he defend the cause of the poor of the people,
  give deliverance to the needy,
  and crush the oppressor!

*   *   *

For he delivers the needy when he calls,
  the poor and him who has no helper.
He has pity on the weak and the needy,
  and saves the lives of the needy.
From oppression and violence he redeems their life;
  and precious is their blood in his sight.
Psalm 72:1-2, 4, 12-14

These themes reverberate throughout the prophetic material.

Before turning to an examination of the pre-exilic prophets, we need to look at the government in the northern kingdom, which seceded in c. 922 B.C.E. and existed till c. 721 B.C.E.. The editor(s) of the Books of Kings condemned every northern king because they followed their founder Jeroboam I in worshipping golden calves. (See 1 Kings 12, 25-33, especially 28-30.) At least two passages, however, have survived this tendentious schema. 1 Kings 11:26-40 attributes the origin of the northern kingdom to the will of God as proclaimed by a prophet Ahijah. Indeed, the promise of God to the new northern monarch very nearly approximates the promise to David:

And I will take you, and you shall reign over all that your soul desires, and you shall be king over Israel. And if you will hearken to all that I command you, and will walk in my ways, and do what is right in my eyes by keeping my statutes and my commandments, as David my servant did, I will be with you, and will build you a sure house, as I built for David, and I will give Israel to you. (1 Kings 11:37-38)

Further, in 2 Kings 9:1-13 a prophet anoints Jehu as the new king of the North. These passages clearly claim divine legitimation of the monarchy in the North as well as in the South. Government was an implementation of divine intention. Significantly, the fierce opposition of Elijah against Ahab (1 Kings 17-19, 21) is presented as opposition to an oppressive monarch, not to the monarchy as such. (Indeed, in 1 Kings 19:16 Elijah is commissioned to anoint a new king, an act carried out by his successor.) The same is true of the prophets of the eighth century B.C.E. (Amos, Hosea, Isaiah, and Micah) and of Jeremiah in the next century. The prophets denounce royal oppression, or royal worship of other gods, but it is rare, if ever, that they reject monarchy *as such*. Little if any attention is given to political theory (Isaiah, with his attachment to the Davidic covenant, may be an exception). The fact of monarchy is accepted; the acts of the monarchs are assailed.

Amos's pronouncement of the doom of the Jehu dynasty (7:10-17) and Jeremiah's declaration that Jehoiachin shall have no heir on the throne of David (22:30) are not directed against the monarchical principle as such. Even the passages in Hosea often cited as opposing monarchy— 7:3-7; 8:4; 10:7; 15; and 13:11—are directed against the kings (and, more often, the nobles and the people) but not against monarchy. The stress in the prophets is on the necessity of the just behavior of kings (as in Isa. 16:5; Jer. 21:11, 22:1-5, 13-19; Mic. 3:1; etc.).

Two themes in the pre-exilic prophets are developed by later writers. There is a hint of the divine legitimacy of foreign rule (e.g. Jer 29:1; cf. 1 Kings 25:24: "Serve the king of Babylon and it will be well with you"). There is also a forward look to an ideal king, or ideal kings, contrasted with the present miserable failures, who in the future will exercise rule in an appropriate manner (e.g. Isa. 7:14, 9:2-7, 11:1-9; Hos. 3:5; Amos 9:11; Mic. 5:2-4).[5]

THE EXILIC AND POSTEXILIC PERIODS

The exilic prophet responsible for chapters 40-55 of the present Book of Isaiah, commonly designated as 2 Isaiah, manifests no interest in government as such. Perhaps 2 Isaiah 55:3—"I will make with you an everlasting covenant, my steadfast, sure love for David"—represents an extension of the Davidic covenant to the community as a whole, but the evidence is slender. Again, the prophet has a high regard for the Persian conqueror Cyrus. God has roused Cyrus (2 Isa. 41:2, 25), Cyrus is loved by God (2 Isa. 48:14), he is called the shepherd or friend of God (2 Isa. 44:18), and he is even hailed as the anointed (Messiah) of the Lord (2 Isa. 45:1). This could be divine validation of foreign rule, but it does not play such a role in later texts.

The other exilic prophet, Ezekiel, mentions elders, chiefs, princes, kings, and shepherds known in pre-exilic Israel, and also foresees the restored community. The northern Israelites and the Judeans will no longer be divided, but "one king shall be king over them all" (Ezek. 37:22). "My servant David shall be king over them; and they shall all have one shepherd" (Ezek. 37:24). For the most part, however, Ezekiel refers to the head of the restored community not as "king" but as "prince," a civil ruler who, in chapters 40-48, is subordinate to the Zadokite priesthood. This anticipates with amazing accuracy the actual state of affairs in succeeding centuries.

Haggai and Zechariah functioned in Jerusalem c. 520-516 B.C.E. Both expected an early restoration of the Davidic monarchy under the Davidic governor Zerubbabel (Hag. 2:20-23; Zech. 6:9-14). The latter passage, however, contains a serious textual problem:

> And the word of the Lord came to me: "Take from the exiles Hekdai, Tobijah, and Jedaiah . . . silver and gold, and make a crown, and set it upon the head of Joshua, the son of Jehozadak, the high priest; and say to him, 'Thus says the Lord of hosts, "Behold the man whose name is the Branch: for he shall grow up in his place, and he shall build the temple of the Lord . . . and shall bear royal honor, and shall sit and rule upon his throne. And there shall be a priest by his throne, and peaceful understanding shall be between them both. And the crown shall be in the temple of the Lord as a reminder to Heldai, Tobijah, Jedaiah, and Josiah and the son of Zephaniah." ' "

Unfortunately, the word "crown" in both verses 11 and 14 is plural in the standard Hebrew text. Further, though the standard text designates Joshua the high priest as the recipient of the crown(s), it also designates the recipient as one who will sit upon the throne, bear royal honor, and have a priest by his side. Finally, the recipient is named "the Branch." ("Branch," in Isaiah 4:2 and Jeremiah 23:5 and 33:15 refers to a future king, and in Zechariah 3:8 surely refers to Zerubbabel.)

Thus the foretold relations between king and priest, Zerubbabel and Joshua, are hopelessly obscure. (We recall those between Moses and Aaron, and later judges and priests.) Some have conjectured that before the exile the authority resided with kings, after the exile with high priests; so Zechariah 6 may reflect a transition. In any event, the monarchy was not restored, and governmental authority was in fact shared between the Jewish priesthood and civil officials appointed by foreign powers.[6]

Jews were under foreign rule for the rest of the biblical period. Such rule, in the preserved books at least, is simply taken for granted. Ezra and Nehemiah are friendly to the Persian authorities. (See, for example, Ezra 7:21-28.) The Book of Esther, though it tells of a potential pogrom, represents the Persian monarch as favorable to the Jews (after he learns that Esther is one). Only with the rise of apocalyptic literature is foreign rule called into question, and even then the issue is not political theory but political practice. As the prophets accepted the monarchy in principle, so postexilic Judaism accepted foreign rule. The question was the ruler's actions. But before turning to the apocalyptic attitude, we must say something of Proverbs.

Proverbs

Systematic analysis of a collection of proverbs is difficult because there is usually no historical reference and often no thematic coherence. The following schema, therefore, has an admittedly artificial flavor.

First, the authors of Proverbs accept monarchy as a fact of life and, on the whole, as a beneficial institution. "When a land transgresses it has many rulers; but with men of understanding and knowledge its stability will long continue" (Prov. 28:2). It is commonly agreed that Proverbs represents the views of the upper stratum of society for whom maintenance of the status quo is ideologically and practically desirable. We thus find admonitions of deference toward rulers: "My son, fear the Lord and the king, and do not disobey either of them; for disaster from them will rise suddenly, and who knows the ruin that will come from both?" (Prov. 24:21-22).

Like the prophets, the authors of Proverbs urge kings to rule with justice and righteousness: "Open your mouth for the dumb, for the rights of all who are left desolate. Open your mouth, judge righteously, maintain the rights of the poor and needy" (Prov. 31:8-9). (See also Prov. 16:12; 20:8, 26, 28; 28:15-16; and 29:2, 4, and 14.)

Finally, in Proverbs there are hints that divine guidance is given to kings/rulers. "By me [wisdom says] kings reign, and rulers decree what is just; by me princes rule, and nobles govern the earth" (Prov. 8:15-16). (See also Prov. 16:10 and 21:1). Not too much should be made of this. The authors of Proverbs were well aware that there could be evil rulers who denied and distorted divine guidance.

Daniel

The Book of Daniel represents a radical shift both in literary genre and ideology: the rise of the apocalyptic. Apocalyptic thinking is often the product of frustrated political and social ambitions and of religious persecution. We cannot here speak of this complex phenomenon except as it relates to the issue of government.[7]

Comments on government in Daniel are of a quite varied nature, but they may be organized under three categories. (1) Human empires exist under the dominion of God, who removes kings and sets up kings (2:21), has given the kingdom to Nebuchadnezzar (2:37), who rules over the kingdoms of men (4:17, 26; 5:18-23), and who must be acknowledged by earthly monarchs (4:34-37). (2) All earthly kingdoms will finally be replaced by God's kingdom (2:44; 4:3, 34; 6:26; 7:13-27). (3) There are hints of the evil, even demonic nature of the world's empires (3:1-23, 7:1-18, 8:5-26). (4) There are oblique references to "princes" (*sarim*) of various kingdoms, including Persia (10:13), Greece (10:20), and Israel (10:21, 12:1). Since the "prince" of Israel is specifically identified as the angel Michael, we may infer that the "princes" of Persia and Greece are the "guardian angels" of those nations. Above earthly kingdoms are heavenly beings supporting and legitimating (?) those kingdoms. We shall return to this theme in comments on Romans 13:1-7.

Deutero-canonical/Apocryphal Writings

These books contain valuable supplementary evidence about the Bible and government but provide little new information. They confirm or augment our knowledge of Greek equivalents of Hebrew terms for governmental leaders already available in the Septuagint, and they allude, albeit indirectly, to Jewish governmental structure in the late Hellenistic period. (See especially Judith 4:8; 6:14, 21; 8:11, 35; 9:3; 15:8). Unfortunately, the function of the elders, the magistrates, the rulers, the princes, and above all the senate (*gerousia*) is no clearer here than in the books of the Hebrew canon.

Esther 16:16-18 claims that the Persian king recognized that the God of the Jews directed his kingdom; Baruch 1:11 calls for prayer for the king of Babylon; and 2 Esdras 11-13, 15-16 and the narratives in 1 and 2 Maccabees reflect a hostile attitude toward foreign rulers opposed to God and his people. All of these views are, in one way or another, in continuity with earlier biblical materials. We may, however, call special attention to two works: Sirach (also known as Ecclesiasticus) and The Wisdom of Solomon.

The former generally shares the outlook of the Book of Proverbs. Rulers are to be respected and obeyed, but rulers are to rule justly, for "The government of the earth is in the hands of the Lord, and over it he will raise up the right man for the time" (Sir. 10:4). Further, Sirach affirms that God has "appointed a ruler for every nation" (17:17). This could imply divine legitimation of monarchy, but it is clear that monarchs must be responsive to the just claims of their people.

A passage in The Wisdom of Solomon has often been adduced to support divine authority for the governing powers:

> Listen therefore, O kings, and understand;
> learn O Judges of the ends of the earth.
> Give ear, you that rule over multitudes,
> and boast of many nations.
> For your dominion was given you from the Lord,
> and your sovereignty from the Most High,
> who will search out your works and inquire into your plans.
>
> (Wis. of Sol. 6:1-3)

The context, however, makes it clear that the divine gift of kingship is dependent upon the proper behavior of kings and rulers (see Wis. of Sol. 6:4-11, 12:14). Good rulers are the gift of God, but not all rulers may claim divine authority.

THE NEW TESTAMENT

Few texts in the New Testament refer directly to government. This is understandable, for two reasons. First, the Christian community in the first century was politically impotent and relatively disengaged from the larger concerns of society and politics. Second, at least until the very end of that century, there remained the conviction that "this age" was about to pass away and be replaced by the "age to come," where earthly institutions, including government, would be of no consequence. Since "this age" did not in fact pass away, the few, sometimes casual New Testament comments about government assumed enormous consequence in the following centuries of Christendom. Therefore, they require careful consideration.

The Synoptic Gospels

Only one passage in the Synoptic Gospels—and it is found in all three—bears directly upon the question of the nature of government:[8]

> And they sent him some of the Pharisees and some of the Herodians to entrap him in his talk. And they came and said to him, "Teacher, we know that you are true, and care for no man; for you do not regard the position of men, but truly teach the way of God. Is it lawful to pay taxes to Caesar or not? Should we pay them, or should we not?" But knowing their hypocrisy, he said to them, "Why put me to the test? Bring me a coin, and let me look at it." And they brought one. And he said to them, "Whose likeness and inscription is this?" They said to him, "Caesar's." Jesus said to them, "Render to Caesar the things that are Caesar's, and to God the things that are God's." And they were amazed at him. (Mark 12:13-17; Matt. 22:15-22; Luke 20:20-26)

All three accounts affirm that Jesus' enemies were attempting to entrap him. If Jesus answers affirmatively, he will lose favor with those who oppose payment. If he answers negatively, he will come into direct conflict with the Roman authorities. Any number of explanations of what he did answer have been proposed, but all still leave us with these questions: What are the things of Caesar? And what are the things of God? The text simply does not provide a sure answer. Taken at face value, it seems to imply that *some* things are Caesar's, and that the civil government has *some* legitimate claims. But for what?

John

Although there are a number of tangential references to government in this gospel, three passages are of special import. After Pilate asks, "Are you the King of the Jews" (John 18:33), Jesus answers: "My kingship [kingdom] is not of this world; if my kingship were of this world my servants would fight, that I might not be handed over to the Jews; but my kingship [kingdom] is not from this world" (John 18:36). In the second passage Pilate says, "Do you not know that I have power to release you, and power to crucify you?" (John 19:10). Jesus answers, "You would have no power over me unless it had been given you from above; therefore he who delivered me to you has the greater sin" (John

19:11). In the final passage Pilate says to the Jews, "Here is your king!" They reply: "We have no king but Caesar" (John 19:14-15).

We may infer that (for John) the Jewish leaders accepted the legitimacy of foreign (Roman) rule. We may also infer, though it is certainly not emphasized, that Jesus (for John) assumed that governmental power was derived from and subject to the sovereign power of God. More important, however, is the affirmation that the kingdom (kingship) of Jesus is of an order different from kingship in this world. (See Paul's comment in Philippians 3:20: "But our commonwealth (colony) is in heaven.") The nature and role of earthly governments are of no real consequence. God's kingdom, in the person of Jesus, is of a totally different order.

Acts

The testimony of Acts regarding government is given by a number of passages favorable towards Roman officials and the Roman state (e.g. 16:35-39, 18:12-17, 19:23-41, 22:22-29, 23:26-30, 25:8-12, 26:30-32). This may fit the author's intention to portray Christianity with compatible to established society, but it says nothing on the issue of government as such.

Romans

Together with the Synoptic references to the payment of tribute to Caesar, the New Testament passage that has exercised the most influence on discussions of the Bible and government is Romans 13:1-7:

> Let every person be subject to the governing authorities. For there is no authority except from God, and those that exist have been instituted by God. Therefore he who resists the authorities resists what God has appointed, and those who resist will incur judgment. For rulers are not a terror to good conduct, but to bad. Would you have no fear of him who is in authority? Then do what is good, and you will receive his approval, for he is God's servant for your good. But if you do wrong, be afraid, for he does not bear the sword in vain; he is the servant of God to execute his wrath on the wrongdoer. Therefore one must be subject, not only to avoid God's wrath but also for the sake of conscience. For the same reason you also pay taxes, for the authorities are ministers of God, attending to this very

thing. Pay all of them their dues, taxes to whom taxes are due, revenue to whom revenue is due, respect to whom respect is due, honor to whom honor is due.

Like the Synoptic passages, this has been interpreted in diverse ways. The crucial issue is, in my judgment, who are these authorities instituted by God?

Paul, in keeping with the dominant Hellenistic-Jewish view, assumes that the civil authorities derive their authority from God. The state has divine legitimation. A few scholars think the "authorities" are the heavenly beings exercising sovereignty over this world. In either case, subjection to the state is a religious obligation. (See C. Morrison, *The Powers*, and the discussion of Dan. 10:13, 20, 21; 12:1 above.)

Since the state has divine legitimation, civil officials are to be considered God's servants. They maintain the fabric of a society willed by God. (Cf. the statement by Rabbi Hanani: "Pray for the peace of the ruling power, since but for fear of it men would have swallowed up each other alive." *Aboth* 3.2, in H. Danby, *Mishnah*, 450.)

I Timothy

One passage from this letter may be cited: "First of all, then, I urge that supplications, prayers, intercessions, and thanksgivings be made for all men, for kings and all who are in high positions, that we may lead a quiet and peaceable life, godly and respectful in every way" (2:1-2). Although submission to the authorities is not required, it is suggested, and the suggestion is confirmed by another letter.

Titus

Titus, probably from the same author, writes

Remind them [the Christians in Titus's care] to be submissive to rulers and authorities, to be obedient, to be ready for any honest work, to speak evil of no one, to avoid quarreling, to be gentle, and to show perfect courtesy toward all men. (3:1-2)

This passage echoes Romans 13:1-7—the Greek words translated "rulers" and "authorities" are the same—and apparently interprets Paul's teaching there as simple advice to be obedient to the civil powers.

II Thessalonians[9]

Since this passage has been adduced as a witness of attitudes toward the state, a brief comment is in order. The author (Paul?) is attempting to convince his readers that the time of the end will be delayed until certain events transpire. These include the coming of the "man of lawlessness," "who opposes and exalts himself against every so-called god or object of worship, so that he takes his seat in the temple of God, proclaiming himself to be God" (2:3-4). The crucial passage for our purposes follows: "And you know what is restraining him now so that he may be revealed in his time. For the mystery of lawlessness is already at work; only he who now restrains [it will do so] until he is out of the way" (2:6-7).

It has been suggested—unreliably—that the restraining force is the Roman state. If so, that government would here be regarded favorably (if the author thought it were restraining the man of lawlessness, not the power coming to punish him). These are only two of the many possible guesses, so this passage provides no solid evidence of New Testament attitudes toward government.

I Peter

A passage of only slightly less importance than Romans 13:1-7 is 1 Peter 2:13-17:

> Be subject for the Lord's sake to every human institution, whether it be to the emperor as supreme, or to governors as sent by him to punish those who do wrong and to praise those who do right. For it is God's will that by doing right you should put to silence the ignorance of foolish men. Live as free men, yet without using your freedom as a pretext for evil; but live as servants of God. Honor all men. Love the brotherhood. Fear God. Honor the emperor.

The subjection to the civil authorities here commanded is remarkable because the letter alludes elsewhere to persecution of Christians (4:12-5:5). Christians should obey the state *even when being persecuted.*

Revelation

All of the New Testament texts examined thus far portray a favorable, or at least a neutral, attitude toward the state. The Book of Revelation does not. Whatever the precise meanings of its esoteric symbolism, its hostility to Rome is clear. We shall limit our examination to those passages thought to refer to the Roman Empire or to the Roman emperor, especially those that speak of the Dragon, the beast(s), and the false prophet. The "dragon" (12:3, 4, 7, 9, 13, 16, 17; 12:2, 4, 11; 16:13; 20:2) is identified as "that ancient serpent, who is called the Devil and Satan, the deceiver of the whole world" (12:9). He and his angels war in heaven against Michael. Defeated, he comes to earth to war on those who bear testimony to Jesus (12:7-17). Defeated again, he is left in a pit for a thousand years (20:2). Let loose for a little while, the dragon is again defeated. With the beast and the false prophet, it is cast into a lake of fire for eternal torment (20:7-20).

The dragon gives authority to the beast (13:1-4), but *which* beast? One comes from the "bottomless pit" (11:7, 17:8), another from the "sea" (13:1), another from the "earth" (13:11). At least two appear together in 13:11-18:

> Then I saw another beast which rose out of the earth; it had two horns like a lamb and it spoke like a dragon. It exercises all the authority of the first beast in its presence, and makes the earth and its inhabitants worship the first beast, whose mortal wound was healed. It works great signs, even making fire come down from heaven to earth in the sight of men; and by the signs which it is allowed to work in the presence of the beast, it deceives those who dwell on earth, bidding them make an image for the beast which was wounded by the sword and yet lived; and it was allowed to give breath to the image of the beast so that the image of the beast should even speak, and to cause those who will not worship the image of the beast to be slain. Also it causes all, both small and great, both rich and poor, both free and slave, to be marked on the right hand or the forehead, so that no one can buy or sell unless he has the mark, that is, the name of the beast or the number of its name. This calls for wisdom: let him who has understanding reckon the number of the beast, for it is a human number; its number is six hundred and sixty-six.[10]

How does all this relate to government? Most commentators have identified the beast as the Roman Empire or the Roman emperor. This identification is made practically certain by the association of the "great harlot" with the beast in chapter 17. The harlot is seated on seven hills (Rome) and is identified as "the great city which has dominion over the kings of the earth," and as Babylon (18:2, 10), often a code name for Rome (cf. 1 Pet. 5:13). The beast, the Roman government, receives its authority from the Dragon, Satan. City and government alike are in no way legitmated by God, but are empowered by his ultimate enemy.[11] This, of course, contradicts the position of Paul, and it can hardly be reconciled with what Jesus said. So just as there is no single Old Testament stance toward government, neither is there one in the New Testament.

NOTES

1. See the discussion by A. D. H. Mayes in *Israelites and Judean History,* 297-308.

2. Modern historical and literary analyses are in general agreement. See B. Anderson, *Understanding the Old Testament,* 206-210.

3. The citation in the text is from the *Revised Standard Edition,* which gives in footnotes the variants "your throne is a throne of God" and "your throne, O God."

4. On sacral kingship in Israel, see A. Johnson, *Sacral Kingship,* and R. de Vaux, *Ancient Israel,* 100-114.

5. Some of these references *may* represent postexilic additions. Be that as it may, they are now what the Bible says. We must recognize here their certain presence, regardless of their conjectural origin.

6. On Haggai and Zechariah, see P. Ackroyd, *Exile and Restoration,* 183-200.

7. On apocalyptic thinking, see P. Hanson, *Interpreter's Dictionary of the Bible: Supplement,* 28-34 (with bibliography).

8. I omit Mathew 17:24-27. In its present form it refers to the payment of the temple tax to which Jesus, if a pious Jew, might have had no objection. If it is a post-70-C.E. composition of the church, when the Romans continued to collect the tax even though the Temple had been destroyed, it might well be considered an analogue to the "render unto Caesar" passage.

9. On this letter, see J. Bailey, *Interpreter's Bible,* vol. 11, esp. 326-330.

10. The letters of the Greek alphabet were also used as numbers, so every name had a numerical value, the sum of those of its letters.

11. For a brief but judicious account, see J. Bowman, *Interpreter's Dictionary of the Bible,* 4, 381-82.

WORKS CITED AND FURTHER READING

P. Ackroyd. *Exile and Restoration*. Philadelphia, 1968.

B. Anderson. *Understanding the Old Testament*. Fourth edition. Garden City, 1986.

J. Bailey. *Interpreter's Bible*. Volume 11. Nashville, Tennessee, 1955. 249-251, 325-330.

J. Bowman. *Interpreter's Dictionary of the Bible*. Volume 1. Nashville, Tennessee, 1962. 368-369.

———. *Interpreter's Dictionary of the Bible*. Volume 4. Nashville, Tennessee, 1962. 381-382.

O. Cullmann. *The State in the New Testament*. New York, 1956.

H. Danby. *The Mishnah*. London, 1933.

R. de Vaux. *Ancient Israel*. Translated by J. McHugh. London, 1961.

P. Hanson. *Interpreter's Dictionary of the Bible: Supplement*. Nashville, Tennessee, 1976. 28-34.

A. Johnson. *Sacral Kingship in Ancient Israel*. Cardiff, 1955.

A. Mayes. In *Israelite and Judean History*. Edited by J. Hayes and J. Miller. Philadelphia, 1977. 297-308.

C. Morrison. *The Powers That Be*. London, 1960.

MARRIAGE AND DIVORCE
Gerald A. Larue

According to the Bible the purpose of marriage is to produce a family and establish a household. In the earliest creation myth, which scholars call the Bible's "J source," Yahweh stated, "It is not good for man to be alone" (Gen. 2:18). The woman who was created and who became the man's mate was the response to that situation. In the Priestly account, called the "P source," humans are instructed, "Be fruitful, multiply, and fill the earth" (Gen. 1:28). Psalmists rhapsodized about large families:

> Behold, sons are a gift from Yahweh,
> The fruit of the womb is a reward . . .
> Happy is the man who has
> his quiver filled with them! (127:3,5)

*　　*　　*

> Your wife will be like a fruitful vine
> within your house;
> your children will be like olive shoots
> around your table. (128:3)

Indeed, the procreative concept was so important that males in biblical times often acquired several mates as a way of guaranteeing large numbers of offspring.

Despite the Bible's emphasis on the importance of reproduction, and despite the acceptance of the joy of sex expressed in the Song of

Solomon, there was expressed in Jewish legislation a notion to the effect that sexual intercourse somehow rendered a couple ceremonially unclean: "If a man lies with a woman and has an emission of semen, both of them shall bathe themselves in water, and be unclean until the evening" (Lev. 15:18). When Moses descended from Mount Sinai to consecrate the Hebrews, he told the males, "Do not go near a woman" (Exod. 19:15). During war, soldiers were not to have sexual contact with women (1 Sam. 21:4-5 and 2 Sam. 11:11). Religious rites and holy wars involved the deity who was, apparently, offended by sexual intercourse.

The terms most commonly used to refer to the family include "house" in the Old Testament (Gen. 14:14; Ruth 4:11) and "household" in the New Testament (John 4:53; 1 Cor. 16:15; Phil.4:22). In addition to those bound by marriage or bloodlines, the family could also include concubines, slaves, servants, resident aliens, widows, and orphans (Gen. 17:23,27; 46:5-7; Isa. 49:43; Matt. 10:35-6; 1 Tim. 5:16). Furthermore, the family was not an isolated unit; it was extended and acknowledged affinity to the larger clan or tribe (Gen. 10:20; Exod. 6:14; Luke 2:4).

So closely knit was the familial unit that it could be said to have composed a "psychic unity" (Pedersen, *Israel,* I-II, 50) or a "corporate personality" (Robinson, "Corporate Personality," 49ff.), by which the group appeared to have an identity of its own. This "corporate unity" could be understood as extending backward and forward in time to encompass the dead and those not yet born. Indeed, the actions of the past could affect the present, just as the present could make an impact on the future (Exod. 20:5, 34:7; Deut. 5:9, 23:2; Jer. 31:29-30; Ezek. 18:2; John 9:2). Injury or misfortune happening to one member implicated the entire body, and called for repayment or redemptive action by the next-of-kin, the "redeemer" or, in a sense, "protector" (Num. 35:19; Deut. 19:4-10; 2 Sam. 3:27).

The father was the head of the family, and he had life-and-death control over family members (Exod. 21:7, 15-17; Deut. 13:6-10; Judg. 11:30-40). The capable parent was one who could manage his household (1 Tim. 3:4), and who would protect (Deut. 1:31), love, nourish (Hos. 11:1-3), and teach his children (Ps. 78:4; Prov. 1:8; Joel 1:2-3), without provocation to anger (Eph. 6:4; Col. 3:22), to lead an acceptable life (1 Thess. 2:11). At the same time, the father was expected to discipline his offspring (Prov. 13:24; Sir. 7:23-24; Eph. 6:1). The mother's influence could be exerted in important decisions (Gen. 21:10; 27:11-17; Judg. 17:2-6). She, too, was to teach (Prov. 1:8, 6:20) and provide a model for her offspring (Prov. 31:28). Children were commanded to honor their parents (Exod. 20:12; Deut. 5:16; Sir. 3:2-16; Eph. 6:1), to heed their instruction (Prov. 1:8; 4:1-4; 5:20, 15:5), to obey (Prov. 6:20, Eph. 6:1, Col. 3:20), to be exemplary and make their parents proud (Prov. 10:1, 15:20), and to be aware of the debt they owed to them (Sir. 7:27-28).

In general, all children were greatly prized (Ps. 127:5, 128:3, Prov. 17:6), but sons were preferred over daughters. After all, it was through sons that a man's name was continued. Moreover, the son's family was expected to care for his parents (Ps. 127:3-5). When daughters married, they became members of their spouse's household, their children continued their husband's family line, and the productivity of the household went to sustain the husband's family. Special laws are preserved concerning the sale of daughters into slavery (Exod. 21:7), although through debt entire families could enter into bondage (Lev. 25:39ff).

Children enjoyed few rights. Rebellious ne'er-do-wells were considered an abomination (Sir. 16:1-3). Should a son curse or strike his parents, he was killed (Exod. 21:15-17; Lev. 20:9; Deut. 27.16; Prov. 30:11). During certain periods children were sacrificed to Yahweh (Judg. 11:30-40; 1 Kings 16:34) or to "Molech" (2 Kings 23:10; Jer. 32:35). The Torah's command to sacrifice the first-born son (Exod. 13:1, 22:29) was modified by provisions for substitutionary sacrifice by which the child was redeemed (Exod. 13:13; Num. 18:15). The legend of Abraham's near-sacrifice of his son, Isaac, may have been composed as a teaching story to justify the substitution of a sacrificial animal for the child (Gen. 22). Ultimately the practice was outlawed (Exod. 34:20, Deut. 18:10).

The notion of child sacrifice was revived in Christianity. The crucifixion of Jesus, who, in Christian theology, was described as the first and only child of Yahweh (John 3:16; Rom. 8:32), was explained as a sacrificial offering in fulfillment of the divine will, despite the fact that this theological interpretation marked a symbolic return to a parental savagery long abandoned by the Jews (Larue, "Surviving," 145, and *Humanism and Easter,* 16).

Marriage and the production of families are not central concerns in the letters written by Paul. Because he erroneously believed that he was living in the end-time and that the miraculous Kingdom of God would soon be instituted by the return of Jesus, he discouraged marriage except in situations where passion could not be controlled (1 Cor. 7:8-9, 25-26).

Marriage

As one might expect in a literature that evolved over a one-thousand-year period, there are differing emphases on the nature of marriage. There is consistency in that the purpose of marriage was to constitute a family and produce offspring and the head of the family was the husband and father.

In the Hebrew scriptures, there is no single word for "marriage." Marriage occurred when a man "took" a wife (Gen. 19:14; 2 Chron. 13:21), or when a man "gave" his daughters in marriage (Gen. 29:19,28; Exod. 2:21, etc.) The Hebrew word translated "betroth" may refer to a woman who was engaged but who had not been "taken" sexually. The term can also signify "wife," in that a betrothed woman could be brought to judgment as a married woman if she engaged in illicit sex before marriage (Deut. 22:23-24). Betrothal was considered the equivalent of marriage (Deut. 28:30, 2 Sam. 3:14). Betrothed men could be recognized as sons-in-law by the woman's father (Gen. 19:14).

In the New Testament, the Greek term for "betrothal" could refer to a promise of marriage (Matt. 1:18; Luke 1:27) and to marriage without sex (Matt. 1:24-5). The root word meaning "to marry" could be used with either sex (1 Cor. 7:33,34), but only the woman was "given" in marriage (Mark 12:25). The New Testament term for "marriage" can refer to the state of being married (Heb. 13:4), to wedding festivities (John 2:1-2), or to the marriage feast (Matt. 22:2, 25:10).

The tenth-century-B.C.E. temple literature, the J source, opens with the story of Adam and Eve, the first couple and the mythical parents of all humankind. Although the account makes no reference to marriage, the story came to be accepted as providing a divine basis for wedlock (Tob. 8:6; Matt. 19:5 and parallels; Eph. 5:31; 1 Tim. 2:13-15). The male, Adam, molded from the earth, was animated by the breath of Yahweh. After innumerable attempts and failures to find an acceptable counterpart and companion for Adam, Yahweh anesthetized him and extracted a rib from his body from which he shaped a female human. The J storyteller, who delighted in assonantal puns, placed the following words in the mouth of the man:

> At last! This is the one!
> Bone from my bones, flesh from my flesh,
> this one shall be called woman ['ishsahah]
> because she was taken from man ['ish]. (Gen. 2:23)

The author then states:

> This is why a man leaves his father and mother and is bonded to
> his wife, and the two become one flesh (2:24).

In general, the word *'ish* means "male" or "a male human being,"
but in particular circumstances it signifies a married man, a husband.
The word *ba'al* may refer to the husband as one who marries or takes
possession of a wife (Deut. 22:22; Prov. 12:4, 31:11, etc.). It may also
signify a man as owner of a slave (Exod. 21:4) or an animal (Exod.
21:28; Isa. 1:3) or property (Exod. 21:34; Eccl. 5:12). The verbal form,
when used to signify marriage, conveys the sense of ownership or possession
(Deut. 21:13, 24:1). A married man can thus be referred to as the husband
or master of a woman (Exod. 21:3,22). A bride or a wife may be designated
as a woman owned or possessed by a man (Gen. 20:3, Deut. 22:22).
She was known by his name (Isa. 4.1). Male dominance and feminine
destiny are stipulated in Yahweh's punishment of Eve:

> I will severely increase your pain during childbearing,
> You shall bring forth children in pain,
> Yet your desire will be for your husband
> And he shall rule over you. (Gen. 3:16)

The same relational pattern is reflected in Genesis 3:20, when Adam
names his wife "Eve" ("life-bearer"), for to be able to name is to possess
the power to determine identity. The primacy of the male, based on
the Genesis story, is validated in the New Testament (1 Tim. 2:13), where
wives are advised to recognize the husband as the family "head" (Eph.
5:22-23). After all, Paul argued, the woman was created out of the man
and for the man's sake, not vice versa (1 Cor. 11:8-9).

Despite the statement in Genesis 2:24, and its reaffirmation in
Ephesians 5:31, there is no biblical evidence that proves it was customary
for a male to forsake his parents at marriage. On the contrary, the practice
was for the wife to break with her family and join her husband's unit
(Ps. 45:14f.). Some scholars have suggested that the Genesis passages
may reflect survival of an early matriarchal cultural pattern. In a matri-
archy, family authority rests with the mother, and kinship or consan-
guinity is traced through her. The mother's family line is dominant, and
she is the name-giver. There are some instances in the Bible where the
woman names the child (Gen. 4:1, 25, cf. 5:3; 16:11, cf. v. 15; 19:37-

8, etc.); in others the father determined the name (Gen. 4:26; 5:3,28-29; 16:15, etc.). Where the mother's family was important, the son's relationship might be traced through her. For example Joab and Abishai are known as sons of Zeruiah, King David's sister (1 Sam. 26:6; 2 Sam. 2:13). All in all, commentators have found insufficient evidence to demonstrate that a matriarchal pattern ever existed in ancient Israel (Gordon, *Introduction,* 22; Baab, "Marriage," 279).

Genesis 2:24 has been interpreted as perhaps reflecting a relationship which has matriarchal overtones (Patterson, "Marriage" 264), in which the married couple remained with the wife's family and the husband severed relationships with his own group. The children would be raised as members of the wife's family. The biblical examples usually cited are those of Jacob (Gen. 29:1-30) and Moses (Exod. 2:21f.), which form part of J's hero fiction. Both men live for lengthy periods with their wives' families. Neither story, however, implies that these living arrangements were anything more than expediency. Jacob lived and worked for his in-laws to pay the bride-price needed for his marriages to Leah and Rachel. Moses stayed with Zipporah's family because it was convenient to do so; he was a murderer, fleeing for his life. In neither case did the living arrangements prevail longer than necessary.

It has also been suggested that Genesis 2:24 refers to a type of marriage that occurred when the woman continued to live with her kinfolk and her husband paid her periodic visits (Smith, *Kinship,* 93-4), which implies a matriarchal pattern. There are only two possible biblical references to such marriage. One concerns Gideon, who lived with his numerous wives in Ophrah, while his concubine, who bore his son Abimelech, lived in Schechem (Judg. 8:27, 31). The other is the legend of Samson, who married a Philistine woman but never sexually consummated the relationship (Judg. 14-15). Samson left the wedding celebration in a fit of pique because, with the help of his bride, the wedding guests solved his riddle. To preserve family dignity, the father gave the now mateless woman to Samson's companion. Much later, his anger having subsided, Samson returned to claim his bride, who was now the wife of another. Apparently the woman still occupied the bridal chamber in her parent's home (15:1). On the assumption that the woman would continue such a living arrangement and that her husband would occasionally visit her, some have suggested that the account may demonstrate such a "visiting husband" marriage.

The term "to be bonded" in Genesis 2:24 cannot be interpreted as concerned with natural "drive" (Von Rad, *Genesis,* 83) but seems to signify a closeness that is both covenanted, as in Israel's relationship to Yahweh (Deut. 10:20), and physical, as in the relationship of skin to bones (Job 19:20). The bonding of husband and wife takes priority over the natural bond of son and parents (Driver, *Genesis,* 43). On the basis of Genesis 2:24, Jesus taught that the marriage covenant created a new, indissoluble familial unit (Mark 10:2-9 and parallels). The notion of "one flesh" in Genesis 2:24 may have been intended to subtly and perhaps humorously imply that through marriage the man becomes a whole person again—regaining, so to speak, his missing rib. The statement cannot be taken as an intentional affirmation of monogamy (Simpson, "Genesis," 500). Nevertheless the union of man and wife was implied by Paul when he advised Corinthian Christians concerning conjugal rites that "the wife does not rule over her body, but the husband does; also, the husband not rule over his body, but the wife does" (1 Cor. 7:4). This same notion, albeit with a metaphorical and mystical interpretation, is reflected in Ephesians 5:28-33.

In Judges 5:30, a captured young woman is referred to as a "womb," that is, a potential child-bearer. The wife who was unable to fulfill her maternal role was a failure. Hannah cried and sulked when she was infertile (1 Sam 1:7). Sarah, in desperation over her barrenness, gave her maid, Hagar, to Abraham as a mate to bear a son (Gen. 16:3). Rachel, angry because she had not given birth, demanded offspring from her husband: "Give me children or I will die" (Gen. 30:1). Her infertility was assumed to be caused by Yahweh. She gave her maid Bilhah to Jacob, saying, "copulate with her, so that she may give birth upon my knees and I will have children through her" (Gen 30:3). Women squatted to give birth; Bilhah would have squatted across Rachel's knees and the child would have been delivered between Rachel's legs. This symbolic birth ritual made it possible for Rachel to claim that she had fulfilled her feminine role: "Elohim judged me, he heard my voice and gave me a son" (30:6).

Monogamy appears to have been the accepted practice in ancient Israel (Gen. 25:20, 41:50; Jth. 8:2; Tob. 2:1, 11.5), but there was also bigamy and polygamy. Lamech, a descendent of Cain, had two wives, Adah and Zillah (Gen. 4:19). Elkanah, a villager, married Hannah and Penninah (1 Sam. 1:2). The fact that the Deuteronomists found it necessary to deal with inheritance problems arising out of bigamy suggests that the practice must have been widespread (Deut. 21:15).

Not only could men of power and wealth support numerous wives, they could also have concubines and copulate with slave women. Abraham sired Ishmael by Hagar, his wife's slave (Gen. 16:1-4). Jacob married both Leah and her sister Rachel; he also produced offspring through his wives' slaves, Zilpah and Bilhah (Gen. 30:1-24). Esau had numerous wives (Gen. 36:1-5), as did Gideon, the hero from the tribe of Manasseh (Judg. 8:30). King David married Saul's daughter, Michal (1 Sam. 18:27), Nabal's widow, Abigail (1 Sam. 25:42), Ahinoam of Jezreel (1 Sam. 25:43), plus four other wives (2 Sam. 3:2-5) while he was in Hebron. When he took control of Jerusalem, he added more wives and concubines to his harem (2 Sam. 5:13-16). These latter appear to have been politically expedient marriages, which helped cement relationships between the leading citizens of Jerusalem and their new foreign monarch. His last wife was Bathsheba, the widow of one of David's soldiers, Uriah the Hittite, for whose death David was directly responsible (2 Sam. 11).

David's relationship to Abishag the Shunnamite cannot be considered a marriage, inasmuch as she was never described as a "wife" and David did not copulate with her. The king was impotent—or, as the text reads, he "could not get warm" (1 Kings 1:1-4):

> Therefore his servants said to him, "Let a search be made for a young virgin for my lord the king, and let her serve the king, nurse him, and let her lie in your bosom that my lord the king may be warm." (1 Kings 1:2-3)

A search was undertaken, and Abishag was chosen:

> The girl was very beautiful, she became the king's attendant and looked after him but the king knew her not [that is: did not have intercourse with her]. (1 Kings 1:4)

Virility was an important aspect of kingship. The king symbolized the nation. As the ruler was virile, so the land, the crops, the herds, and the nation were fertile. An impotent monarch threatened the health of the people. It is not surprising that when David's impotence became known, his eldest son, Adonijah, reached for the crown (1 Kings 1:5). His plans failed, and Solomon joined David on the throne to form a diarchy. After David's death, Adonijah asked Solomon for the hand of Abishag in marriage (1 Kings 2:17). To possess a woman belonging to another man was to assume his place and title. For example, when David's rebellious son Absalom forced David out of Jerusalem, the young man publicly engaged in sexual relations with each of the ten concubines David had left to care for the palace, thereby establishing his role as successor to David's possessions—including the crown (2 Sam. 15:16,

16:22). When David recaptured the city, the ten women were isolated and denied intercourse with the king. They had been befouled through sexual contact with another man (2 Sam. 20:3). In view of this protocol, it is not surprising that Solomon interpreted Adonijah's request to marry Abishag as another bid by his elder brother for control of the kingdom. Adonijah was murdered (1 Kings 2:22-25).

Solomon is the most married individual in biblical narrative. His harem consisted of seven hundred wives (some of whom were princesses) and three hundred concubines (1 Kings 11:1-3). Many of the marriages were designed to form political alliances; but in the light of the rebellion provoked by David's impotency, there may also have been an intention to demonstrate Solomon's royal virility.

Solomon's marriages to foreign women came under judgment in the theologized Deuteronomic history (1 Kings 11:1-13). Deuteronomic law prohibited marriage with foreign women because of fear of apostasy (Deut. 7:3-4; also see Exod. 34:16; Judg. 3:6). However, despite the examples set by patriarchal legends (Gen. 24; 27:46-29:30), such marriages took place both before and after the code was written. Esau married three Canaanite women (Gen. 36:2); Joseph married an Egyptian (Gen. 41:45); Moses married a Midianite; and a Hebrew woman, who was among those who fled Egypt had a child by an Egyptian (Lev. 24:10). Gideon married a Canaanite woman (Judg. 8:31), and Boaz married Ruth, a Moabitess who became one of King David's ancestors (Ruth 1:4, 4:13-17). Some marriages with foreigners came through capture of women in wars (Deut. 21:9-13, Judg. 5:29).

During the postexilic period an elitist attitude, fostered by the Jews who returned from exile in Babylon, led to the proscription of marriages between Jews and foreigners. Nehemiah, as governor, designed an agreement in which the signers promised, "We will not give our daughters to the people of the land or take their daughters for our sons" (Neh. 10:30). Nehemiah feared divine disfavor. Had he read the Deuteronomic claim of Yahweh's reactions to the Solomonic marriages (1 Kings 11:9ff)? He was also angry over the bastardization of the Hebrew language (Neh. 13:23f). Ezra went further and demanded that Israelite men divorce their foreign wives and their children (Ezra 10:3ff). The story of Ruth, which may have been composed in reaction to the harshness of the rulings by Ezra and Nehemiah, pointed out that King David's ancestry included the union of a Moabitess and a Jew.

Just as Jewish religious leaders sought to protect the faith from contamination, so Christian leaders attempted to protect the early church from unbelievers. Paul forbade marriage with non-Christians (2 Cor. 6:14-16). If a Christian was already married to a non-Christian, Paul sanctioned the continuation of the marriage because the non-Christian could somehow magically be sanctified or made holy by the union and there was also the possibility that the non-Christian could be converted (1 Cor. 7:12-16). The author of the first letter of Peter advised wives married to nonbelievers: "Be submissive to your husbands, so that some, though they do not obey the word, may be won without a word by the behavior of their wives, when they see your reverent and chaste behavior" (1 Pet. 3:1-2). Hope for such conversions was increased by belief in the indissolubility of marriage.

Incest

Incestuous relationships are forbidden in the seventh-century-B.C.E. Deuteronomic law (22:30; 27:20,22-23), and in the Levitical codes written one or two centuries later (18:6-20, 20:11-23). Reports of incestuous behavior among Christians angered Paul (1 Cor.5:1-2). Children of incest were known as "bastards" and restricted from religious assemblies (Deut. 23:2). Marriage or sex between a brother and a half-sister was specifically prohibited (Deut. 27:22; Lev. 18:11,20:17).

Different rules seem to have prevailed in earlier times. Before King David's son Amnon raped Tamar, his half-sister, she begged him to refrain and asked that they marry before engaging in sex saying, "Please ask the king, he will not keep us apart" (2 Sam 13:13). Tamar's concern was with the onus of rape and loss of virginity, not with a taboo against married sex with her half-brother. The rules pertaining to incest propounded later in the Deuteronomic and Levitical codes apparently were not part of Hebrew sexual regulations in David's time.

According to Genesis 12:10-20, Sarah was Abraham's sister, but in Genesis 20:12 she is described as a half-sister, sharing the same father but not the same mother. In Genesis 26:6-11 Rebeccah, Isaac's wife, who was also his cousin (Gen. 24:15), posed as his sister. In each of these folkloric parallels, we are told that fear lest their wives' beauty (Sarah was ninety) might prompt someone wishing to possess the woman to kill her husband and render her free for marriage led the patriarch to lie and to pretend that his wife was his sister and therefore unmarried.

Both Genesis 12:10-20—the story in which Sarah enters the harem of the Egyptian pharoah—and Genesis 26:6-11—which tells of King Abimelech of Gerar discovering Isaac fondling Rebeccah in anything but an acceptable brother-sister fashion—are part of the J folklore. The stories are doublets. Each focuses on the same theme: the attempt at deception by pretending that a wife was a sister, but they have different characters and different locales. A third account, from what is called the "E source," merges facets of the two stories (Gen. 20:1-18). The key figures are Abraham and Sarah, the king is Abimelech; but here Sarah is said to be Abraham's half-sister. In E, Abraham and Sarah were, according to the Levitical code, in a forbidden incestuous marriage. In J, the patriarchs simply lied.

The J source includes a rather crude but amusing folktale relating the incestuous origin of the Moabites and Ammonites (Gen. 19:30-38), with a play on the names "Moab" and "Ammon." Following the destruction of Sodom and Gomorrah, Lot's daughters, believing that their world was destroyed and fearing that they would be unable to find husbands, fulfilled their female role as childbearers by engaging in sexual intercourse with their drunken father. Their offspring become the progenitors of the Moabites and Ammonites. Despite Von Rad's notion that "Without doubt the narrative now contains indirectly a severe judgment on the incest in Lot's house, and Lot's life becomes inwardly and outwardly bankrupt" (Von Rad, *Genesis,* 219), the J writer displays absolutely no condemnation of the incest. The child of the first daughter was called "Moab" on the basis of an inaccurate but punning etymology suggesting that the name meant "from a father" (*me-ab*). The second daughter's son was named "Ben-ammi," which means "son of my people," and which Driver (*Genesis,* 204) suggested means "of my father's kinsman."

Incestuous sexual relationships were common in Jerusalem prior to the total destruction of the city by the Babylonians in August 586 B.C.E. (Ezek. 22:10-11). Despite Deuteronomic prohibitions, men copulated with their stepmothers, daughters-in-law, and half-sisters. Ezekiel thought this behavior triggered the ultimate destruction of Jerusalem. The Apostle Paul condemned incestuous relationships between a man and his stepmother in a Christian home in Corinth (1 Cor. 5:1).

Levirate Marriage

The importance of producing offspring is reflected in a marriage regulation known as "levirate," from the Latin *levir,* meaning "brother-in-law." In Hebrew thought, the importance of a name was amplified by the belief that in the shadowy afterlife in Sheol there was no true identity. Without offspring to carry on the man's name, it would be as if he had never existed. Having a son guaranteed a kind of immortality.

Deuteronomic law (25:5-10) provided that if a married man died without leaving a son to carry on his name, it was the duty of his brother to take the dead man's widow as a wife, to have intercourse with her, and to name the first son born of this union as if it were the child of the dead man:

> When brothers live together and one of them dies without leaving a son, his widow shall not marry outside the family. Her husband's brother shall have intercourse with her; he shall take her in marriage and do his duty by her as her husband's brother. The first son she bears shall perpetuate the dead brother's name so that it may not be blotted out from Israel.

By law, the widow was forbidden to marry outside of the dead husband's family. She was considered to be a possession, a chattel (Exod. 20:17), not free to remarry, and compelled to perform her wifely duty of bearing a child in the name of the dead man. Brothers lived with their parents until the elder brother married. Then the younger brother could remain at home or live with the married brother. The law recognized, however, the living brother's right to refuse the obligation:

> If the man is not willing to take his brother's wife she shall go to the elders at the town gate and say "My husband's brother refuses to perpetuate his brother's name in Israel; he will not do his duty by me." Then the town elders shall summon him and reason with him. If he remains adamant and says "I will not take her," his brother's widow shall approach him in the presence of the elders; she shall pull his sandal off of his foot, spit in his face and declare: "This is the way we repay the man who will not build up his brother's family." His family will be known in Israel as The House of the Desandaled Man. (Deut. 25.7-10)

Both the removal of the sandal and the act of spitting in the man's face were clearly designed to humiliate the person who failed his familial responsibility.

Two additional purposes, however, for the levirate have been suggested by T. and D. Thompson: caring for the widow and keeping property within the husband's family ("Legal Problems," 90). The plight and vulnerability of the widow is known from prophetic protests (Isa. 1:17,23; Jer. 7:6) and protective legislation (Exod. 22:23; Deut. 14:29,

16:11, 14, etc.). The dead man's property passed under the control of the widow; should she remarry or return to her family, the property could be lost to the son's family.

Only two examples of the levirate appear in the Jewish scriptures; the stories of Tamar (Gen. 38) and Ruth. Tamar was widowed when her husband, Er, the first son of Judah, died. Inasmuch as she was childless, it became the duty of Er's brother, Onan, to fulfill the levirate requirement. But Onan refused to produce a child that would not bear his name. He chose instead to masturbate and "spilled his semen on the ground." For his disobedience, Yahweh killed him. The levirate responsibility passed to the next brother, Shelah, who was at that time too young for marriage. The youth matured, but Judah, the father of the three boys did not permit the marriage to be consumated. Tamar therefore tricked her father-in-law, Judah, into having intercourse with her, thereby fulfilling the familial responsibility to raise up a child in the name of her dead husband. As in other J stories, there is no condemnation of this incestuous sex. In fact, Judah, on learning what Tamar had done, declared, "She has been more righteous than I" (Gen. 38:26).

Ruth, a Moabitess, was the childless widow of a Hebrew. His mother had some family land that should have gone to her deceased son, as family estate. Since he had died, the right to buy it from her devolved on the nearest male relative, as did the duty of taking Ruth to wife and begetting a child who would inherit her former husband's name and property. The relative was willing to buy the land but refused to take Ruth as a charge on his own property. Therefore he had to renounce his right to purchase and the next in line took over. The ritual of the removal of the shoe, apparently performed by the man himself, is explained as a mode of affirming a transaction. The Bible says nothing of Ruth's having to spit in her in-law's face. The next in line, Boaz, took possession of the land and the woman.

In the Tamar story, the persons responsible for the levirate marriage were close kin of Er, and the sexual union occured only once (Gen. 38:26). In the story of Ruth, both Boaz and the unnamed man were distant relatives of the dead man's father. The sexual relationships involved in the Tamar story and as required by Deuteronomic law constitute a unique form of legalized incestuous sex. All other forms, as we have seen, were prohibited in the Priestly code (Lev. 18:16), but the levirate still functioned in Jesus' lifetime. The Sadducees posed a question involving a widow who married a succession of seven brothers-in-law after her husband died, without producing offspring. The question was, whose wife would she be in the afterlife? Jesus responded that relationships like marriage did not exist in the afterlife (Matt. 22:23-32 and parallels).

Paul had no interest either in the levirate or in the continuation of a man's name. He believed in the immediate return of Jesus and taught that sexual relationships could interfere with preparation for that momentous event. He advised marriage only for those whose sexual passions were uncontrollable (1 Cor. 7:9). Widows were told that they were better off to remain unmarried (1 Cor. 7:8,40). If widows did remarry, however, they should unite with a Christian only (1 Cor. 7:39). No concern for the levirate regulation was expressed.

Marriage Rites

Couples generally married young. It has been estimated that some members of the royal family, whose lengths of reign are listed in 1 and 2 Kings, married as young as fourteen (Amon and Josiah) or sixteen (Jehoiachin). Some middle-aged and older men took young wives. Isaac was forty years old when he married Rebeccah (Gen. 25:19ff). She was a virgin, probably in her teens, inasmuch as when Isaac is quite old and feeble she was spritely enough to play an active role in the rivalry that developed between her sons. When Ruth slept at the feet of Boaz, his comment that she chose him rather than one of the available young men implied that he was considerably older than the young widow. David appears to have been in late middle-age when he married Bathsheba, who had been the wife of one of his young soldiers. When Sarah died at the age of 127 (Gen. 23:1), Abraham, who was ten years older (Gen. 19:17), remarried. In addition to his wife Keturah, who was presumably a young virgin, he took concubines and produced offspring.

Jesus' mother, Mary, was supposed to have been pregnant before Joseph married her (Matt. 1:18-25). According to Deuteronomic law, she should have been stoned to death (Deut. 22:20-21). The Gospels explain: her pregnancy was due to impregnation by the Holy Spirit, who was supposed to have "come upon" her (Luke 1:35). Miraculous birth by divine impregnation of a virgin is not uncommon in hero legends (Raglan, *The Hero;* Rank, *The Myth*). For Mary to be a suitable bride for God she had to be a virgin. Thus the fiction of the virgin birth developed (Larue, *Ancient Myth,* 108).

Marriages usually were arranged by fathers on behalf of their children, although the mother might have had something to say (Gen. 24:55, Judg. 14:2, Tob. 7:14). The groom's father was involved inasmuch as it was his family line that would be maintained. The bride's father was concerned with the price he could get for a worker as well as the loss of a child-bearer who would leave his familial household to strengthen that of another. Daughters did, however, maintain relationships with kin-groups. Tamar, after the death of her husband, returned to her father's house (Gen. 38:11). Ruth's desire to remain with her husband's family can be interpreted as an unusual expression of loyalty (Ruth 1:8, 15-18).

The father instituted the search for a suitable bride for his son, preferably among families of the same tribe or clan, and met with the bride's father on behalf of his son (Gen. 34:8). The bride's father "gave" (i.e. sold) his daughter in marriage (Gen. 29:23,28; Exod. 2:21). In some situations the mother was involved. Samson's parents together negotiated with the Philistine parents for their son's bride (Judg. 14:5). Hagar arranged for the marriage of her son, Ishmael (Gen. 21:21).

There were other ways to obtain brides. Daughters could be given as a prize in war (Josh. 15:16). The Benjaminites captured brides during a vintage festival (Judg. 21:23). A nonbetrothed virgin who was raped was compelled to become the wife of the rapist. The rapist was required to pay the woman's father fifty silver pieces as the bride price (Deut. 22:28-29).

The aged Abraham sent a servant to distant kinfolk to find an acceptable bride for Isaac (Gen. 24). According to the J fiction, the servant relied in part on supernatural guidance and in part on an established protocol in selecting Rebeccah. The approach to betrothal included the presentation of a gold nose-ring and bracelets to Rebeccah (perhaps to demonstrate both affluence and seriousness of intent), a dialogue concerning his purpose, and the sealing of an agreement with Rebeccah's father. Following the sealing of the betrothal the servant presented gifts to Rebeccah, her mother, and her brother Laban. The concluding ritual was the sharing of a meal that the servant had refused to eat until the betrothal had reached closure.

The wedding feast was both a celebration and a commensality rite. Sharing food constituted a binding of relationships. Isaac and Abimelech, having solved their difference, made a covenant which they finalized by eating and drinking (Gen. 26:28-30; see also Gen. 31:54; 2 Sam. 3:20). Perhaps the salt in the food constituted the binding element (Smith, *Lectures,* 270), since salt was used in conventional offerings uniting Yahweh and his people (Lev. 2:13, Num. 18:19, Ezek. 43:24). The implication of its contractual nature is reflected in the admonition "Have salt in yourselves and be at peace with one another," (Mark 9:50).

Before Rebeccah left her family, her father and brother blessed her and expressed their hope for an abundance of offspring (Gen. 24:60). She accompanied the servant to Isaac's home, but she veiled herself before Isaac could see her. The servant told Isaac what had transpired and Isaac took Rebeccah into his tent and consumated the marriage sexually. Apparently the betrothal formalities, completed when the servant reached an agreement with Bethuel, negated the need for any elaborate ritual when Rebeccah met Isaac. J noted that "she became his wife and he loved her" (v. 67). In this instance, the bride and groom enjoyed no personal courtship—they married and then fell in love.

Children appear to have had little say in the choice of their mates. Sirach commented, "A woman will accept any man, but one daughter is better than another" (36:21). But there were exceptions. In J's story of Jacob's marriages, Jacob chose Rachel. He fell in love with her, and worked seven years to pay the marriage price (Gen. 29:20), before approaching her father, Laban, saying, "Give me my wife that I may go into her, for my time is completed" (29:31) by which he signified that the betrothal was the equivalent of marriage except for cohabitation. A full day of feasting followed. In the evening, Leah, the veiled substitute bride whom he did not choose, copulated with Jacob as his wife. The account demonstrates how little husband and wife knew of one another prior to their first sexual encounter and the binding nature of the sexual act. Jacob and Leah had one week in which to celebrate or complete their union. At the end of that time, he was given Rachel as a second wife and began another seven years of servitude to pay for her (29:27-28). Apparently there was no ceremony or celebration accompanying the acquisition of Rachel.

What is most obvious in the above story is that women are regarded as commodities. Marriage was recognized as a business, not a religious, transaction. Rachel and Leah referred to themselves as having been sold by their father (Gen. 31:15).

The amount of the bride price varied with the status of the bride's family and, in some situations, with what the groom or the groom's family could afford. Jacob paid in labor for Leah and Rachel (Gen. 30:15-30). Shechem offered to pay any amount for the hand of Dinah (Gen. 34:12). In other settings there appears to have been an established rate (Exod. 22:17; Deut. 22:28f.). David's payment for Michal was set by her father, King Saul, at one hundred Philistine foreskins—inasmuch as David was relatively poor. David paid double that amount (1 Sam. 18:25-17).

The ritual transference of authority over the woman from the father to the husband is briefly outlined in Tobit 7:13-8:1. First, having agreed to the marriage, Raguel, the father, took the hand of his daughter, Sarah, and gave her to Tobias, saying:

> Take her. In accordance with the ordinances decreed in the book of Moses, I give her to you to wed. Possess her and lead her in peace to your father and may the God of heaven grant you peace and prosperity.

Having symbolically transferred authority over Sarah to Tobias, the father blessed them. Next, on a scroll brought by his wife, he wrote out the cohabitation contract that legalized the transfer. The familial ritual progressed to the sharing of food and drink. During the festivities, the mother prepared the bridal chamber and comforted her daughter. The marriage feast cemented the relationship between the two families and at the same time bound those who were guests. When the feast was over, Tobias was led to the bedroom, where the marriage was sexually consummated.

The wedding feast was a lavish celebration, with an abundance of wine (John 2:1-10) and, for the wealthy, expensive meats (Matt. 22:4). To decline an invitation was interpreted as an insult (Matt. 22:1-7). Needless to say, guests were expected to be suitably attired (Matt. 22:11).

A royal epithalamion described the entrance of the virgin bride as she left her father's home and, accompanied by her bridesmaids, was led, with shouts of joy, into the palace and the presence of the king (Ps. 45). She, chosen for her beauty, was garbed in robes woven with gold thread and may have worn a jeweled crown (Isa. 49:18). Throughout the ceremonies she was veiled, which explains how Laban was able to substitute Leah for Rachel as Jacob's bride (Gen. 29:23). The king's garments were scented with ceremonial oil and spices. We may suppose that in private marriages, too, the couple were given special honors and regal status in imitation of more elaborate state functions.

It was important that the bride in her first marriage be a virgin. The first sexual encounter ordinarily took place in quarters provided by the bride's family. As proof of her virginity at the time of marriage, the bride's family kept the sheets from the wedding night, which were expected to reveal blood from the tearing of the hymen (Deut. 22:13-21). Should there be no blood evidence, the woman was stoned at the door of her father's house by the men of the city. Should the husband falsely deny her virginity, he was whipped and fined (Deut. 22:18-19). There were no virginity requirements for men.

A women suspected by her husband of having an adulterous relationship could be brought before the priest in the temple and subjected to a series of magical procedures—including offerings, the use of holy or blessed water mixed with the sweepings from the temple floor, the invocation of curses, and so on (Num. 5:11-28). The woman was obviously presumed guilty until proven innocent; and, because she was under her husband's control, she had no choice but to obey. Should she be found innocent, there was no condemnation of the husband.

The State of Being Married

Some marriages were marked by happiness, some were marred by unhappiness. The unmarried man was pitied, for he was without a home (Sir. 36:24-26). Marriages arranged by parents did produce couples who loved one another. Where there was love, the sharing of a meal in poverty was preferable to dining in affluent but hate-filled mansions (Prov. 15:17, 17:1). Throughout the Bible there is emphasis on the virtues of loyalty and fidelity, but there is evidence that there was infidelity.

The married state as portrayed by the wisdom writers is described from a male perspective. So far as these men were concerned, there were two kinds of married women: good and bad (Prov. 12:6, 18:22). The good wife was diligent and hard-working, trustworthy and industrious. She labored in the field and the home as a manager and business woman (Prov. 12:24, 31:10-31). Her affection was a source of delight for her husband (Prov. 5:19). As he sat with his male companions on the benches in the city gate, he could be sure that all was well at home because of his hard-working wife (31:23,31). The good wife was silent and disciplined. She charmed her husband and put fat on his bones (Sir. 26:13-18). She made him happy and enabled him to age in peace (Sir. 26:1-4).

Similar emphases appear in Christian writings. Women were "the weaker sex" (1 Pet. 3:7)—after all, it was the woman who was beguiled by the serpent in Eden, not the man (1 Tim. 2:14)! Wives were expected to be submissive to their husbands (Eph. 5:22; Col. 3:18; 1 Pet. 3:1), and the model for this role was Sarah "who obeyed Abraham and called him 'master' " (1 Pet. 3:6).

In references to conflict between husband and wife, it is the woman who is faulted (Prov. 12:4, 19:13, 21:19, 25:24, 27:15; Sir. 25:16-20). Men could be warned not to be jealous of their wives and be advised of the dangers of becoming interested in singers, harlots, virgins, and other men's wives (Sir. 9:1-9); but no listing of husbands' faults is provided. Evil wives brought shame to their husbands (Prov. 12:4). Some wives were too vocal (Prov. 9:13; Sir. 26:6); some were drunkards (Sir. 26:8); some were promiscuous (Prov. 9:13-18; Sir. 26:9-12). Strife between wives occurred in bigamous marriages (Gen. 29:30-31; 1 Sam. 1:6), particularly when one wife was barren (Gen. 16:4, 30:1-2; Deut. 21:15-17).

The wise men warned their pupils against involvement with women of loose morals (Prov. 5:3-23) and adultery (Prov. 2:16-17, 6:32, 7:6-27; Sir. 26:9-12, etc). Adultery was explicitly prohibited in the Decalogue (Exod. 20:14; Lev. 18:20; Deut. 5:18); and should a couple be caught in the act, they were both killed (Lev. 20:10, Deut. 22:22). The adulteress, with her make-up and smooth tongue, could bring about her partner's death at the hands of her angry husband. There appears to have been no condemnation or punishment of men who associated with harlots, although men were warned that such diversions could cost them their inheritance (Sir. 9:6). A married woman or widow who acted as a harlot could be sentenced to death (Gen. 38:15-24).

Jesus and Paul, by both example and teaching, placed celibacy above marriage. The saying attributed to Jesus (Matt. 19:10-12) was given in response to a comment by the disciples after Jesus had stated his opposition to divorce (except for unchastity). They suggested that if divorce was practically outlawed, then it might be better not to marry. Jesus' response centered on the role of the ascetic eunuch who was celibate not because of some birth defect, nor through castration, but by voluntarily eschewing marriage for "the sake of the kingdom of heaven." He noted that only those "to whom it was given" could accept this role (Matt. 19:11). Apparently, Jesus considered himself to be one such person.

The Apostle Paul's ascetic inclination—which he, too, considered a benefit not bestowed on all (1 Cor. 7:7)—led him to favor celibacy over marriage (1 Cor. 7:25-6). He "regarded marriage and married life as an emergency measure" (Bornkamm, *Paul,* 208) providing protection against "the temptation to immorality" (1 Cor. 7:2). Marriage brought with it concerns for involvement with "worldly problems" (1 Cor. 7:28,33).

Although Paul appears to place no restraints on sexual activities within marriage, his statement about mutuality of sexual behavior can be interpreted as promoting a mechanical sexuality, which Manson (*Studies,* 199) labeled "a peculiar form of marriage . . . in which couples lived together in a relation of brother and sister rather than husband and wife." Manson noted that this Pauline doctrine opposed "Jewish sentiment, for which the normal sex-relation of husband and wife is a real good, a privilege accorded and a duty imposed by God." Paul's concern was with anything that distracted the believer from the Christian commitment that prepared one for the second coming of Jesus. He believed that "the form of this world is passing away" (1 Cor. 7:31).

Paul's recommendations for celibate marriage did not become the Christian norm. 1 Peter, written shortly after the Corinthian letter, reflected hope for "the revelation of Jesus Christ" (1 Pet. 1:13, 4:7), but focused on the demeanor of the married couple (1 Pet. 3:1-7). By the end of the first century and the middle of the second century, when 1-3 John, Revelation, and 2 Peter were written, although expectations of the *parousia* were still central (1 John 2:18; Rev. 1:1, 22:20), so that scoffers could mock "Where is the promise of his coming?" (2 Pet. 3:4), the focus of these writings was on theological issues, not on sex and family. Paul's stringent recommendations appear to have been bypassed.

Parents were to raise their children strictly (Prov. 13:24, 23:13-14, 29:17). Daughters could be especially worrisome burdens for the fathers, who were concerned lest they prove to be unmarriageable, become pregnant out of wedlock, make a bad marriage, be barren, or unfaithful in marriage (Sir. 7:24-25, 42:9-11).

Tension could arise between parents and their offspring. Children did not always honor or respect their parents. Jacob lied to his father, Isaac, and conspired with Rebeccah to aquire dishonestly Esau's blessing (Gen. 27). David's son Absalom attempted to overthrow his father (2 Sam. 15).

Nor does the story of Jesus as told by gospel writers, reflect the highest familial precepts. Joseph and Mary do not emerge as ideal parents, and Jesus' relationship to them appears to have been tangential. Luke recorded a legend of the family's journey to Jerusalem, when Jesus was twelve years old (Luke 2:41-51). One might accept as boyish thoughtlessness Jesus' stay at the Temple without informing his parents, and one might also accept as parental thoughtlessness the parents' assumption that Jesus was travelling with kinfolk. The fact that that a whole day passed without the parents checking on the boy seems irresponsible. Jesus' dismissal of their three-day search appears flippant. The writer noted, however, that Jesus was obedient after they returned to Nazareth.

The sparsity of references to Joseph in the New Testament (John 1:45) raises questions about the importance of father-son relationships in the holy family. Luke's genealogical account phrases the relationship as "Jesus, . . . being the son (as was supposed) of Joseph" (Luke 3:23). Matthew's list concludes with "Joseph, the husband of Mary, of whom Jesus was born" (1:16). This reading is based on Alexandrian and Byzantine texts. Other ancient sources read: "Jacob begot Joseph, to whom virgin Mary, having been bethrothed to him, bore Jesus"; and

"Joseph, to whom the virgin Mary was betrothed, begot Jesus" (Huck, *Synopsis,* 2). The last version, favored by many translators, was so controversial when printed in the footnotes of first editions of *The Revised Standard Version of the Bible* that pressure from religious groups led to its removal.

The citizens of Nazareth may have recognized Jesus as "the carpenter's son" (Matt. 13:55), but due to the myth of Mary's divine impregnation, Joseph's role in Christian tradition became that of a stepfather who dutifully married Mary when she was pregnant out of wedlock (Matt. 1:18-25) to save her from punishment under Jewish law (Deut. 22:23-24). Jesus used the term "Father" with reference to his relationship to God but not to Joseph (Luke 2:41-51). Some commentators have suggested that Joseph died before Jesus commenced his public activities, and inasmuch as the Gospels focus on these years of Jesus' life, it is understandable that Joseph was ignored.

Mother-son relationships do not fare much better. When a woman calls out "blessed is the womb that carried you and the teats you sucked" (Luke 11:27), Jesus dismissed the reference to his mother and replies, "Rather, blessed are those who hear and keep God's word." A pericope in Mark 3:19b-35 describes an event that occurred in Nazareth when members of Jesus' family, who were with the crowd that had gathered about him, expressed concern for Jesus' mental stability. This interpretation depends upon linking the phrase in Mark 3:21 "those with him" to verse 31 which mentions Mary and Jesus' brothers, thus implying that his mother may have considered him to be emotionally disturbed. On the other hand, the phrase may be translated "his (Jesus') friends" (RSV) suggesting that friends, not family, raised the question of mental illness. Jesus, when informed of Mary's presence, ignored her and announced that "Whoever does the will of God is my brother and sister and mother" (3:31-35).

At the wedding feast in Cana, Jesus addressed Mary not as "Mother" but by the impersonal term "Woman" (John 2:4)—just as he did when, from the cross, he committed her to the care of his beloved disciple (John 19:26). Jesus used this same impersonal form of address when he spoke to Mary Magdalene in the post-resurrection scene (John 20:13).

Indeed, Jesus is purported to have stated that his purpose was to set children against their parents (Matt. 10:35). He demanded that those who would be disciples hate "father and mother and wife and children and brothers and sisters, and even his own life" (Luke 14:25) and love him more than one's family (Matt. 10:37). Such teachings accord with the requisition in Mishnah *Baba Mezia* 2:11 that a man honor God and the Torah more than his teacher, and his teacher more than his parents. The young man who approached Jesus had kept the Decalogue regulations, including the command to honor parents, but he was rejected as a disciple because obedience to Jewish law was inadequate; he had to abandon all that he had acquired to follow Jesus, trusting in the promise that his earthly wealth would be replaced by "treasure in heaven" (Matt 19:16-21).

The fact that Jesus was still unmarried at an age when most Jewish men would have been, suggests that his focus was upon his teaching role rather than upon the Jewish ideal of a family. Indeed, Jesus had little to say about marriage and the family.

Divorce

The centrality of the male in biblical culture is made clear in regulations concerning divorce. Pedersen notes, "It seems as if the husband, without further ado, can dissolve the marriage—whereas we hear nothing of women possessing the same freedom" (Pedersen, *Israel* I-II, 71). Despite the denunciation of divorce and the claim that God hates divorce (Mal. 2:16), divorce was a male privilege that was rather lightly regarded. A wife could be divorced for adultery (Jer. 3:8, Matt. 19:9) but also for vague and trivial reasons: if she "finds no favor" in her husband's eyes, if he "finds some indecency in her" (Deut. 24:1), or "if she doesn't obey" his orders (Sir. 25:26). The reference to the husband being unfaithful to the "wife of his youth" (Mal. 2:16) might refer to men divorcing older wives so that they might marry younger women. There is no biblical evidence on the subject of financial settlements.

Perhaps the Deuteronomic legislation pertaining to divorce sought to place limitations on the male's sweeping powers. Once the man had determined to divorce his wife, he was required personally to serve her with a written decree prior to dismissing her from the home (Deut. 24:1; Jer. 3:8; Isa. 50:1). This divorce certificate not only indicated that the husband had no further claim on the woman and could not, should he change his mind, reclaim her, but it had the effect of making it clear that she was available for remarriage to someone else (Deut. 24:2). If she remarried and her second husband died or divorced her, the first husband could not take her back as his wife. This law did not apply to David, however, who reclaimed his wife Michal (1 Sam. 18:20-27)— after her father had given her to another man (1 Sam. 25:44)—because he had never divorced her (2 Sam. 3:14-16). Hosea apparently was able to remarry his wife after he divorced her when she left him to become a cult prostitute for Ba'al. The reclamation was possible because she had not remarried. Hosea's declaration—"she is not my wife and I am not her husband" (2:2)—has been interpreted as the statement made during the presentation of the divorce decree, but this suggestion has no support within the Bible.

By the time of the New Testament, a woman of power could divorce her husband. Josephus states that Salome, sister of King Herod, sent her husband, Costabarus, governor of Gaza and Idumea, a bill of divorce despite the fact that this was not in accord with Jewish law (*Antiquities* XV.vii.10). Paul's reference to the Lord's ruling that "the wife should not separate from the husband . . . and the husband should not divorce his wife" (1 Cor. 7:10) echoes the traditional Jewish pattern: the wife might leave her husband, but only the husband could divorce (Daube, *New Testament,* 362). If the woman separated from her husband, she was not free to remarry; she could only remain single or be reconciled to her husband.

Having stated that divorce was unacceptable, Paul immediately made an exception in the case where a Christian was married to an unbeliever. He urged continuance of the marriage if possible, in the hope that the unbelieving partner might be converted; but simultaneously he did not rule out the possibility of divorce (1 Cor. 7:12-15). The question put to Jesus by the Pharisees—"Is it lawful for a man to divorce his wife?" (Mark 10:2)—reflected current controversy. Having established that the Torah sanctioned divorce, Jesus stated that Mosaic legislation was a divine concession to "the hardness of your heart" (Mark 10:5), by which he seemed to refer to human difficulties in reconciliation. Jesus taught that marriage could not be dissolved and that divorce was not acceptable— a position that accorded with and originally may have been drawn from the Qumran code (CD iv.21). He referred to the J creation myth (Gen. 2:24) and insisted that the two became indissolubly one. Jesus distinguished between what he believed was the divinely ordained intent of marriage and Jewish legal practice. His teaching was rigid.

> Whoever divorces his wife and marries another, commits adultery against her; and if she divorces her husband and marries another, she commits adultery. (Mark 10:11-12)

This saying is paralleled in Luke 16:18, but modified in Matthew 5:31 and 19:9 by the addition of a phrase "except for unchastity." The term

98   *Gerald A. Larue*

used could refer to premarital unchastity or to adultery. The Matthean addition completely changes the emphasis of the Markan and Lukan sayings. When the apostle Paul wrote to the Corinthian Christians, he drew on the Jesus tradition later found in Mark, forbidding divorce for any reason (1 Cor. 7:10-12), but, as we have seen, he then went on to exceptions in the spirit later dominant in Matthew (1 Cor. 7:12-15).

BIBLIOGRAPHY AND FURTHER READING

O. Baab. "Marriage." *The Interpreter's Dictionary of the Bible.* Vol. 3. Nashville, Tenn., 1962. 278-287.

G. Bornkamm. *Paul.* Translated by D. Stalker. New York, 1971.

S. R. Driver. *The Book of Genesis.* London, 1948.

C. Gordon. *Introduction to Old Testament Times.* New Jersey, 1953.

A. Huck. *Synopsis of the First Three Gospels.* Revised edition. Oxford, 1954.

S. Johnson. "Jesus Teaching on Divorce." In *Five Essays on Marriage.* Louisville, Ky., 1946. 18-66.

G. A. Larue. *Humanism and Easter.* Amherst, N.Y., 1985.

——. *Ancient Myth and Modern Life.* Long Beach, Calif., 1988.

——. "Surviving the Apocalyses." In *Neo-Fundamentalism.* Buffalo, N.Y., 1988. 135-152.

T. Manson. *Studies in the Gospels and Epistles.* Edited by M. Black. Philadelphia, Pa., 960.

W. P. Patterson. "Marriage." *A Dictionary of the Bible.* Volume 3. Edited by J. Hastings. New York, 1908. 262-271.

J. Pedersen. *Israel, its Life and Culture.* London, 1946-47.

L. Raglan. *The Hero.* London, 1946-47. New York, 1956.

O. Rank. *The Myth of the Birth of the Hero.* New York, 1964.

H. W. Robinson. "The Hebrew Conception of Corporate Personality." *Werden und Wesen des Alten Testaments.* Edited by J. Hempel. B.Z.A.W., LXVI, 1936. 49ff.

C. Simpson. "Genesis: Exegesis." In *The Interpreter's Bible.* Volume 1. Nashville, Tenn., 1952. 439-829.

W. R. Smith. *Kinship and Marriage in Early Arabia.* Edited by S.A. Cook. London, 1903.

T. and D. Thompson. "Some Legal Problems in the Book of Ruth." *Vetus Testamentum,* 18 (1968). 79-99.

R. de Vaux. *Ancient Israel.* Translated by J. McHugh. New York, 1961.

G. Von Rad. *Genesis.* Translated by J. H. Marks. Philadelphia, 1961.

MIRACLES
Stevan Davies

To ask what the Bible really says about miracles is to beg the question. After all, are we referring to what *we* think miracles are or to what *the Bible* thinks they are? To define them in modern terms, as "events produced by supernatural intervention and contrary to natural laws," is really to end the discussion, since the Bible knows nothing of natural laws. It *does* know of laws and rules given by Yahweh to various objects, for instance the sea: "He gave it a rule not to cross its boundaries" (Prov. 8:29). But this law is Yahweh's, not nature's, and there is no "natural law" that it violates or supersedes. In fact, the Bible recognizes no distinction between the "natural" and the "supernatural." Consequently, we must stop trying to impose our ideas on the Bible and consider what *it* says.

The Bible has several terms to describe amazing or otherwise incredible events: miracles, signs, wonders, marvels, prodigies and so forth. These events elicit awe usually because they are extraordinary. When an angel appears to Moses "in a flame of fire out of the midst of a bush," Moses says, "I will turn aside now to see *why the bush is not burnt*" (Exodus 3:23). The authors of the Old Testament assumed that the world was produced, and might at any time be rearranged, by the arbitrary will of an invisible person. This view is completely contrary to our present understanding of nature.

Pre-eminently the Old Testament speaks of miracles in the homiletic passages of Exodus and Deuteronomy as events that took place during the exodus from Egypt. I will discuss them first and follow with a discussion of some of the many references the Old Testament makes to them. It is tempting to say that the miracles of the Exodus story are so central and important that they alone are "what the Old Testament means by miracle"—all the other miracles mentioned in it being at best of secondary importance. This, however, would be to suppose that the Old Testament was written as a whole, with a single set of ideas, a supposition ruled out by its manifest diversity and contradictions, which show that it was composed from many different sources. We must listen to the Bible closely, as to a symphony, to hear what each of its different voices says.

The sequence begins with God's creation of the heavenly bodies. "And God said, 'Let there be lights in the firmament of the heavens to separate the day from night; and let them be for signs and for seasons and for days and years' " (Gen. 1:14). The moon and stars will not only determine the Earth's cycles, they will be the source of "signs," portents of marvelous changes. Similarly in Genesis 9: The rainbow Noah sees is not a natural phenomenon but a miraculous "sign" created by God after the flood to appear after rainstorms throughout the rest of history as a way of reminding mankind of its duty to him.

For the editors of the Pentateuch, however, the greatest and most marvelous sign of Yahweh's power and purpose was the deliverance of Israel from Egypt. Therefore, in the rhetorical reports of this great wonder, we find the Bible's first and largest concentration of words commonly translated as "miracle." The account begins in Exodus 3:19-20, where the whole motif is summarized. Yahweh says to Moses, "I know that the king of Egypt will not let you go unless compelled by a mighty hand. So I will stretch out my hand and smite Egypt with all the wonders which I will do in it; after that he will let you go" (Exod. 3:20).

In Exodus 4:1-7 the wonders commence when God tells Moses to pick up a rod and cast it upon the ground. Moses does so, and it becomes a serpent. Moses picks up the serpent and "it became a rod in his hand." Next Moses is told by God to put his hand into his bosom. Moses does so, and when he takes it out, it's leprous; he puts it back into his bosom and it returns to normal. God then says, "If they will not believe you, or heed the first sign, they may believe the latter sign. If they will not believe even these two signs or heed your voice, you shall take some water from the Nile and pour it upon the dry ground; and the water which you shall take from the Nile will become blood upon the dry ground" (4:8-9). Moses is told to take the rod "with which you shall do the signs" (4:17). And, when he goes back to Egypt, "see that you do before Pharaoh all the prodigies which I have put in your power"

(4:21). Shortly thereafter, Moses tells Aaron of "all the signs" that Yahweh "had charged him to do" (4:28). Then Aaron relates these things to the people of Israel and does "the signs in the sight of the people. And the people believed" (4:30). In chapter seven Yahweh informs Moses, "I will harden Pharaoh's heart, and though I multiply my signs and wonders in the land of Egypt, Pharaoh will not listen to you . . ." (7:3). Then he says, "When Pharaoh says to you, 'Prove yourselves by working a miracle,' then you shall say to Aaron, 'take your rod and cast it down before Pharaoh, that it may become a serpent' " (7:9). In this section of Exodus we are apparently to understand that all of Moses' and Aaron's magical works, as well as the sending of the plagues, are to be thought of as a sustained set of miracles, "signs and wonders." The sequence concludes with the parting of the Red Sea, which, while not labeled "a sign" in Exodus, is included in the sequence in Deuteronomy 11:3-4.

Indeed, the events of Exodus are more often described as miracles in the commentaries about them than in their narration. Most often the terms for miracles are used to describe those events in advance, or to reflect on their significance. Consequently the individual incidents are of relatively little importance in themselves. It is the whole program of the events of the Exodus that counts. Therefore, too, in telling the details the story-teller is not concerned with verity, nor even with verisimilitude. (For example, all cattle of the Egyptians die in Exodus, 9:6, all cattle left in the field in 9:25, and all firstborn cattle in 12:29. Obvious folkloristic overkill, but it makes a nice story.)

The miracles of the Exodus have a function quite different from what they appear to have. They are presented as a means to frighten Pharaoh and compel his obedience, but the story more importantly serves as a paradigm of the activity of God, a paradigm to be recited in the communities of Israel. Their main importance is in their retelling. For example, when God says to Moses in Exodus 10:1-2, "Go in to Pharaoh; for I have hardened his heart and the heart of his servants, that I may show these signs of mine among them, and that you may tell in the hearing of your son and your sons' sons how I have made sport of the Egyptians and what signs I have done among them; that you may know I am Yahweh," it is clear that the purpose of the magical acts and the plagues is not solely, not even mainly, to facilitate the escape of the Israelites. The key purpose is to give the Israelites a story they will retell through all generations. Admittedly, according to the story the marvels *do* eventually persuade Pharaoh to permit the Israelites' departure, but they also persuade the reader that Yahweh could have got them out without so elaborate a program. Why, then, are there so many disasters and delays? To give Yahweh an excuse to show off his power, yes, but in the long run to make the people believe in Yahweh's power and give them a story for annual repetition. This is even clear *prior* to the performance of the miracles, for they are first displayed to the Israelites, "and the people believed" (Exod. 4:30).

One might assume that the miracles are done to convince Pharaoh. But, in fact, God *precludes* them from having this effect, for he says " 'Pharaoh will not listen to you; that my wonders may be multiplied in the land of Egypt.' Moses and Aaron did all these wonders before Pharoah; and the Lord hardened Pharaoh's heart" (10:9-10). In a sense, Pharoah's hardened heart is a good device. After all, the more quickly Pharaoh was convinced, the shorter and less impressive would be the story in its retelling.

The purpose of the Exodus miracle stories must therefore be found in the social functions served by their retelling, and the Old Testament states those functions clearly. For instance, in Deuteronomy 4:34-35 Yahweh asks, "has any god ever attempted to go and take a nation for himself from the midst of another nation, by trials, by signs, by wonders, and by war, by a mighty hand and an outstretched arm, and by great terrors, according to all that Yahweh your God did for you in Egypt before your eyes? To you it was shown, that you might know that Yahweh is God; there is no other besides him." Here the Exodus miracles are used to establish the foundation for belief that Yahweh is God. Shortly thereafter, in Deuteronomy 6:21-22, Yahweh says "When your son asks you in time to come, 'What is the meaning of the testimonies and the statutes and the ordinances which Yahweh our God has commanded you?' then you shall say to your son, 'We were Pharaoh's slaves in Egypt; and the Lord brought us out of Egypt with a mighty hand; and the Lord showed signs and wonders, great and grievous, against Egypt and against Pharaoh and all his household, before our eyes. . . .' " Here the retelling establishes the significance of the commandments of Yahweh. All this is gone over again in Deuteronomy 11:3-8, and again elsewhere. The author of these passages evidently conceived this deliverance, including the reported "signs and prodigies," as *the* events by which Yahweh's divinity and power were proved and his claim on his people established.

The miracles also have a paradigmatic function: "As it was done once, so it can be done again." When the Israelites begin to doubt their ability to campaign against superior forces, for example, Yahweh tells them in Deuteronomy 7:17-20, "If you say in your heart, 'These nations are greater than I; how can I dispossess them?' you shall not be afraid of them, but you shall remember what Yahweh your God did to Pharaoh and to all Egypt, the great trials which your eyes saw, the signs, the wonders, the mighty hand, and the outstretched arm, by which Yahweh your God brought you out; so will Yahweh your God do to all the peoples of whom you are afraid. Moreover, Yahweh your God will send hornets among them, until those who were left to hide themselves from you are destroyed." Not only does this passage use the Exodus miracles as a general paradigm; the more specific theme of Yahweh's sending of plagues is used as a paradigm for a future plague. Another paradigmatic use of the story is found in Joshua, chapter three. As the Red Sea was in the Exodus story, so the Jordan river is parted that all Israel may cross it. Joshua in announcing this event says, "Sanctify yourselves, for tomorrow Yahweh will do wonders among you" (3:5).

When Joshua subsequently demands that the people choose between Yahweh and the gods of the Amorites, "the people answered, 'far be it from us that we should forsake Yahweh, to serve other gods; for it is Yahweh our God who brought us and our fathers up from the land of Egypt, out of the house of bondage and who did those great signs in our sight. . . .' " (Josh. 24:17). The basis of their faith is supposed to have been the story of those miracles, the story told them by their fathers. And the contrary also can be true: The basis of a *loss* of faith can be loss of confidence in the Exodus miracles, for in Judges 6:13 Gideon complains to an angel of the Lord, "Pray, sir, if Yahweh is with us, why then has all this befallen us? And where are all his wonderful deeds which our fathers recounted to us, saying, 'Did not Yahweh bring us from Egypt?' But now Yahweh has cast us off, and given us into the hand of Midian." To indicate that the miracles of the Exodus can be replicated, the angel sets fire to a pile of meat and cakes with the tip of his staff and vanishes. Here the Exodus miracles remain the basis of trust in Yahweh; another miracle is performed not only to inspire faith by itself but also to reassure Gideon that the trust based on the Exodus miracles is valid.

The consequences of loss of trust in those miracles, and so in God, is discussed in Psalm 78:9-12: "The Ephraimites, armed with the bow, turned back on the day of battle. They did not keep God's covenant, but refused to walk according to his law. They forgot what he had done, and the wonders that he had shown them. In the sight of their

fathers he wrought marvels in the land of Egypt, in the fields of Zoan."
This theme is reiterated in Psalm 78:42-43: "They did not keep in mind
his power, or the day when he redeemed them from the foe; when he
wrought his signs in Egypt, and his miracles in the fields of Zoan."
If one bases trust on the Exodus miracles, loss of trust comes from
loss of belief in them. Accordingly, as breaking with God's covenant
is the consequence of forgetting, it is essential for that covenant that
they be remembered and recited.

Another use of the Exodus miracles in the Old Testament deserves
attention. In Psalms of praise the Exodus miracles are described alongside
significant cosmic events. Psalm 136 speaks of the Lord "who alone
does great wonders," then lists events of creation, the making of the
heavens, the establishment of the sun, the moon, and the stars. The
psalm suddenly shifts to "him who smote the first-born of Egypt . . . and
brought Israel out from among them." After Psalm 105 urges people
to "remember the wonderful works that he has done, his miracles and
the judgments he uttered," it outlines the events of Genesis from Abraham
through the conquest of Canaan. The wonderful works are described
in verses 26-27: "He sent Moses his servant, and Aaron whom he had
chosen. They wrought his signs among them, and miracles in the land
of Ham." These signs and prodigies were done so as to be retold by
Israel, not only to account for the escape from Egypt but to bolster
trust in Yahweh, to justify obedience to Yahweh's commandments, and
to show what may be expected of Yahweh in the future. They are not
in a category by themselves—other events were also such signs—but
these have a particular importance to the national myth.

It is necessary to remember, given the great importance of the Exodus
miracles in the Old Testament, that they most probably never happened.
A modern, scientific attitude cannot help but regard them as impossible,
often absurd. They were invented to establish a national myth for the
people of Israel. Nonetheless, in the minds of those peoples who populate
the Old Testament, the world was surrounded and permeated by miracles.
Signs, wonders, and prodigies were everywhere. Why? The Israelites did
not and could not distinguish between "natural law" and divine intervention breaking natural law, which is our usual idea of the miraculous.
Rather, they attributed both common events (sunrise, the natural year)
and uncommon events (our "miraculous") to the same source: God. Only
rarely were events considered to be so unusual that they had to be explained
as communication from God: his signs, his wonders, his prodigies. In
the books of the prophets particularly, we hear of such "signs" and

"prodigies" that were conceived to be special messages from God from which people were to learn lessons.

This popular belief in "signs" and "prodigies" was combined with early forms of the national and creation myths. Since the national myth described the way the Israelites received their law and their land, the "miraculous" confirmation of it was especially important. However, the confirmation of the creation myth by its marvelous results was also important, and the two systems existed independently, as shown by the two versions of the justification of the sabbath (Exod. 20:11; Deut. 5:14f.). Presumably the practice of Sabbath observance was far older than either mythical justification. The national myth had greatest popular appeal, and so we find a predominance of references to its probative "signs" and "prodigies" in Psalms.

In several of the books of the prophets the Lord is said to send a sign. For example, "As my servant Isaiah has walked naked and bare-foot for three years as a sign and a portent against Egypt and Ethiopia, so shall the king of Assyria lead away the Egyptians captives and the Ethiopians exiles . . ." (Isa. 20:3). Another example from the same book: "This is the sign to you from the Lord, that the Lord will do this thing that he has promised: Behold, I will make the shadow cast by the declining sun on the dial of Ahaz turn back ten steps. So the sun turned back on the dial the ten steps by which it had declined" (Isa. 38:7-8). And again:

> "And you, O son of man, take a brick and lay it before you and portray upon it a city, even Jerusalem; and put siegeworks against it, and build a siege wall against it, and cast up a mount against it; set camps also against it, and plant battering rams against it round about. And take an iron plate, and place it as an iron wall between you and the city; and set your face toward it, and let it be a state of siege, and press the siege against it. This is a sign for the house of Israel. Then lie upon your left side, and I will lay the punishment of the house of Israel upon you; for the number of the days that you lie upon it, you shall bear their punishment. For I assign to you a number of days, three hundred and ninety days, equal to the number of the years of their punishment" (Ezek. 4:1-4).

Here what we should call a "miracle" (the backward movement of the shadow on the sundial) has a different function than the deliberate "symbolic actions" taken by the prophets, for in the case of the sundial the prophet predicts a most unlikely/impossible event, not in his power to produce, and it happens, thus implicitly giving credence to his other predictions. The effect depends on the incredibility of the occurrence. In the case of the prophet's deliberate, symbolic action, the prophet himself does some unlikely but possible things, as symbols of what he predicts. The symbolic expression may be useful as a publicity device, but to our mind it does nothing to increase belief in the likelihood of the prediction coming true. To the minds of the ancients, however, since they believed that things done, said, or heard might be "omens" that *caused* the happenings of the events they foreshadowed—Ezekiel's symbolic actions might have seemed more effective than Isaiah's turning back the sun.

The use of miracles, not just unconventional behavior, as evidence of truth shows the rudimentary development of a concept of *natural order*. Hebrew had as yet no words to express this concept, but the concept must be there to make "unnatural" events prodigies or signs of the divine will, and so of the future. Not all signs were miracles, and not all miracles were signs. Since the Israelites had no clear concept of "miracle," they could not state the difference, but they were dimly aware of it. Sometimes a verifiable prediction is made, and then its verification demonstrated, to support the prophet's credibility. In 1 Samuel (10:1-10), for example, the sign that the Lord has anointed Saul to be prince is that a set of carefully specified events will occur, events that are then shown in fact to occur. This sort of miracle is basically identical in nature with the miracles recounted in the Exodus narrative, for their purpose is to demonstrate the credibility of Moses. Moses asks for them and Yahweh gives them for that purpose explicitly (Exod. 4:1-9). First the people must be made to trust him, then Pharaoh must be made to fear him, at least to the extent of letting the people go. Thus the primary purpose of these miracles (according to the story in the Bible) is not directly to show the power of God but to verify the message of prophets. Samuel, Elijah (the Carmel sacrifice), and Elisha (the food prophecy) all are represented as using such verifications, and Deuteronomy probably followed common belief in making these the test of a true prophet (18:18-22). But it certainly went beyond common belief in making its own law the limit of the authority of a prophet so accredited (13:2-6). It is likely that a prophet capable of producing "signs and wonders" and verified predictions would convince ordinary people of his divine mission—even if his instructions and perspectives differed substantially from those of the authors who composed Deuteronomy.

There is another type of miracle in the Old Testament: the miraculous activity of God throughout creation. This type is often depicted in Psalms. For example, in Psalm 107:23-28, "Some went down to the sea in ships, doing business on the great waters; they saw the deeds of Yahweh, his wonderous works in the deep. For he commanded and raised the stormy wind which lifted up the waves of the sea, they mounted up to heaven, they went down to the depths. . . ." And in Job 9:6-10 we read of God, "who shakes the earth out of its place, and its pillars tremble; who commands the sun, and it does not rise; who seals up the stars; who alone stretched out the heavens, and trampled the waves of the sea; who made the Bear and Orion, the Pleiades and the chambers of the south; who does great things beyond understanding, and marvelous things without number."

In such passages the "miraculous" blends into the order of the universe, using God's control of the sea and the monsters within the sea as the most visible and striking example of his power. But even in this kind of passage (though not in Job) one can find reflections of what most writers of the Old Testament believed the most important signs:

> Thou art the God who workest wonders, who has manifested thy might among the people, the sons of Jacob and Joseph. When the waters saw thee, O God, when the waters saw thee, they were afraid, yea the deep trembled. The clouds poured out water; the skies gave forth thunder; thy arrows flashed on every side. The crash of thy thunder was in the whirlwind; thy lightnings lighted up the world; the earth trembled and shook. Thy way was through the sea, thy path through the great waters; yet thy footprints were unseen. Thou didst lead thy people like a flock by the hand of Moses and Aaron. (Ps. 77:14-20)

Thus even such lyric exaltation of God's power is sometimes subordinated to the Exodus narrative. God's power over the seas is exemplified most certainly in the story of the parting of the Red Sea.

Insofar as the Old Testament speaks of miracles as "signs," "prodigies," and "marvels," only a few main points are made: (1) that the world in general, especially the activities of God in regard to the seas, are signs of his wondrous power; (2) that on occasion prophets performed miracles or "signs" to verify their prognostications; and (3) that the Exodus narrative is the paradigm and central example of God's power. There is not a great deal else to say.

But there is something *not* to say. There is a myriad of marvels in the narratives of the Old Testament: Angels intervene in human affairs; the hand of God does this and that; prophets (notably Elisha in 2 Kings 4:1-44) raise the dead, cure lepers, feed a hundred with food enough for only a few, and so forth. But to call these "miracles," "signs," or "prodigies" is to add to the Old Testament something it does not say. It does not call them "miracles" because it *could* not; it did not call them "signs" or "prodigies" because most of them *were* not—these were done for their own sake, not as signs of things to come. And even those events that were signs of things to come were not signs of Israel's destiny, which was the main concern of most biblical authors who wrote about "signs" and "portents."

Indeed, the authors of the Old Testament seem to be far less interested in miracles than most of the people who read it are. Its prevailing view is that Yahweh is in charge of all creation. *Everything,* therefore, is miraculous in the sense of being the "mighty acts of Yahweh." Since everything is in this sense miraculous, little is made of particularly unusual events that today we might single out as miraculous. Our singling them out comes from the belief that there is a natural order, which God has supposedly established and normally maintains, and a supernatural order (or disorder?), which becomes evident to us when the natural order is altered. In other words, "miracles" are God's special acts, and the "natural" is the set of events in accord with "natural law." If, however, the "natural" is assumed to be the creation of God (as the Old Testament assumes), there is no great contrast between the acts of God that are regular and the acts of God that are unusual.

Take for example a few passages from Joshua 10:11-14:

And as [the Amorites] fled before Israel, while they were going down the ascent of Beth-horon, Yahweh threw down great stones from heaven upon them as far as Azekah, and they died; there were more who died because of the hailstones than the men of Israel killed with the sword. Then spoke Joshua to Yahweh in the day when Yahweh gave the Amorites over to the men of Israel and he said in the sight of Israel, "Sun, stand thou still at Gibeon, and thou moon in the valley of Aijalon." And the sun stood still, and the moon stayed, until the nation took vengeance on their enemies. Is this not written in the Book of Jashar? The sun stayed in the midst of heaven, and did not hasten to go down for about a whole day. There has been no day like it before or since, when Yahweh hearkened to the voice of a man; for Yahweh fought for Israel.

These events are *not* labeled "miracles." In fact, the odd thing about them is said to be that Yahweh hearkened to the voice of a man. The uniqueness of the occasion is mentioned, rather matter-of-factly, but no special conclusions are drawn. Yahweh has been fighting for Israel throughout the book of Joshua—this is nothing new. To single out this kind of story as a miracle, to use it especially to exemplify the power of God, may be our idea of what the Old Testament should be saying about the power of God, but it is not what the Old Testament does say.

THE NEW TESTAMENT

In the New Testament we find whole books, the Gospels, that are sometimes thought to be principally about miracles. Jesus, some argue today, can be known to be the Son of God on the grounds that no one other than the Son of God could have done the miracles he did. We occasionally find that perspective in the New Testament. Passages in the Gospel of John argue that Jesus' miracles, called "signs," serve as evidence of his special status. After he turns water to wine at the Cana wedding, the gospel reports that "this, the first of his signs, Jesus did at Cana in Galilee, and manifested his glory; and his disciples believed in him" (2:11). Nicodemus greets Jesus by saying to him, "Rabbi, we know that you are a teacher come from God; for no one can do these signs that you do, unless God is with him" (3:2). Toward the conclusion of John's gospel we find a passage probably retained from an early collection of miracle stories: "Now Jesus did many other signs in the presence of the disciples, which are not written in this book; but these are written that you may believe that Jesus is the Messiah, the Son of God, and that believing you may have life in his name" (20:30-31). Such passages imply that miracles serve as valid evidence for the proposition that Jesus is "the Christ, the Son of God."

Surprisingly, much of the New Testament's commentary on the miracles of Jesus is written *in explicit opposition* to this very theory. Miracles, it is said, do *not* constitute reliable evidence that Jesus is Christ, and those who follow him should *beware* of evidence drawn from miracles. Some sayings attributed to Jesus himself cast doubt on the validity of miraculous signs. In Mark's gospel, for example, "the Pharisees came and began to argue with him, seeking from him a sign from heaven, to test him. And he sighed deeply in his spirit, and said, 'Why does this generation seek a sign? Truly, I say to you, no sign shall be given to this generation' " (8:11-12). In John, Jesus is quoted as saying, in apparent exasperation, "unless you see signs and wonders you will not believe" (4:48).

The problem, as the New Testament presents it, is that miracles—signs and wonders—are by no means unique to Jesus, and to take them as proof that he is the Messiah would lend credence to *other* miracle-workers who *falsely* claim to be messiahs. This problem is evident in Mark's gospel, where believers are warned that "false messiahs and false prophets will arise and show signs and wonders, to lead astray, if possible, the elect" (13:22), a passage Matthew also quotes (24:24). Similarly, in 2 Thessalonians readers are warned that "the coming of the lawless one by the activity of Satan will be with all power and with pretended signs and wonders, and with all wicked deception for those who are to perish, because they refused to love the truth and so be saved" (2:9-10). Even Revelation reports, in wild and imaginative language, that "the beast was captured, and with it the false prophet who in its presence had worked the signs by which he deceived those who had received the mark of the beast and those who worshiped its image" (19:20). "Signs and wonders," if taken as valid evidence, can mislead.

Jesus' followers in the early church claimed to do miracles—signs and wonders—just as Jesus did. While passages in Acts indicate that Jesus should be regarded as one "attested to you by God with mighty works and wonders and signs which God did through him in your midst" (2:22), other passages indicate that the apostles should similarly be regarded. In Acts 8:13 Simon of Samaria is amazed by the "signs and great works of power performed" by the apostle Philip. Stephen "did great wonders and signs among the people" (6:8), as did Barnabas and Paul (15:12) and others. The dead are raised by apostles (see 9:36-43), the sick are healed, prison doors are opened, and believers are delivered from dangers at sea. "God did extraordinary works of power by the hands of Paul, so that handkerchiefs or aprons were carried away from his body to the sick and diseases left them and the evil spirits came out of them" (19:11).

The New Testament regards the ability to do miracles as evidence of special power received from spirits—either God or Satan. While such special power was considered uncommon, it certainly was not considered unique to Jesus. In fact, in outlining the order of precedence in the Christian church Paul announces that "God has appointed in the church first apostles, second prophets, third teachers, then *those who do wonders,* then healers, helpers, administrators, speakers in various kinds of tongues"

(1 Cor. 12:28). Workers of wonders and healers are, respectively, fourth and fifth in precedence!

Our exalted idea of one who can work a miracle is in conflict with the far less exalted idea found in the New Testament. In the first century healers were found throughout the ancient world. Their diagnoses and healing techniques were, obviously, quite different than diagnoses and healing techniques today. Often a diagnosis of a mental or physical ailment would be based on the presumption that the ill person had fallen under the power of some evil spirit. That spirit might have been operating on its own, or sent by a greater evil spirit, like Satan, for malevolent purposes, or sent by a greater good spirit, like God, as a punishment for ritual or moral misbehavior. Indeed, the environment was thought to be filled with spiritual beings, both beneficent and maleficent. As today we believe that invisible germs inhabit our environment and occasionally enter us and bring us disease, so they believed that invisible spirits did the same thing. As we believe that experts can identify the specific germ responsible for an illness (streptococcus, hepatitis B virus, etc.) and then manage to rid us of it, so they believed that experts could identify specific spirits and manage to drive them out. To be sure, today we know how important it is for patients to believe in their physician's expertise. In fact, people who truly believe in their physician are not infrequently cured by taking a placebo; their faith cures them. Similarly, in the ancient world a healer who could engender faith in his abilities would increasingly, perhaps even at a geometric rate, attract the sick, cure some or many of them, and hence, as word spread, attract more who, with even greater faith in his abilities, would also be cured.

The accounts of Jesus' miracles of healing in the New Testament testify to the fact that during his time he was regarded as outstanding in his ability to heal. As his fame spread throughout the region, "they brought to him all who were sick or possessed with demons. . . . And he healed many who were sick with various diseases, and cast out many demons" (Mark 1:29-31). Such reports are common. But, like all healers, Jesus was not always successful. He healed "many"—but not "all." As his fame spread, faith in his abilities spread, and his accomplishments increased. But when there were skeptics around, his accomplishments were few. In his hometown for example, those who had known him since childhood did not think so highly of him, and "he could do no mighty work there, except that he laid his hands upon a few sick people and healed them. And he marveled because of their unbelief" (Mark 6:5-6). For this kind of work the term "faith healer" is apt. Jesus was apparently a great healer, but he was one among many other contemporary faith healers.

Although faith in the power of the healer was crucial in most cases in the ancient world (as it is in most today), the healer had to be more than simply one who inspired trust. As the spirits of disease were powerful entities sent, it was assumed, by even more powerful spirits, the ancient healer usually claimed to be assisted by a powerful spirit of his own. A healer with possession of a spirit more powerful than the spirits of disease could thereby drive out inimical spirits in a kind of supernatural battle. Mark reports that Jesus was accused of being possessed by the higher demon Beelzebub (3:22). The gospel calls this accusation an unforgivable sin; by contrast it declares that Jesus is possessed by, and drives out demons through, the higher holy spirit (3:29-30 and 1:10-12). The question is not whether Jesus is possessed by a spirit; this is assumed. The question is whether he is possessed by the holy spirit (affirmed), Beelzebub (denied), or the spirit of an ancient prophet (denied in Mark 8:27-33). Many of the healings and exorcisms done by Jesus were attributed by some to the spirit. Acts 2:22, for example, makes this clear, when we are told that God worked miracles through Jesus (not that Jesus did them on his own).

On occasion Jesus relied on magical *techniques,* not the power of faith or of the spirit. Jesus' use of magic is described in considerable detail. In Mark 7:33-35 for example, people bring to Jesus a deaf man who has a speech impediment. "And taking him aside from the multitude privately, [Jesus] put his fingers into his ears, and he spat and touched his tongue, and looking up to heaven, he sighed, and said to him, 'Ephṗhatha,' that is, 'Be opened.' And his ears were opened, his tongue was released, and he spoke plainly." Similarly, in John 9:6-7 Jesus encounters a blind man. He "spat on the ground and made clay of the spittle and anointed the man's eyes with the clay, saying to him, 'Go, wash in the pool of Silóam' (which means Sent). So he went and washed and came back seeing." These are actions of magical technique, not healing by faith alone, not healing through the activity of a spirit. Indeed, Jesus apparently used all three methods successfully, as did countless other healers of his time. So did his followers (as Acts reports). If Jesus' healings and exorcisms were sometimes done with practices used by other healers, we can understand why some Christians found it inadvisable to argue that these abilities could prove that Jesus was the Christ.

Besides Jesus' miracles of healing, the Gospels report other miracle stories of a legendary nature—such as turning water into wine—and stories that today we might regard as miracles but which are not labeled so in the Bible. There is nothing in the New Testament to indicate that its authors held the present concept of natural law (and so would understand a miracle as something breaking that law). Paul, it seems, does believe that there is a natural *moral* law, which people should utilize to govern their behavior (see Romans 1:26, 2:14). But to Paul, as to other New Testament writers, worldly events are caused by divine or demonic instigation. Accordingly, if God gives Jesus power over wind and sea (Mark 4:41), this is not a miraculous intervention into a natural order. When he stills that storm, his followers are afraid, amazed, and curious; but it never occurs to them that Jesus has transcended some natural law. His followers simply didn't think in those terms.

Because the authors of the Gospels, like all other people of antiquity, had no precise concept of "the miraculous," nor any specific term for "miracle," they depicted the extraordinary events that attended Jesus' life and the life of the early churches in a variety of ways. Sometimes they merely reported such events without comment, expecting that readers would understand from the reports the extraordinary character of what had happened. When they wanted more specifically to indicate an event's extraordinary nature, they often took over language from the Old Testament. So we occasionally read of "signs and marvels"; but these writers usually dropped the word "marvels" and they rarely made any reference either to the Exodus or to Israel (Acts 7:6-7 is the only exception). The new Christians were more concerned about their private lives than the life of their "nation." Though a good Greek term for the Old Testament's "wonder" was available to them (*thauma*), New Testament authors rarely used it directly, more often indicating amazing events by reporting that the people "wondered." After "signs," their favorite term for such events was "powers," which appears with this sense in pagan usage at about the same time, and for which neither the Old Testament nor modern English has a good equivalent; we might say "acts of power."

Deeds designated by these terms are represented by all the gospels as evidence of Jesus' miraculous power and thus, by implication, of the conclusion to which the writers wished to lead their readers: that Jesus was the Messiah, the Son of God. The purpose of the evangelists was not only to report wonders, but to *cause* wonder, to make the reader ask himself, "Who can this being have been?" and so to come gradually to the desired conclusion. In the same way, both Paul and Acts describe miracles as evidence that Jesus and God were working in the apostles and other members of the early churches. But, because the early Christians thought that "false prophets" and "false messiahs" were capable of performing similar "works of power," and that they would indeed continue to do so down to the apocalypse, the fundamental role of miracles in the career of Jesus and in the creation and propagation of the early Christian churches was treated with caution.

FOR FURTHER READING

R. M. Grant. *Miracle and Natural Law in Graeco-Roman and Early Christian Thought*. Amsterdam, 1952.
Ernst Keller. *Miracles in Dispute*. London: SCM Press, 1984.
C. F. D. Moule, editor. *Miracles: Cambridge Studies in Their Philosophy and History*. London, 1965.
Gerd Theissen. *The Miracle Stories of the Early Christian Tradition*. Philadelphia: Fortress Press, 1983.

SEGREGATION
AND INTOLERANCE
Bernhard Lang

Is it possible to find in the sacred scriptures of Judaism and Christianity an alternative to the religious segregation and intolerance that fills our modern world? Or, put conversely, to what extent is the animosity between religious groups rooted in the Bible itself? If we look closely and honestly at the Hebrew Bible and the Christian New Testament, we will see that the dominant attitude toward nonbelievers is not one of integration and tolerance, but of segregation and intolerance. While both attitudes can be found—from the idea of religiously sanctioned genocide to the acceptance of social outcasts—ancient societies were not generally open and accepting. Religious leaders insisted that their people separate themselves from the gentiles. Social segregation and the prohibition of intermarriage were accompanied by strict control over apostasy. In order to strengthen separate existence and the boundary between Jew and non-Jew, ancient authors published their fantasies about a militarily powerful people who would annihilate polytheistic nations that threatened its unique religion. To the regret of the modern mind, such fantasies became part of the Bible.

The preaching of the charismatic Jewish reformer, Jesus of Nazareth, must be seen only as a brief respite in this history of intolerance. His association with tax collectors and prostitutes, as well as his willingness to heal those who were not Jewish, indicate his reluctance to abide by established cultural norms. He asked only that the sick trust him; all else—gender, profession, and nationality—were irrelevant. That very emphasis on trust, however, would eventually re-establish in the young Christian church the intolerance of traditional ancient life. Indeed, "faith" would soon become the basis by which believer and unbeliever would be divided. As early as the letters of Paul, Christians continued the Jewish tradition of self-segregation, religious intolerance, and rigorous internal control. Religious conviction provided a harsh environment for tolerance and integration.

RELIGIOUS SEPARATION IN THE HEBREW BIBLE

Approximately eight hundred years before the birth of Christ, the Judaism pictured in biblical texts began. Our historical knowledge of earlier Israelite religion—the creed of Abraham, Moses, David, or Elijah—remains vague and problematic. Scholars postulate that the Hebrews may have worshiped many gods and goddesses at first, but that one god, Yahweh, came to be known as the national god. While families and clans honored local gods, Yahweh presided over state concerns: kingship, war, and peace. Eventually the polytheism of Israelite religion was condemned and new beliefs were advocated. By the eighth century B.C.E., the prophet Hosea preached to his people that in the ideal past their nomadic ancestors honored no other god but Yahweh. Hosea reminded the people of the legend that, during their days in Egypt, Yahweh alone was their protector. Yahweh was Israel's state god, and Hosea urged the people to worship him exclusively.

As Israel struggled to maintain its existence against the powerful Assyrian empire, the worship of Yahweh became increasingly important. As small vassal kingdoms, the Israelite states of northern Israel and southern Judah paid heavy tribute and lived under military supervision. Their overlords noted any delay of payment, and attempts at rebellion were crushed immediately. In this situation of continual crisis, the prophetic movement, which advocated the exclusive worship of Yahweh, expanded. Scholars call those who condemned the worship of other gods and goddesses the "Yahweh-aloneists." According to the "aloneists," not only were the people to worship Yahweh exclusively, they were to avoid anyone who continued to honor many deities. Hosea assured the Israelites that in the past they were always isolated from all other people and had no other god but Yahweh. He bemoaned the change he saw in his own day: "Ephraim [i.e. northern Israel] mixes himself with the peoples.

. . . Aliens devour his strength, and he knows it not. . . . The pride of Israel witnesses against him, yet they do not return to Yahweh their God, nor seek him, for all this" (Hos. 7:8-10). With the movement toward monotheism came religious separation and intolerance.

The difficulties the biblical people had with their powerful neighbors eventually led to the annihilation of northern Israel in 722 B.C.E. The state in which Hosea had lived was destroyed and colonized by the Assyrians. This severe dislocation of Israelite culture and religion gave the Yahweh-alone party a more vivid character. For the first time, the aloneists became politically influential. During the reign of King Hezekiah of Judah (722-699 B.C.E.) they convinced the king to enact religious reforms. What remains of those reforms survives as the "Covenant Code," now part of the book of Exodus.[1] In an appendix to that code, a prophetic oracle insists on the separation of Israelites (i.e. true members of the aloneist movement) from their neighbors:

> When my angel goes before you, and brings you in to the Amorites, and the Hittites, and the Perizzites, and the Canaanites, the Hivites, and the Jebusites, and I blot them out, you shall not bow down to their gods, nor serve them, nor do according to their works, but you shall utterly overthrow them and break their pillars in pieces . . . I will not drive them out from before you in one year . . . Little by little I will drive them out before you, until you are increased and possess the land. . . .They shall not dwell in your land. (Exod. 23:23-33)

The Israelites might be forced to live among nonbelievers, but they must not embrace any alien religion or culture. Yahweh will protect his followers, rid the land of all gentiles, and give it over to the aloneist Israelites.

This oracle was put into the mouth of Moses, so the author made it refer to the Palestinian peoples who actually lived *before* the Israelite invasion—the Amorites, Hittites, and Perizzites, for example. Most of these cultures had collapsed by the time the oracle was written, six or seven hundred years later; the writer used their names only for stage dressing.[2] What he was really writing about were two opposing factions: those who followed the one God, Yahweh, and the others who were polytheists, Israelites and gentiles both. The battle going on between these two groups, though presented as actual warfare, was in reality a political and spiritual struggle. The "gentiles," i.e., the polytheists, had to be annihilated because they were religiously dangerous. Their presence in the land would be a constant temptation. "They shall not dwell in your land, lest they make you sin against me; for if you serve their gods, it will be surely a snare for you" (Exod. 23:33). The unbelievers must eventually disappear from Israel. The Covenant Code enunciated its basic conviction unambiguously: "Whoever sacrifices to any God, save to Yahweh only, shall be utterly destroyed" (Exod. 22:20).

King Hezekiah's cultic reforms and the earlier prophecies of Hosea paved the way for another reform, which was enacted in the time of King Josiah of Judah (641-609 B.C.E.). In 622 B.C.E. a scroll was brought to King Josiah and read aloud to him. Allegedly discovered during some repairs to the Jerusalem temple, the book contained a code of law. Supposedly no one knew about this hidden code, which overthrew many of the previous ritual practices. Except for Yahweh's, all religious cults were to be abolished. Yahweh was to be the only god worshiped in the Jerusalem temple. The high priest Hilkiah, high-ranking officials, and a prophetess all supported this code, which reflected their aloneist policy. Josiah eventually made the book into the law of the state, and Judea now had codified religion. Modern scholars generally agree that this reforming code of law constitutes the basis of the book of Deuteronomy. While the exact age and origin of the text are hard to determine, the code is significant because of its monolatrous nature. Interestingly the code did not deny that other gods and goddesses might exist, but it said Judah was to worship only its national god, Yahweh.

The biblical narrative presents King Josiah's reform as the culmination of attempts to establish aloneist orthodoxy as the exclusive form of Israelite religion.

Like the Covenant Code, the book of Deuteronomy again voices aloneist themes. Rather than assert in its own name that the Israelites must remain faithful to Yahweh and not associate with worshippers of other gods, Deuteronomy uses Moses to justify religious intolerance and self-segregation from all non-Israelites. Yahweh tells Moses, and Moses tells his people, that in distant places, far away from the promised land, peace will be offered to those cities given to the "chosen people." Cities in Palestine, however, must be treated differently: "But in the cities of these peoples that Yahweh your God gives you for an inheritance, you shall save alive nothing that breathes, but you shall utterly destroy them, the Hittites and the Amorites, the Canaanites and the Perizzites, the Hivites and the Jebusites, as Yahweh your God has commanded" (Deut. 20:16-17). Again, Yahweh states the reason for this genocide succinctly:

". . . that they may not teach you to do according to all their abominable practices which they have done in the service of their gods, and so to sin against Yahweh, your God" (Deut. 20:18). The residents living in the land given to the Israelites must be utterly destroyed because their religion is seen as something attractive, something to which the followers of Yahweh could be easily seduced.

This text again refers to some gentiles whose names had lost any ethnic connotation—the Amorites, Hivites, and so on—in order to symbolize the stranger and polytheist. In another deuteronomic text, the author mentions two authentic enemies of Israel, the Ammonites and Moabites. These two eastern neighbors of Israel lived in what is now the kingdom of Jordan. Just as with the mythical Amorites and Hivites, "no Ammonite or Moabite shall enter the assembly of Yahweh; even to the tenth generation none belonging to them shall enter the assembly of the Lord for ever" (Deut. 23:3). Both kings Saul and David had fought against these people, and the prophets had pronounced numerous oracles against them. They were Israel's archenemies. However, David lived before the Deuteronomist, and when it came to practical measures, economic considerations modified his zeal. He needed serfs to work the conquered lands. So, instead of exterminating Moabites, he "measured them with a line, making them lie down on the ground; two lines he measured to be put to death, and one full line to be spared" (2 Sam. 8:2) There could be no peaceful existence between Israel and her enemies.

From the perspective of the aloneist Israelites, the uncompromising law laid down by Moses was not heeded by the ensuing generations. Consequently, polytheism survived within Israel. The influence of the aloneist party was weakened because of the continual worship of other goddesses and gods. "Ephraim did not drive out the Canaanites who dwelt in Gezer; but the Canaanites dwelt in Gezer among them" (Judg. 1:29). Other tribes who disobeyed the intention of Yahweh and his messenger, Moses, are listed in the Book of Judges: Manasseh, Zebulun, Asher, Naphtali, Dan, and Joseph (ch. 1). Yahweh recalled that he had promised never to break his covenant *if* the Israelites made no other covenant with the local inhabitants and if they broke down all alien altars. "But you have not obeyed my commandment," he reproached them. "What is this you have done? So now I say, I will not drive them out before you; but they shall become adversaries to you, and their gods shall be a snare to you" (Judg. 2:1-13). Now the disobedient Israelites would be punished by the continuing presence of pagans in their midst. And living among the gentiles would cause them much suffering.

The deuteronomistic history of the aloneists also contains inflated accounts of the massacres of polytheists. The prophet Elijah, commanded by Yahweh, reportedly slaughtered numerous prophets of the pagan deity Baal (1 Kings 18)—probably a reflection of a local conflict of the ninth century B.C.E. While Elijah is reported to have slain 450, the military captain Jehu allegedly killed "*all* the prophets of Baal, all his worshipers and priests" (1 Kings 10:18-27). Both massacres are reported as good things; they showed how aloneist ideals should be successfully carried out. Another passage tells how, at the instigation of the Jerusalem priest Jehoiada, a mob "went to the house [temple] of Baal and tore it down." At the same time the mob killed "Mattan the priest of Baal before the altars" (2 Kings 11:18).

It is difficult to determine what actually happened in the ninth century between groups who worshiped Baal and groups who worshiped Yahweh. Did opposition to Baal originate in the idea that Yahweh should receive *exclusive* veneration? Although this possibility cannot be ruled out completely, it seems more likely that the early conflict had to do with the rival economic and personal claims of various priesthoods. In the ninth century, *both* groups, despite their differences, were most likely polytheistic. What we have in the deuteronomistic history of the aloneists is an effort to read back into history the values and reforms of monolatrous Israel.

Historically, we are on better ground in late seventh-century southern Judah. In the report on King Josiah's aloneist reform in Jerusalem, no Baal priests are mentioned at all—although we do hear of "idolatrous priests whom the kings of Judah had ordained to burn incense in the high places at the cities of Judah and round about Jerusalem; those also who burned incense to Baal, to the sun, and the moon, and the constellations, and all the host of the heavens" (2 Kings 23:5). These priests are said to be "deposed" by the king, and this account is historically reliable. It is more difficult to say whether, when the northern Israelite territory of Bethel was annexed, "all the priests of the high places" were actually "slain" (2 Kings 23:20). Perhaps Josiah's reform was vigorously opposed by the priests of that area, which made the king's reaction even more vigorous. Although there are many stories of slain prophets and priests, the history of the conflict between the Yahweh-alone movement and the supporters of polytheistic Israel cannot be reliably constructed. The biblical text is not always the best *historical* guide to what happened in history. It does, however, reveal much about the attitude of the authors.

THE PROHIBITION OF INTERMARRIAGE

A more peaceful form of segregation was the prohibition of marriage between Israelites and their pagan neighbors. The Book of Deuteronomy prohibits intermarriage with seven fictional gentile nations: the Hittites, Girgashites, Amorites, Canaanites, Perizzites, Hivites, and Jebusites. Since these names are symbolic for *all* pagan nations, marriage with all of them was forbidden. Yahweh himself is said to have issued this law: "You shall not make marriages with them, giving your daughters to their sons or taking their daughters for your sons. . . ." The religious reason for this prohibition is explicitly stated: "for they would turn away your sons from following me [Yahweh], to serve other gods" (Deut. 7:3-4). There is no provision for conversion in the text. At this point in history, the Israelites had a national religion in which one's *birth* determined religious identity. People did not *choose* their religion, they assumed the ritual, cultural, and political allegiances of their community. Religious and national commitments were too fundamental to change.

The aloneists had difficulty in imposing the "divine" prohibition of intermarriage on their fellow Israelites. "So the people of Israel dwelt among the Canaanites, the Hittites [etc.] . . . and they took their daughters to themselves for wives and their own daughters they gave to their sons; and they served their gods. And [thus] the people of Israel did what was evil in the sight of Yahweh" (Judg. 3:5-7). Evidently, intermarriage was common, but the aloneists would not go with the herd. Only when an Israelite man sought to marry a *captive* gentile woman could she be accepted into the Israelite community. The procedure prescribed by the Book of Deuteronomy involves a careful separation of the captive from her family and, implicitly, from her religious affiliation:

When you go forth to war against your enemies, and Yahweh your God gives them into your hands, and you take them captive, and see among the captives a beautiful woman, and you have desire for her and would take her for yourself as wife, then you shall bring her home to your house, and she shall shave her head and pare her nails. And she shall put off her captive's garb, and shall remain in your house and bewail her father and mother a full month; after that you may go in to her, and be her husband, and she shall be your wife. (Deut. 21:10-13)

Shaving the head, paring the nails, changing clothes, and mourning were all parts of the *death* ritual. Before the captive could become a member of an Israelite tribe, she first had to accept the symbolic death of her old family and nation. Only after this period of mourning and acknowledgment of a new life could a pagan woman no longer be a threat to Israelite religious culture. There could be no intermingling of the life of Israel and the life of the foreign nation.

Men who had acquired gentile wives through other circumstances were enjoined to divorce them. Radical aloneists insisted on divorce as a means of cleansing the Israelite people. Divorce, however, could not easily be imposed on someone unwilling to send away his wife. In biblical Israel, marriages were arranged between two families intent mainly on making good economic and political matches for their children. Neither religious authorities nor the community had any means of controlling marriage. We know of only one occurrence, after the Babylonian Exile in mid fifth-century Jerusalem, when Ezra tried to make the Judaeans divorce their foreign wives. Whether the scribe Ezra was actually successful is far from clear. Instead, the Judaeans seem to have got rid of *him*. His account stops in mid-air, with the divorces not yet final. Even so, his rhetoric was remembered. "You have trespassed and married foreign woman, and so increased the guilt of Israel. Now then make confession to Yahweh the God of your fathers, and do his will; separate yourselves from the peoples of the land and from the foreign wives" (Ezra 10:10-11). This record surely came from the Yahweh-aloneists, who perpetuated Ezra's ideal.

Nehemiah, a contemporary of Ezra, dealt with the same issue of mixed marriages. "In those days I saw Jews," he reports,

> who had married women of Ashdod, Ammon, and Moab; and half of their children spoke the language of Ashdod, and they could not speak the language of Judah, but the language of each people. And I contended with them and cursed them and beat some of them and pulled out their hair; and I made them take oath in the name of God, saying, "You shall not give your daughters to their sons, or take their daughters for your sons or for yourselves. . . . Shall we then listen to you and do all this great evil and act treacherously against our God by marrying foreign women?" (Neh. 13:23-27)

Even though governor of Jerusalem, appointed by the Persians who then controlled the country, Nehemiah had no legal power to dissolve marriages. He therefore had to use his police power tyrannically—by cursing, beating, and pulling out hair, for example. Although his report is not very specific, Nehmiah claims to have been successful in driving out of Jerusalem a high priest's son who married a foreign woman and in making the heads of the families swear that they would permit no such marriages in the future (Neh. 13:25-8). While this may have been true, his further claim—"I have cleansed them from everything foreign" (Neh. 13:30)—is certainly an exaggeration. The boast betrays, however, the intention of cleansing all foreign culture from Israelite life.

From the point of view of the orthodox monotheists, it is quite understandable why the high priest's son was sent away. Since the priesthood was passed on from father to son, a priest's mixed marriage could result in strong foreign connections of someone serving in the Jerusalem temple. These connections would certainly involve such an individual in cultic activities other than those of Jewish orthodoxy. That a priest's marriage to a foreigner met with opposition is also clear from the book of Malachi, dating from about 450 B.C.E. "Judah has been faithless, and abomination has been commited in Israel and in Jerusalem," exclaims the prophet, "for Judah has profaned the sanctuary of Yahweh, which he loves, and has married the daughter of a foreign god" (Mal. 2:11). The prophet's oracle seems to refer not to mixed marriages in general, but to one controversial marriage in particular, which explains the reference to the Temple. Possibly it was the high priest who had married a foreign woman whom the prophet calls "the daughter of a foreign god."[3] According to Malachi, there can be nothing more offensive than a priest's mixed marriage: The sanctuary must not be polluted.

INTERNAL CONTROL, PUNISHMENT, AND PERSECUTION

Corresponding to external separation—exemplified both in the prohibition of intermarriage with gentiles and the abolition of polytheistic cults—was a high level of internal control and intolerance. Followers of Yahweh should not only limit their contact with the outside world, but they should also tightly control their own communities. According to biblical texts, the Israelites were frequently unfaithful to the one God. Inclined to apostasy, they had to be prevented from falling prey to the snares of pagan religion by both a tight system of supervision and the threat of severe punishment. The Book of Deuteronomy sets only one kind of punishment for apostasy: death by stoning.

According to Deuteronomy, when a man or a woman was discovered worshiping other gods (like the sun, the moon, or stars), and when two witnesses confirmed the crime, the idolator was to be stoned to death (Deut. 17:2-7). Prophets and visionaries were not accorded any special privilege: If their revelations incited people to worship other gods, they too were to be punished by death (Deut. 13:1-5). If an entire city as a community decided to worship other gods, that city had to be annihilated. Everything, including the animals, had to be burnt; no booty could be taken into a believing community. Cities of apostates were to be treated like enemies—the notorious Canaanites, Amorites, Jebusites, etc. —and not be permitted to exist (Deut. 13:12-18).

Individuals or communities who succumbed to foreign beliefs had to be discovered and severely dealt with. Believers were bound by law to report all apostasy, even in the case of close relatives and friends:

> If your brother, the son of your mother, or your son, or your daughter, or the wife of your bosom, or your friend who is as your own soul, entices you secretly, saying, "Let us go and serve other gods" . . . you shall not yield to him or listen to him, nor shall your eye pity him, nor shall you spare him, nor shall you conceal him; but you shall kill him; your hand shall be first against him to put him to death, and afterwards the hands of all the people. You shall stone him to death with stones. (Deut. 13:6-10)

If the idolator tried to seduce someone of equal position (brother of the same mother, friend) or an inferior and dependent (son, daughter, wife), the person being seduced to idolatry had to notify the authorities. An echo of this uncompromising rule can be heard in a New Testament description of the struggles against synagogue members who were of Christian—and therefore heretical—persuasion: "Brother will deliver up brother to death, and the father his child, and children will rise against parents and have them put to death" (Matt. 10:21). This passage goes beyond Deuteronomy in implying that children were supposed to supervise their parents' religious behavior. Nonbelievers would not be tolerated in a community dedicated to Yahweh.[4]

Such passages on apostasy emphasize how religious commitments should take precedence over family ties or clan allegiances. In a community where the extended family was crucial for economic and social survival, the idolator wanted to use the family network to facilitate his or her conversion efforts. Those kin or friends who felt that they were being seduced sought to evade the conflict between religious and kin loyalties by hushing up the affair. Against this, the law proclaimed the clear priority of religion—a drastic measure in a kinship-based society. Family feelings were to be utterly ignored. Indeed, if the relative reported the apostasy, he or she had to throw the death sentence's first stone.

During the time of the Second Temple (the one built after the Babylonian exile, in the late sixth century B.C.E), early Judaism saw a proliferation of religious movements and sects. The dichotomy of Jews and gentiles was complicated by the assimilationists (who were neither real Jews nor real gentiles) as well as by competing and mutually exclusive groups *within* Judaism. In practical life, these groups often compromised and sometimes achieved remarkable tolerance of each other. We know that the Sadducees, who did not believe in the resurrection of the dead, were not banned from the synagogues or punished for their disbelief. Nor did the Sadducees punish others for their superstition. So far as we know, the debate between the Pharisees and Sadducees remained at the level of verbal exchange (Acts 23:6-9). Such tolerance was restricted, however; not everything was tolerated by everyone. For instance, the book called "The Wisdom of Solomon" (which Solomon never dreamt of) reports tensions between assimilationists, dubbed "law-breakers," and orthodox followers of traditional Jewish custom (Wisd. of Sol. 2:10-20). On the eve of the Maccabean uprising of the 160s B.C.E., a certain Mattathias established himself as a religious terrorist, destroyed pagan altars, killed Jews who were favorably inclined to Hellenistic ways, and circumcised children by force (1 Macc. 2).

While the Book of Deuteronomy envisions tight social control only in connection with the capital crime of idolatrous worship, early Judaism developed a more complete list of both major and minor religious offenses and corresponding forms of punishment. Although we have no way of telling to what extent these rules were actually carried out, it cannot be doubted that to some extent they were practiced. It was in line with such rules that Paul, in his pre-Christian days, persecuted the new Jewish sect of Christians. A self-appointed heresy hunter, Paul "laid waste the church and, entering house after house, he dragged off men and women and committed them to prison" (Acts 8:3). Later, when converted to Christianity, Paul himself suffered from the measures taken by vigilant synagogue officials. "Five times," he reports, "I have received at the hands of the Jews the forty lashes less one" (2 Cor. 11:24). According to the ancient Jewish book of law, this penalty sometimes led to the death of the person thus punished.[5]

The deuteronomic tradition underlying ancient Judaism insisted on the people's divine election: "You are a people holy to Yahweh your God; Yahweh your God has chosen you to be a people for his own possession, out of all the people that are on the face of the earth" (Deut. 7:6). Election entails separation. Israelites had to separate themselves culturally and religiously from the gentiles. This segregation could include, at least in theory, the violent annihilation of local populations and the strict prohibition of all social contact. If contact was inevitable, then no marriage could take place between the followers of Yahweh and the others. On the condition that Israel venerated only one God, it would become the leading nation of the earth: "And the peoples of the earth shall see that you are called by the name of Yahweh; and they shall be afraid of you. . . . Yahweh will make you the head and not the tail" (Deut. 28:10-13). The aloneist tradition as seen in Hosea, Deuteronomy, and Judges emphasizes the fundamental structure of monolatrous Judaism. Israel's one God has covenanted with his one chosen people. This one God controls the one people's history and provides blessings. To observe the wishes of Yahweh is to bring prosperity, fertility, peace, and order. Other peoples and other gods are alien to the one God and one people. To worship other gods or to embrace the culture of other peoples is to reject the one God of the one people. To turn away from that God, and to follow the gods of the gentiles, is to turn from order to chaos, from safety to danger, from blessing to barrenness. Only through segregation—which often entailed violence and intolerance—could the holiness of the Jews be preserved.

This attitude of the separatist faction of postexilic Judaism was not shared by all worshipers of Yahweh in Palestine. While real assimilationist voices—those who advocated the complete assimilation to the gentile world—are not represented among the canonical writings of the Bible, we can at least point to a trajectory that, although not opposing separatism, was more tolerant. The Book of Ruth seems to demonstrate the permissibility of marriage with Moabite women, and the Judith story allows for an Ammonite man's conversion to the Jewish faith (Jth. 14:10). In the Book of Esther, a Jewish girl marries the Persian king. These voices, however, appear to be relatively isolated and are not accorded the status of the Book of Deuteronomy. It can also be argued that the seemingly tolerant stories make use of poetic license, telling about the rare exception rather than the rule. The normal situation or course of events would not make for a good story. In the Old Testament, the separatist attitude prevails.

JESUS: A MORE TOLERANT FIGURE

Jesus was a first-century Galilean whose audience was mostly Jewish. According to the gospels, he told his followers, "I was sent only to the lost sheep of Israel" (Matt. 15:24). It was to the Jews that Jesus preached the love of the one and only God. Both the restriction to Israel and the emphasis on God certainly originate in the Book of Deuteronomy. (Mark 12:29-30 almost exactly restates Deuteronomy 6:4-5.) But Jesus' intention was not to follow simply the paradigm established by Deuteronomy. As a charismatic preacher and miracle-worker, Jesus rejected deuteronomic norms of religious segregation and intolerance. Although the gospels were written by second or third-generation Christians, we can discern his openness to non-Jews. Both the unique relationship he claimed to have with God and the magic powers he knew he possessed made him independent from Jewish traditions and institutions.

In one gospel story, Jesus responds generously to the needs of a Phoenician woman (Matt. 15:21-28). The woman—referred to in deuteronomic style as a "Canaanite"—asks Jesus to save her daughter from possession by a spirit. At first Jesus refuses to grant her request. In his dialogue with the woman, he refers to his powers as "bread" not to be fed to the non-Jew. "It is not fair to take the children's [Jews'] bread," Jesus initially concludes, "and throw it to the dogs [gentiles]." The mother counters by saying that "even the dogs eat the crumbs that fall from their masters' table." Considering the woman's faith and per-sistence, Jesus heals the possessed girl. While Jesus seems sure that his message and powers should be experienced only by the Jews, he also seems willing to counter the deuteronomic intolerance toward gentiles.

In a parallel story Jesus is reported to have performed a similar miracle for another pagan, a Roman centurion. In this story the Roman shows intense faith in the healing power of Jesus (Matt. 8:5-13). On yet another occasion, we hear about a dialogue Jesus had with a Samaritan women (John 4:7-30). In spite of the fact that "Jews have no dealings with Samaritans," Jesus not only talks to her but also lumps the Samaritan cult on Mt. Gerizim with the Jewish cult in Jerusalem as destined to be replaced by the true worship of God in the spirit (4:21-23). Although Jesus' conversation with the Samaritan woman may not be historical, the story reflects his opinion on the differences between Jews and Samari-tans: Both denominations are in the process of being superseded by the new order of the messianic age. That age, of course, is inaugurated by

Jesus himself.

The message of all these reports is identical. While Jesus defined his mission as restricted to the people of Israel, he could occasionally be more tolerant of other people. This attitude, though, must not be misunderstood. Jesus neither advocated the possibility of Moabites becoming Jews (as the biblical story of Ruth seems to do, in opposition to Deuteronomy), nor did he preach about God's concern for the Ninehvites (as does the biblical book of Jonah). Jesus is rarely shown as interested in saving pagans from damnation or promising them a place in God's coming kingdom. His tolerant, more liberal attitude was also not based on the idea that all people are somehow equal due to a natural law. This modern, enlightenment idea was foreign to a first-century Jew. Jesus simply recognized that sincere trust in him overruled national and religious boundaries. Ultimately, for Jesus it was *trust* that defined people. For a religious enthusiast, all other definitions—of class, gender, nationality—were of less importance.

Even more striking than Jesus' rejection of religious separation was his tolerance of heretofore unacceptable moral behavior. While Deuteronomy wants all "sinners" to be eradicated from Israel, Jesus made them the first members of his own community. He freely associated with people who notoriously disobeyed the Jewish law or were hated because of their collaboration with Roman authorities. One group of such people were the tax collectors, the "publicans" of the King James Version. In the Hellenistic and Roman worlds, taxes were not collected by state officials. Local men of wealth and influence contracted with their city or district to gather the taxes it paid to Rome. The hostile references to them in the gospels rather reflect their equivocal position between their fellow Jews and the Romans than describe their honesty or dishonesty.

One of Jesus' disciples, a man called Matthew or Levi, was a tax collector (Matt. 9:9; Mark 2:14). Matthew apparently gave up his profession because he could not easily wander about with Jesus and collect taxes. Another of Jesus' tax collector associates, however, Zacchaeus of Jericho, did not give up his business (Luke 19:1-10). Although Zacchaeus reportedly repaid those he had treated unfairly, Jesus did not urge him to do so. We can speculate that these rich tax collectors supported Jesus financially and that their faith and wealth helped popularize his mission.

Jesus rejected the traditional codes of separation by associating freely with the socially unacceptable. He "ate with the tax collectors and sinners"

(Mark 1:16). To those of his contemporaries who stood on the upper rung of the social ladder—the "chief priests" of the Jerusalem Temple and "the elders of the people" (Matt. 21:31)—Jesus insisted that even "the tax collectors and harlots go into the kingdom of God before you." Whether prostitutes were actually among the women who belonged to Jesus' immediate following (Luke 8:2-3) is unknown. Here tradition may have suppressed evidence that was thought to be offensive to later, more settled Christians. Mary Magdalene, a woman "healed of evil spirits and infirmities" (Luke 8:2), was certainly a leading figure among Jesus' friends. Her profession as a prostitute, however, cannot be ascertained from the New Testament. The "woman of the city, who was a sinner," perhaps a wealthy prostitute, is the only person of that trade referred to in the gospels (Luke 7:37ff.). She once came in while Jesus was reclining at dinner, knelt at the side of the couch by his feet, wept over them, dried them with her hair, kissed them, and poured perfume over them. When some disciples challenged the propriety of this, Jesus took her part. As with the tax collectors, Jesus did not condemn prostitution or urge harlots to leave their profession. He told the woman that her trust had saved her and "go in peace." Jesus did not ask marginal people to conform to the social norm, only to trust in him.

Jesus summarized his attitude to sinners—in the Gospels exemplified by tax collectors and prostitutes—by his injunction not to judge others. "Judge not, that you be not judged. For with the judgment you pronounce will be judged, and the measure you give will be the measure you get" at God's impending universal judgment (Matt 7:1-2). In the case of an adulteress, Jesus explicitly challenged the traditional law by urging others not to stone her to death. When Jesus said, "Let him who is without sin among you be the first to throw a stone at her," no one of those present dared to start. Left alone with the woman, Jesus told her that he would not condemn her (John 8:3-11). Although Jesus is reported to have told her "sin no more," his stance was not one of moralism. Not only does Jesus associate with those popularly defined as sinners, he does not make it a prior condition of their pardon that they give up what many considered to be immoral behavior.

Jesus' tolerance of sinners must be understood in the context of his role as a wandering charismatic. A charismatic is captured by the spirit and sees him- or herself as having divine gifts that give authority over others. Charismatic leaders are able to motivate people to change their lives and beliefs radically. Free from any need for institutional legitimation, the charismatic is unconcerned about everyday codes of behavior. Even normal family life and occupational commitments are scorned. Among Jesus' followers were a significant number of outsiders or outcasts: those with a dishonest trade or a profession not approved of by Jewish society. Since Jesus believed that these outcasts had more trust than more conventional Jews, it was to them that he promised special places in God's kingdom (Matt. 21:31). The relationship between Jesus and social outcasts was reciprocal. They loved and supported him, and he responded with the charismatic's gratitude, promising them spiritual rewards. As a charismatic teacher, Jesus was not interested in their occupations or past histories. He was only touched by their willingness to acknowledge his divine power and authority. Tolerance could be granted to those who at least by implication accepted Jesus as someone endowed with unsurpassable power.

PAUL'S REESTABLISHMENT OF SEGREGATION AND INTOLERANCE

Jesus established a precedent: Righteousness was more important than profession or nationality. Sinners could be saved by trust alone. Paul, an uncompromising, dedicated, and zealous follower of Jesus, made this the central point of his teaching. What had remained implicit in Jesus' own message now became clearly expressed and unambiguously practiced. Whether Jew or gentile, everyone was called to join the new community of believers. To join the Christian community, one did not have to be a Jew first. Christian baptism made circumcision, the hallmark of Jewish religious identity, superfluous. "For as many of you as were baptized into Christ have put on Christ. There is neither Jew nor Greek, there is neither slave nor free, there is neither male nor female; for you are all one in Jesus Christ" (Gal. 3:27-28). The Christian identity is so strong that it supersedes and obliterates all other identities. A baptized person is "a new creation." The early Christian communities founded by Paul in Asia Minor and Greece were open, welcoming, and accommodating. In that sense, Paul transcended the narrowness of traditional deuteronomic separatism.

Once a convert had joined the Christian group, however, he was confronted with much less tolerance. Within the group, Paul strove to establish a sense of order. In his own letters, as well as those ascribed to him, we can see the return to deuteronomic notions of stern religious segregation and intolerance.

"Do not be mismated [or: do not associate] with unbelievers," says an inserted fragment of text found in a Pauline letter. "For what partnership have righteousness and iniquity? Or what fellowship has light with darkness? What accord has Christ with Belial [Satan]? Or what has a believer in common with an unbeliever? What agreement has the temple of God with idols? For we are the temple of the living God" (2 Cor. 6:14-16).[6] Paul sets up a distinction between believer and nonbeliever that reflects his familiarity with Jewish history and law. Christians belong to light and Christ, the others to darkness and Satan. Experiencing Christ sets the believer apart from the disbeliever.

In the generation of Paul, the new Christian community developed a growing sense of separate identity. What started as an enthusiastic movement inside Judaism had experienced so much opposition that sectarian, separate existence was the logical outcome. One could speak of Christians as "the sons of light"; the others—*all* the others—were *the sons of darkness.*

The letters of Paul reveal a community in which special bearers of the spirit of Christ compete with one another for authority and influence. Paul asserted his unimpeachable position as leader, since he thought he shared in the supreme authority of Christ himself. "If any one thinks that he is a prophet, or spiritual," he told the Corinthians, "he should acknowledge that what I am writing to you is a command of the Lord [Jesus Christ]. If any one does not recognize this, he is not recognized [as a prophet]" (1 Cor. 14:37-38). In matters of doctrine Paul often used persuasion, but at other times he refused to tolerate other viewpoints: "If any one is preaching to you a gospel contrary to that which you received [from me, Paul], let him be accursed" (Gal. 1:9). Paul, like Jesus, assumed that his connection to the divine enabled him to speak with authority and conviction, and that authority included the power to separate Christians from non-Christians and to condemn certain behavior.

Paul knew that Christians could not separate themselves completely from people whose behavior or beliefs they did not endorse. If one really wished to do so, he wrote, "then you would need to go out of the world." What is possible, he thought, is to keep the Christian community itself free from dubious individuals. "Those inside the church" are urged "not to associate with any one who bears the name of [Christian] brother if he is guilty of immorality or greed, or is an idolator, reviler, drunkard, or robber—not even to eat with such a one" (1 Cor. 5:10-12). The idolator may be the liberal Christian who feels free to continue worshiping in the Greek style of his or her ancestors, a cult that actually involved images or "idols."[7] To the preceding list the apostle adds the homosexual and the one who "joins himself to a prostitute" (1 Cor. 6:9, 16). Jesus' "eating with tax collectors and sinners" seems long forgotten. It is quite logical that Paul should refer to the deuteronomic law to round off his argument. "Drive out the wicked person from among you," Paul writes in 1 Corinthians 5:13, closely echoing this demand of Deuteronomy 17:7: "purge the evil from the midst of you."

When a case of incest ("a man living with his father's wife") was reported to Paul, he ordered immediate punishment: "When you are assembled, and my spirit is present [Paul probably means: my letter is read in public], with the power of our Lord Jesus, you are to deliver this man to Satan for the destruction of the flesh, that his spirit may be saved in the day of the Lord Jesus" (1 Cor. 5:4-5). While we cannot be certain what "handing over to Satan" means, it does imply that the criminal has to leave the community. A later, pseudo-Pauline letter uses similar language. "Hymenaeus and Alexander" and others "have made a shipwreck of their faith" and were therefore, by Pseudo-Paul, "delivered to Satan that they may learn not to blaspheme" (1 Tim. 1:20). In this case the excommunication excludes not an immoral person, as in 1 Corinthians, but people who committed the specifically religious crime of blasphemy, perhaps by cursing the name of Jesus.[8]

AFTER PAUL

The Christian community, no longer a group of wandering Jewish sectarians, eventually developed a firm structure of offices and apostolic control. In a peculiar and perplexing story told in the Acts of the Apostles, the implications of community control is frightfully vivid. In the early church, the text explains, all Christians held their possessions in common. No one owned private property. When, however, the couple Ananias and Saphira sold a piece of property, they laid only part of the proceeds at the apostles' feet. When Peter confronted him with his sin, Ananias instantly fell down and died. "After an interval of about three hours his wife came in, not knowing what had happened," the report continues.

And Peter said to her, "Tell me whether you sold the land for so much." And she said, "Yes, for so much." But Peter said to her, "How

is it that you have agreed to tempt the Spirit of the Lord? Hark,
the feet of those who that have buried your husband are at the door,
and they will carry you out." Immediately she fell down at his feet
and died. When the young men came in they found her dead, and
they carried her out and buried her beside her husband. And great
fear came upon the whole church, and upon all who heard of these
things. (Acts 5:7-11)

This is almost certainly not an incident that actually happened. It was
probably a story told in communities where private property was outlawed, a story that warned of the consequences of secretly hoarding
wealth. Nevertheless, the account reveals the spirit of apostolic authority.
The very term "apostle," it must be remembered, denotes the authority
of someone who is commissioned by the Lord himself and acts as his
representative. The leadership claimed by the apostles and their succes-
sors aimed at *total control*—not only over the faithful's belief, but also
over all their possessions. That control could take on Orwellian dimen-
sions, extending to their very lives. Religious segregation, intolerance,
and internal control had found their way into Christianity.

CONCLUSION

Segregation and religious tolerance must be understood in terms of the
development of social institutions. In the beginning of biblical history,
we see a society dominated by concerns of family and kin. With the
growth of the state and the increasing influence of religious institutions,
freedom became more and more restricted. Public institutions began to
invade domains that were previously considered private. The more
vigorous and prophetic religion became, the more it sought to control
even the private lives of its members, so that religious enthusiasts could
sometimes deny the relevance of kinship altogether. While Jesus tolerated
the social outcast, he set the stage for later intolerance. His insistence
on the importance of "trust" would encourage later Christians to condemn
those who did not exemplify "the faith," since in Greek a single word,
pistis, means both "trust" and "faith." While Jesus appeared reluctant
to condemn the sinner or to separate the righteous from the unrighteous,
Paul used his authority to control Christian behavior. As a Jewish teacher
schooled in the law, Paul could not resist appropriating deuteronomic
policies of segregation and intolerance. New Testament Christianity, like

the Yahweh-alone movement, sought isolation from other groups and suppressed whatever pluralistic tendencies or idiosyncracies emerged in the community. Except for rare instances in the Hebrew scriptures and brief examples in the gospels, religious tolerance and openness to people with different lifestyles and opinions are absent from the Bible.

NOTES

1. Exod. 21-23; for the dating, see M. Smith, *Palestinian Parties* 107, with n. 69.

2. The list of people Israel supposedly encountered when entering Palestine is a stock item of separatist rhetoric, which sometimes appears in a military context (Deut. 7:2; Exod. 3:8; Josh. 3:10; etc.). In King Hezekiah's days these names lacked any geographical or ethnic connotation. One of the lists also includes the Rephaim, most likely the name for mythical giants (Gen. 15:20)! Modern scholarship, moreover, has profoundly modified the notion of early Israel's military conquest of Palestine. It seems therefore likely that the archaic ethnic names are used symbolically for everything foreign to Israel.

3. This is only one of two possible interpretations. If mixed marriages in general are referred to, then the underlying idea would be that all sins committed in Israel pollute its Temple (which was ritually cleansed every year).

4. The Book of Deuteronomy apparently based its policy of control on ancient Near Eastern models. According to these, a subject was bound by oath to denounce anyone suspected of treason, including close relatives. For a relevant text, see *Ancient Near Eastern Texts Relating to the Old Testament,* ed. J. B. Pritchard, 3ed., Princeton 1969, 535.

5. *Mishnah,* tractate Makkot 3:10-14. This text can be found in H. Danby, *The Mishnah,* Oxford, 1933 and later, 407ff.

6. Whether interpolated (as some commentators argue) or not, this text was taken as Pauline in spirit.

7. On the Corinthian cult of "idols" as ancestor worship, see the suggestive paper by C. A. Kennedy, "The Cult of the Dead in Corinth," in *Love and Death in the Ancient Near East,* ed. J. H. Marks and R. M. Good, Guilford, Connecticut, 1987, 227-36 (M.H. Pope volume).

8. Cf. "Cursed be Jesus!" (1 Cor. 12:3).

FOR FURTHER READING

J. D. M. Derrett. "Cursing Jesus (1 Cor XII 3): The Jews as Religious Persecutors." *New Testament Studies* 21 (1975) 544-554.

P. Garnsey. "Religious Toleration in Classical Antiquity." In *Persecution and Toleration*. Edited by W. J. Sheils. Oxford, 1984. 1-27.

A. E. Harvey. "Forty Strokes Save One: Social Aspects of Judaizing and Apostasy." In *Alternative Approaches to the New Testament*. Edited by A. E. Harvey. London, 1985. 79-96.

W. Horbury. "Extirpation and Excommunication." *Vetus Testamentum* 35 (1985) 13-38.

B. Lang. *Monotheism and the Prophetic Minority*. Sheffield, 1983.

G. Shaw. *The Cost of Authority: Manipulation and Freedom in the New Testament*. Philadelphia, 1983.

M. Smith. *Palestinian Parties and Politics that Shaped the Old Testament*. Second edition. London, 1987.

M. Weinfeld. "The Ban of the Canaanites and Its Development in Israelite Law." *Zion* 53 (1988) 135-147.

SLAVERY
Morton Smith

The Hebrew word for "manservant" could be used of anyone from a king's minister to a slave; and the words for "maidservant" were likewise ambiguous. One must therefore proceed cautiously when writing of slavery in the Hebrew Bible.

Slavery makes its first biblical appearance in the story of Noah and his sons. According to Genesis 6-9 Noah was the only man God liked well enough to save from the flood (Gen. 6:8, 13f.). After the flood, however, he took to drink and lay drunk and naked in his tent. His son Ham saw him there and told his two brothers, Shem and Japeth. They took a cloak, walked backward into their father's tent, and covered Noah without looking at him. When Noah woke up, he learned what Ham "had done to him." Whatever that was thought to have been—guesses have ranged from castration to tale-bearing—he cursed Ham's descendants in the person of Ham's son, Canaan, saying, "Let him be a slave of slaves" (Gen. 9:18-27). As often in Genesis 1:11, the story became a rule for all time thereafter, in this case for all Canaan's descendants, if not all of Ham's.

Obviously something is wrong here. After all, Ham's "sin" seems to have been Noah's fault. Indeed, even if one accept *Ham's* sin, why curse Canaan? Perhaps an early folk tale explaining the origin of slavery has been spliced with a curse made as the Israelites were consolidating power and enslaving the Canaanites. Such a curse would probably have been made later than Solomon, who carried through the enslavement (1 Kings 9:20ff.), and earlier than Deuteronomy 7 (the sixth or seventh century B.C.E.), which commanded that all Canaanites be exterminated.

Whatever happened, the result is a muddle that has been made worse by translation. The Greek translation did not follow the Hebrew exactly and used a somewhat odd expression that *could* mean "slave," but need not. Jerome, who knew Hebrew, translated bluntly, "slave of slaves." The King James translators softened this to "servant of servants," and the American revisers perpetuated their blunder. Since the saying is a curse, the meaning is surely "slave of slaves."

What slavery meant in the biblical world can best be shown by a few famous examples. Let us first look at the story of Abraham, Sarah, and Hagar, which shows how a tenth- or ninth-century-B.C.E. author thought his pious hero would treat a slave girl (Gen. 16:1-16; 21:8-21). As everyone knows, Abraham and his half-sister Sarah had been living in, shall we say, half-incestuous marriage. Sarah, however, was childless. She had some property of her own, including some slave girls, and she decided to give one of them to Abraham so that he could have children from her former property. She thought this would, as she put it, "build her up" (16:2). Her choice was an Egyptian girl, Hagar, whom she may have bought while visiting Egypt some ten years before. Abraham was well on in years—Gen. 16:16 makes him 85. If so, he must have been unusually gifted, but that would hardly have made him seem attractive. Attractiveness, however, was unimportant; nobody thought of asking the girl how she would like him. Sarah simply put the proposition to Abraham, he agreed, she gave him Hagar, and Hagar conceived. But then Hagar became contemptuous of Sarah, who complained to her husband. So Abraham said, in effect, "I give her back to you. Do as you like with her." Sarah treated Hagar so badly that she ran away, but when she got out into the desert she saw an angel who advised her to go back, take her medicine, and keep her place. After all, she had Abraham's child in her, so she could not be treated too badly; indeed, the child might grow up to avenge her. (It is remarkable how often angels give down-to-earth advice). She obeyed and had the child— a boy who was called Ishmael—and then, some thirteen years later, Sarah had a son. No sooner was Sarah's son weaned than she saw Ishmael as a possible competitor for a share of Abraham's property. She then pressed Abraham to drive Hagar and Ishmael out of the camp. At first he refused "because of his son" (nothing is said of any concern about Hagar, 21:11), but another prudent angel advised him to do as Sarah demanded, so he did. Hagar had probably been a slave in the family for more than twenty years (Ishmael was about fifteen), so when

Abraham sent her away he generously gave her some bread and a jug of water so large that she had to carry it on her shoulder (21:14). With these, she and her son were sent into the desert on foot.

This story indicates clearly the social status of what the Authorized Version politely called Sarah's "handmaid." The proper term is *slave,* and the social practices that the Bible takes for granted, without any criticism, are those of chattel slavery. Hagar was simply a piece of property, to be used as needed and thrown out when needed no longer.

Strong's *Exhaustive Concordance* indicates that, in the whole Bible, The Authorized Version uses "slave" only twice, and the Revised Version only twice more, but there are hundreds of biblical uses of Greek and Hebrew words that mean "slave."

Domestic slavery, of the sort illustrated by the Abraham story, was supplemented by enslavement of entire societies, sometimes by economic measures, sometimes by conquest. Social groups enslaved this way might, if peasants, be left on the lands formerly theirs and made to pay a sizable share of their crop, or they might be drafted and used as work gangs for various purposes. The clearest case of mass economic enslavement is the legend of Joseph's purchase of the Egyptians.

The Joseph legend dramatizes an ancient commodity trader's daydream. By God-given insider information the hero, Joseph, persuaded the Pharaoh of Egypt that seven years of good crops were to be followed by seven years of famine, and that the government should accumulate grain in advance by taxing the crops of the good years. He was therefore put in charge of the taxes and the grain supply, and when the famine came he was able, by selling the grain, to acquire first all the money of the people, then all their livestock, and finally their lands, their families, and themselves. "He made slaves of them from one end of Egypt to the other. . . . Then Joseph said to the people, 'Behold, I have today bought you and your land for Pharaoh. Now . . . sow the land, and at the harvest you shall give a fifth to Pharoah" (Gen. 47:21-24).

According to the legend, Joseph provided his father's family, who had come to join him, with food and pasturage; they were not enslaved with the natives of the country. At some time later, however, they seem to have been reduced to slavery, since at the beginning of Exodus we find them and their children subject to taskmasters and "put to work as slaves" on royal building projects "with hard labor in mortar and bricks and all kinds of field labor" (Exod. 1:14). The people came to remember Egypt as a "slave house" (Exod. 13:3, 20:2; Lev. 26:13; Deut. 5:6, 6:12, etc.)

With the conquest of Canaan it became Israel's turn to enslave, but the account of how they did it has been sacrificed, in Joshua, to the legend that they *exterminated* their enemies. (See the details in the chapter "War.") However, the compiler of Joshua felt he had to account for the survival of some pre-Israelite Palestinians as slaves of the Jerusalem temple, so he reported or made up the story that they had sent to Joshua, when he was massacring the entire populations of Palestinian cities, a delegation whose members pretended to come from a far-off country. By this misrepresentation they persuaded the Israelites to make a treaty and swear not to kill them. When they then turned out to be neighbors, the Israelites were much disappointed that they could not kill them, and Joshua blamed them for their dishonesty: "Why did you deceive us? . . . So now you are accursed and there shall never cease to be some of you who shall be enslaved and wood cutters and water carriers for the Temple of my God" (Joshua 9.23; in his righteous indignation Joshua forgot that the Temple would not be built for two hundred years).

Given such a record, we should probably describe most of the victims—those not drafted for temple service—as "tributaries" rather than "slaves." The same term might be used for those Moabites who survived David's slaughter of two-thirds of his captives and "became slaves for David, bringing tribute" (1 Kings 8:2), as did the Syrians after David killed 22,000 captives (8:6), and the Edomites, after 18,000. On the other hand, we are told that Solomon, famous for his justice, "conscripted for corvée labor the descendants of all the people who were left of the . . . (Palestinians) who were not Israelites . . . (and) whom the people of Israel were not able to destroy utterly," and they remain corvée labor "to this day" (1 Kings 9:20–21). Here we should probably speak of the victims as a permanent class of slave-laborers, much as the Israelites are said to have been in Egypt. Solomon also assigned slaves (probably many) to the service of the Temple. Their descendants were still attached to it after the exile, along with others called "those given" (Neh. 7:46-60, 11:3, etc.).

Of such state and temple slaves we have little information, but a good many biblical laws regulate the acquisition and treatment of private slaves, mainly enslaved Israelites whom the biblical legislators wanted to protect. To non-Israelite slaves the alleviating provisions usually do not apply.

According to the Bible, slaves could be acquired by capture in war (e.g., Deut. 20:10ff.) or purchased from slave dealers, resident or neighboring aliens, or fellow Israelites. The author of Leviticus much preferred purchase from aliens (25:44ff.): "From the gentiles who are round about you, from them you shall buy male and female slaves, and also from the descendants of the natives who are living with you, from them you shall buy and from their descendents . . . and [the slaves thus purchased] shall be your [permanent] possessions, you shall bequeath them to your children after you as a permanent possession forever; you shall treat them as slaves."

While prescribing this treatment for gentiles, Leviticus discouraged the purchase of Israelite slaves, but did not prohibit it. The context of the passage just cited, and many other texts, makes clear that there were poor men willing to sell off their children, or even to sell themselves, into slavery; and even Israelites and their children might be purchased, though their condition after purchase was mitigated by some special laws—above all by the provision that according to the older law, the males—and according to later laws, the females also—must be released after seven years (Exod. 21; Deut. 15; Num. 25). Defaulting debtors could be seized by creditors and sold into slavery (2 Kings 4:1; Neh. 5:1-5)—sometimes, reportedly, for as little as the price of a pair of shoes (Amos 2:6—but prophetic rhetoric, then as now, is not wholly trustworthy). Similarly, thieves who could not pay for what they had stolen were enslaved (Exod. 22:2). Finally, an owner could breed slaves from his own stock. The Bible says, "If [an Israelite slave's] master gives him [a slave woman as] a wife and she bears him sons or daughters, the wife and her children shall belong to the master." If the Israelite slave is set free, "he shall go out by himself" (Exod. 21:4). (This might be a way to persuade him to stay; the text goes on to provide: "And if the slave shall firmly declare, 'I love my master, my wife, and my children; I will not go free,' then his master shall bring him to the gods [probably, to the household shrine], and shall make him stand by the door or the door-post, and his master shall pierce his ear with an awl [driving it through into the wood] and he shall serve him forever"— Exod. 21:5f.) In the same way, any other property a slave might acquire belonged to the master. For instance, after David became king he gave to the son of Jonathan, his former lover, all that remained of Saul's property, including one of Saul's slaves named Ziba. Ziba had fifteen sons and twenty slaves of his own, so all these, along with him, became slaves of Jonathan's son (2 Sam. 9:1-10).

The extent of the master's property rights is perhaps best shown by the law on manslaughter. If two free men fight and one kills the other during the fight, the winner is also to be killed; but, if the loser survives for a day or two and gets up and walks about, the winner need pay him only for his loss of time. On the other hand, if a man beats his slave so that the slave dies during the beating, the law prescribes only that the slave "shall be avenged" (Exod. 21:20)—the vengeance is not specified, but presumably was not death, since in the preceding case the death penalty was taken for granted, without any mention, from the general rule, "Whoever strikes a man so that he dies, shall surely be put to death" (21:12). Moreover, the text goes on in 21:21 to say: "If [the slave] survives for a day or two he shall not be avenged, for he is his [master's] property" (and it is a general rule of biblical law that damages to property are not punished by death). Similarly, if a man keeps an animal known to be dangerous, and it kills a free man or woman, the owner is to be put to death (21:29), but if it kills a slave the owner must pay the slave's owner thirty shekels to compensate for the damage to his property (21:32). Again, the *lex talionis* ("An eye for an eye and a tooth for a tooth") did not hold for slaves. If, however, a slave was mutilated by his master, he had to be set free in compensation (21:26f.). Similarly, an owner who cohabits with an Israelite slave girl must give her the privileges due a wife, or else set her free (21:7-11).

What the New Testament has to say, it says in Greek, and therefore fairly clearly, because the Greek word for slave, *doulos,* has little of the ambiguity of the equivalent Hebrew words. So far as I know, until Christianity got control of the Roman Empire, *doulos* was never used of a king's minister, nor by a free man in self-deprecation, except in translations of Near Eastern texts (among them, the Old Testament) and in speaking of enslavement to the gods. When otherwise used of free men it is pejorative, indicating subjugation, usually moral or political—a "slave" of the passions, a "subject" of the Persian king, and the like. While slaves and free men can both be referred to as "servants," "helpers," and so on, the difference of legal status remains sharp. When a free servant is called a *doulos* the speaker is either abusing him or is mistaken. This clarity has been completely obscured by the Authorized and Revised Versions of the New Testament, which commonly translate *doulos* as "servant" or the like, as part of their attempt to make the Word of God suitable for good society.

Once the texts are translated correctly, we can see that Jesus lived in a world where slavery was common. There were innumerable slaves of the emperor and the Roman state; the Jerusalem temple owned slaves; the High Priests owned slaves (one of them lost an ear in Jesus' arrest); all of the rich and many of the middle classes owned slaves. Slave-owning was the order of the day and, so far as we are told, Jesus never attacked the practice. He took the state of affairs for granted and shaped his parables accordingly. In these as in real life, the great men, whether they represent God or the devil, are usually slaveowners, and the main problem for the slaves, as Jesus presents things, is not to get free, but to win their master's approval. There seem to have been slave revolts in Palestine and Jordan in Jesus' youth. A miracle working leader of such a revolt would have attracted a large following. If Jesus had denounced slavery, we should almost certainly have heard of his doing so. We hear nothing, so the most likely supposition is that he said nothing. (The silence cannot plausibly be explained by supposing that he kept the teaching secret, or that his followers suppressed it. We know that he and they employed both secrecy and suppression regarding his magical practices and his claim to be King of the Jews. Nevertheless, reports of both Messianic claims and magical rites have come down to us. Had there been any considerable teaching or significant action about libera-tion of slaves, reports of that would have reached us, too. The issue was a hot one.)

Also, if he had advocated liberation, his adherents would probably have followed his teaching. But the Gospels and Acts say nothing of this, and Paul, our earliest Christian writer, not only tolerates slavery but orders Christians to continue it. He has the notion, perhaps from Jesus' magical practices, that all those baptized "into Jesus" are united with him, so that "in" him "there is neither slave nor free, there is neither male nor female, but all . . . are one in Messiah Jesus" (Gal. 3:28; cf. Rom. 10:12; 1 Cor. 7:22, 12:13; Col. 3:11). However, Paul recognizes that this internal union does not obliterate either sexual differences or differences of social position in the present world. Although he thinks these differences relatively unimportant, he insists that they continue. Of slavery, in particular, he says, "If you, as a slave, were called [by God, to become a Christian], don't worry [about your slavery], but if you can also become a free man, you had better . . . [As a general rule, however,] let each man remain in that [social position] in which he was called" (1 Cor. 7:21, 24).

What this meant in practice was shown when one of the slaves of Philemon (a convert) ran away, came to Paul, and was converted by him. The conversion put Paul in a tight spot. To conceal a runaway slave was legally a theft, and the penalties were severe. So he sent the slave back to Philemon with a letter to him, asking him as a favor to keep the slave "forever, no longer [as] a slave, but . . . [as] a beloved brother." The letter concludes, "Confident of your obedience, I have written you, knowing that you will do even more than I say. And at the same time prepare accommodations for me, for I hope to visit you soon." This was a gentle way of telling Philemon that Paul intended to check up on what would be done to the slave. The whole letter, in fact, is wonderfully tactful and careful, and this increases the significance of what it carefully *does not say*. It does *not* say, "Christians are not allowed to own slaves, least of all to own each other as slaves; therefore, by his conversion your slave has become free of you. Consequently you should recognize this state of affairs and make it legal by legally setting him free at once." On the contrary, it recognized the validity of Philemon's ownership of the slave and hopes that he will continue to own him forever. But it asks him, please, as a special favor, to treat *this* slave as a brother. Philemon's ownership and treatment of his other slaves, particularly those who are pagans, are not questioned. Paul probably had in mind (but significantly did not cite) the passage of Leviticus from which 25:44ff. was quoted above. It distinguishes sharply between Gentiles, who are to be enslaved and treated as slaves, and "your brother" the Israelite, who, even if enslaved, is to be treated kindly. Philemon was a Gentile first and had become a Christian only recently. His reverence for that particular passage of the Mosaic law might have been somewhat less than Pauline, so Paul chose not to test it. Neither did he say anything to question slavery as an institution; in fact, its validity is implicitly recognized.

If there was any doubt about the meaning of the letter to Philemon, it would be settled by the letter to the Colossians—if only we were sure that Colossians was genuine. But, even if it is not, it is certainly the earliest, closest, and most perceptive imitation and interpretation of Paul. After laying down the Pauline rule that "in Christ" "there is neither Greek nor Jew . . . barbarian, Scythian, slave [or] free man" (3:11), Colossians goes on to give rules of behavior for persons in different social positions: Wives, husbands, children, parents. Then: "Slaves, be obedient in all things to your masters according to [the law of] the physical [world]. [Serve] not with pretended obedience like those trying to please men, but sincerely, fearing the Lord. . . . You serve the Lord Messiah and any cheater will get what [he deserves]" (3:22-25). Whether or not the master is a Christian is not asked. Simply as an owner by civil law he is in the place of God—though the text goes on to warn owners that they must be just and evenhanded in dealing with their slaves, knowing that they, themselves, have a master in heaven (4:1).

This picture of the entire world as an estate in which all the inhabitants are the slaves of God, the owner, had appeared already in Leviticus, 25:55, where Yahweh, prohibiting the Israelites to sell in perpetuity their ancestral landholdings, justified the prohibition by claiming that the land belonged to him, "For all the Israelites are my slaves. They are my slaves because I brought them out of the land of Egypt." The conqueror owns the spoils. By Paul's time the notion was moving towards legal implementation in the Roman Empire; the emperors were beginning to take the title *dominus* proper to the head of a household and owner of its slaves. The triumph of Christianity did much to strengthen the trend, and, among the elements of Christianity, Paul's habitual designation of himself as "Paul, the slave of Christ" (Rom. 1:1; Gal. 1:10; Phil. 1:1; imitated in Titus 1:1;) was particularly influential. (Note the papal title, "Slave of the slaves of God," *servus servorum Dei*). Another important factor in shaping the picture of men as slaves and God as slaveowner was of course the Gospels; the parables often use the relation of slave to master as an example of the relation of a man to God.

From this edifying theory we go back to the objective question, What does the New Testament say about actual slavery?

Colossians was often imitated, so there are a number of letters generally recognized as pseudo-Pauline forgeries. Three of these, Ephesians, 1 Timothy, and Titus, contain passages on slavery (1 Tim. 6:1-2; Eph. 6:5-8; Titus 2:9-10) to the same effect as the one we have just seen. Of these, 1 Timothy is most interesting, because it not only enjoins Christian slaves to treat their pagan masters respectfully, "in order that the name of God and the [Christian] teaching shall not be badly spoken of," but also warns those who have Christian masters that "they should not be contemptuous of them because they are brothers, but rather serve them because they are believers."

With all these clear passages, there is no reasonable doubt that the New Testament, like the Old, not only tolerated chattel slavery (the form prevalent in the Greco-Roman world of Paul's time) but helped to perpetuate it by making the slaves' obedience to their masters a religious duty. This biblical morality was one of the great handicaps that the emancipation movement in the United States had to overcome. The opponents of abolition had clear biblical evidence on their side when they argued. As one said in 1857: "Slavery is of God" (F. Ross, *Slavery Ordained of God,* Philadelphia, 1857, 5).

FOR FURTHER READING

W. Westermann. *The Slave Systems of Greek and Roman Antiquity.* Philadelphia, 1955.

M. Finley, editor. *Slavery in Classical Antiquity.* Cambridge, 1960.

I. Mendelsohn. *Slavery in the Ancient Near East.* New York, 1949.

K. Hopkins. *Conquerors and Slaves.* Cambridge, 1978.

T. Wiedemann. *Greek and Roman Slavery.* Baltimore, 1981. (Sources in translation, with brief comments and a good introduction.)

WAR
Robert P. Carroll

To everything there is a season . . .
a time of war and a time of peace (Eccl. 3:1,8).

War has always been a part of the general context in which human communities live, and the Bible has much to say about it. The Hebrew Bible in particular—as a product of the Iron Age period, and from an area of the ancient world overshadowed by the great empires of Egypt, Assyria, Babylon, Persia, Greece, and Rome—reflects many aspects of warfare and its consequences. As a means of expanding territory or of defending the homeland, war was a normal cultural and social activity for many of the biblical writers, and military achievements were celebrated. It should, therefore, not be surprising that a longing for peace also appears as a recurrent theme. Biblical writers dreamed of a time when the Israelites would no longer be subordinated to foreign powers and when shattered communities and wrecked economies might be healed. No overall ideology or strategy of war or peace is to be found in the Bible, so no easy judgments can be made concerning whether the Bible favors war or peace. Sometimes the defense of the realm, the opportunity for conquest, or occasionally even the demands of justice could give rise to war, and on these occasions the biblical writers approved of the necessary military actions taken. On other occasions, going to war was recognized as folly and the disastrous consequences were recorded.

The New Testament is less concerned than the Hebrew Bible with such matters. The New Testament was composed over a more brief period, when the Jewish and Christian communities had no land to defend. Nonetheless, it often shares the values of the older book, using the language and ideology of warfare in many different ways. Altogether, the Bible, both Hebrew and Christian, is a book soaked in the language and imagery of warfare, and no short essay can do justice to the diversity of material on war in it. What follows is therefore only a short outline of the subject; not every nuance will be caught.

METHODOLOGICAL CONSIDERATIONS

Given the amount of material on war in the Bible and the diversity of viewpoints expressed by its different writers, it is wise to note the limitations of any such study. How, for example, does one read texts that come to us from alien ancient cultures, which have a long history of editing? Such problems of analysis and interpretation make it difficult to render a balanced account of what is going on in the Bible. The cultural and theological roles of the Bible in Western civilization have been such that there is also the temptation to simplify diversity and to read into the ancient documents modern views more amenable to the reader's own way of thinking.

In military matters, this temptation has not always been resisted successfully! Equally formidable problems of interpreting biblical texts can complicate matters when war in the Bible is discussed. A good example of this need for interpretation is the contradictory material about the conquest of Palestine by the Israelites, in Deuteronomy, Joshua, and Judges. Deuteronomy represents Yahweh, the national god, as commanding the annihilation of the seven nations of Canaan (7:1-5, 20:16-18); and Joshua 1-11 reports the successful carrying out of this command in Joshua's campaigns of annihilation against the Canaanite cities. Judges, on the other hand, tells a rather different story about the failure of the Israelites to wipe out the Canaanites and the consequent corruption of the nation under the influence of Canaanite culture. Between these two accounts of the Israelite response to the divine command of annihilation, there is a serious contradiction—either they did or they did not annihilate the Canaanites! One account, at least, is wrong. The historian may ask, "Which is correct?", or "Which story is the more accurate historical account?" The interpreter of all the texts needs to ask further questions about how the texts are to be related to one another, i.e.

the question of their intertextuality. To decide which, if any, represents a historically accurate picture is a very complex interpretive question, whereas taken at face value, the texts simply contradict one another. One interpretive approach would explain the contradiction in terms of different sources (the classical theory of the composition of the Pentateuch and other biblical books would assist here). Put together, at some later stage, the different stories contradict each other. A different explanation would say that the Judges text reflects an ideological account of how Israel failed to obey the divine command of annihilation and how this disobedience led to continual warfare with the Canaanites. Yet another analysis might say that Judges represents a more accurate historical account and Joshua is more ideological. But questions of interpretation can hardly be avoided on this issue.

Making allowances for the ideological holdings of the biblical writers, and reading the text as representing more what the writer believed than what objective historical events actually were, are very important rules for reading the Bible. Theological aims and values that have interfered with the text should also be recognized as part of the interpretive task confronting the reader. In many ways, the Bible is a book in which various writers have tried to impose their viewpoints on older texts in order to reinterpret them for subsequent purposes.

An example of this practice may be seen in the story of the Israelite military defeat of the Egyptians at the Red Sea in Exodus 14. The military aspects of the story can still be detected in the text (see Exod. 12:41, 13:18, 14:25), but the dominant aspect of the narrative as it now appears is a miraculous, divine attack on the Egyptians in which the Israelites become passive witnesses of their enemy's destruction. Here, theological concerns take over the story and play down what may once have been a legend of the military defeat of the Egyptians. Less developed elements of this phenomenon can be seen in the two accounts of the defeat of Sisera in Judges 4-5. A more blatant theologizing of a military act is evident in the famous story of how David killed Goliath, the Philistine giant, in an idealized combat between the representative of Israelite religion and the champion of the uncircumcised (1 Sam. 17). In 2 Samuel 21:19, the matter is very simply stated: "And Elhanan the son of Jaareoregim, the Bethlehemite, slew Goliath the Gittite" (corrected in 1 Chronicles 20:5 by a writer familiar with the David legend). The Chronicler's tendency to turn battles into miracles is also illustrative of this principle.

ISRAEL'S ORIGINS

The extent to which the stories of Israel's origins, narrated in the books of Exodus to Deuteronomy and Joshua-Judges, contain any reliable historical information is too complex a subject for discussion and need not concern us here. Whether partly historical or entirely fictional, the narratives include numerous stories of battles, skirmishes, and tactics employed to avoid conflict. (In the Genesis stories, only Abram the Hebrew appears as a warrior—in Gen. 14:13-16.) Although the exodus from Egypt is mainly presented as a miraculous escape due to the plagues sent on Egypt, one line of the story represents the people marching out of Egypt in battle formation (Exod. 13:18), and another strand of the narrative tells of the defeat of the Egyptian chariot battalion (Exod. 14:7) in the marshes of the Red Sea. Religious ideology has colored the telling of the story, so we cannot determine whether a real battle was ever fought between the Israelites and the Egyptians, but traces of such a story may be detected in the text.

The trek through the desert between Egypt and Palestine occupies the bulk of the Pentateuch and provides the occasion and location of many encounters with hostile forces. The military defeat of Amalek, in Exodus 17, is made into an etiology of permanent war between Yahweh and Amalek: "Write this as a memorial in a book . . . that I will utterly blot out the remembrance of Amalek from under the heaven. . . . Yahweh will have war with Amalek from generation to generation" (17:14,16).

The telling of this story reflects an ideology of "total war" against a persistent enemy and belongs not only to the stories of Joshua's conquests (17:13), but also to a strand in the Bible of religious war. Different strategies and tactics of war may be seen in the other desert stories, where Israel comes into conflict with neighboring states: the avoidance of war with Edom (Num. 20:14-21); the annihilation of Arad and the Negeb cities (Num. 21:1-3); echoes from the "Book of the Wars of Yahweh" (Num. 21:14-30); the destruction of the Ammonites (Num. 21:3-35); and conflict with Moab involving the internationally famous "seer," Balaam (Num. 22-24).

The conquest and settlement of Palestine by the Israelite tribes is told in very different ways by the books of Joshua and Judges. Joshua presents an ideological myth of almost instant military conquest. Beginning with the legendary circumambulation of Jericho thirteen times in seven days (including the sabbath!), and with trumpets blasting on the seventh day, Joshua lays hold of "the whole land" (11:23) in a few chapters (6-11).

A rather different perspective on the conquest of Palestine appears in the Book of Judges (epitomized in Judg. 1). Throughout that book the tribes struggle, sometimes in vain, against their Canaanite opponents. The theological overwriting in the Book of Judges (sometimes termed "deuteronomistic" because of its similarity to the language and ideology of the Book of Deuteronomy) sets the narratives into an ideological framework that distorts the individual stories within the book. Perhaps the best known battle in Judges is the one fought between the tribes of Naphtali and Zebulun against the Canaanites, in which Deborah and Barak defeated Sisera, the Canaanite general. The story is told both in a prose version (Judg. 4) and in the famous poem "The Song of Deborah" (Judg. 5). In the prose account, the Israelite forces defeat their superior and better equipped opponents by engaging the Canaanite chariots near the river Kishon on ground utterly unsuitable for chariots (Judg. 4:7; in verses 12-16 the Canaanite forces appear to be routed on the slopes of Mount Tabor). One of the few permanent rules of war is this: If you have ill-equipped soldiers or are facing a more professional army, never meet them on open ground—always have recourse to guerilla tactics and choose your own ground to fight on. The poem that celebrates this famous victory over the Canaanites tells the story in a stylized and ideological manner, although both accounts are given from a woman's viewpoint. Thus, complex interpretive issues are raised by Judges 4-5 that obscure the military aspects of the story.

The Book of Judges is much taken up with narratives of battles and accounts of strategies whereby the enemy was defeated (e.g., Gideon's ruse for alarming the Midianites so that they could be defeated by the Ephraimites in Judges 7). Samson's campaigns against the Philistines are told with much humor and depict a strong man with no military finesse wreaking havoc on the enemy. Here, war is more folk tale than military strategy, and little useful historical or social information may be gleaned from the text. The internecine conflict between the Israelites and the Benjaminites depicted in Judges 19-21 may or may not reflect reliable details of fighting strategy among warring clans. The editorial conclusion to the section may indicate the reason why such appalling stories were included in the Book of Judges: "In those days there was no king in Israel; every man did what was right in his own eyes" (Judg. 21:25).

WHEN KINGS GO FORTH TO BATTLE

The story of the kings of Israel and Judah set forth in the books of Samuel and Kings (with parallels, revisions, and alternatives in Chronicles) can be regarded on one level as the story of the wars of the kingdoms. From persistent defeat by the Philistines to the emergence of individual kings who effectively expanded territory and defeated opposing nations—until the time of the great empires of Assyria and Babylon, when the monarchies of Israel and Judah met defeat and extinction—these books focus on the military exploits of the kings within a highly ideological framework. On occasion, battles are described in detail, but more generally the writers prefer stereotypical phrases such as "there was war between . . ." or "there was war again . . ." (see 1 Kings 14:30, 15:7; 1 Sam. 19:8). The narrative styles used in these books are such that stories of war between opposing factions are more often used to develop *religious* themes. Thus, the stories of King Saul the warrior (1 Sam. 11-19) quickly move from depicting Saul as a great fighter to presenting him as a haunted religious fanatic caught up in the coils of his own overzealous personality. Conflict between him and the prophet Samuel, and then between him and the younger warrior David, determine the shape of the stories much more than his status as Israel's kingly warrior. Nonetheless, Saul remains a warrior throughout the story of his life, and he meets his death fighting the Philistines on Mount Gilboa (1 Sam. 31). But it is David the warrior who is the dominant figure in the stories, and little is portrayed that does not discredit Saul.

David is the great warrior figure of the Hebrew Bible. Whatever historical material may be concealed behind the stories of his exploits (1 Sam. 16 to 2 Sam. 24)—and it is possible that there is no history at all behind the text—the narrated figure of David is a splendid work of dynamic action and military achievement. Even the legend of his having killed the Philistine giant Goliath is of a piece with his heroic status in biblical storytelling. Only when he ceases to fight his nation's battles does he begin to decline as a heroic figure—his illicit rendezvous with Bathsheba takes place when he should have been out of the city fighting the enemy! (2 Sam. 11:1)—and much of his subsequent fighting is done in retreat from his own family. In the conflict with his son Absalom, his men persuade him to remain behind in the city (2 Sam. 18:1-5). But his many wars are represented as giving Israel and Judah territory and security in a period when the kingdoms were getting established. Perhaps in the listing of his mighty warriors (2 Sam. 23:8-39) there is an alternative tradition about who *really* did the heroic fighting, and this may represent an attempt to cut his legend down to size. Our final image of David is of an old and dying man giving one of his favorite sons instructions on who should be murdered after his death (1 Kings 2:1-12)—a scene that recalls Lenin's purported last words about Stalin.

The many stories of war in the Books of Kings serve various purposes in the overall plan of the story of the kings of Israel and Judah. Often, the ideological handling of the stories presents the battles as divine means of retribution for past offenses or rewards for fidelity to principles congenial to the writers. Whether this reflects a mode of story-telling in which disparate accounts are interwoven or some form of archival record of the kings' wars as enhanced by stories of the prophets is a matter for scholarly debate. A good example of this style of story-telling is the account given of King Ahab (1 Kings 16:29-22:40), in which his reign is more often the background for the exploits of the prophet Elijah; even his wars are occasions for prophetic deeds rather than kingly action (see 1 Kings 20). The outbreak of war between Syria and Israel becomes an occasion of disputing prophets (1 Kings 22), in which the Israelite king remains anonymous throughout the story until a concluding stereotypical note identifies him as Ahab (1 Kings 22:39). Here, a prophet is more than a match for a king or for many warriors (see 2 Kings 1), so it would be unwise to read the Books of Kings as providing reliable information concerning the history of Israel and Judah's kings or of the history of biblical warfare.

The closing chapters of 2 Kings reflect on the monarchies in the period of the Assyrian and Babylonian empire and depict the collapse and disappearance of both states. Here, war means invasion by the empires, sieges of the cities, defeat followed by deportation, and the general despoliation of land and people. The writers continue their denigration of the kings and present their reigns as the corruption of Israelite religion by means of imported cultural activities. War is no longer the triumph of Israel over its enemies but divine defeat of the nation for offenses commited by the kings. The second Book of Kings ends with the defeat and devastation of Jerusalem, deportations to Babylonia, and a momentary glimpse of the last Judean king on release from prison.

SECOND TEMPLE PERIOD

Although the Hebrew Bible is the product of the "second temple period" (c. 516 B.C.E. to 70 C.E.), there is a tendency among many scholars to attribute the literature about the first Temple to the period of the first Temple (the sixth century B.C.E. and earlier). Hence, in order to talk about the literature of the Persian and Greco-Roman periods, the category "second temple period" is usually used.

In this period, the Jewish communities in Jerusalem, Judea, Babylonia, and Egypt lacked a political structure that could operate independently of the imperial authorities or make war against its opponents. Yet a number of texts depict warlike activities, and in the Greco-Roman period wars against the foreign imperial power did sometimes break out. The Chronicler's version of the history of the kings of Israel and Judah is similar to what we find in Kings, though there is an increased tendency to depict fighting as a *religious* activity. Thus, in 2 Chronicles 20, the conflict with the Moabites and Ammonites is represented as a great victory for prophet-inspired religious belief and piety: "And when they began to sing and praise, Yahweh set an ambush against the men of Ammon, Moab, and Mount Seir, who had come against Judah, so that they were routed" (20:22).

The Book of Esther, set in the Persian period, portrays the Jewish communities of the imperial provinces under threat of extermination from hostile elements within the empire. In a reversal of this threat, the Jews rise up against their enemies and put them to the sword. Throughout the cities and provinces of the empire, more than seventy-five thousand Persian opponents of the Jews were slaughtered (Esther 9:1-16). The holiday inspired by this massacre later became a great occasion of feasting and celebration, and it has passed into the annals of Jewish festivals as the "days of Purim" (Esther 9:23-32). The role of the Jewish woman Hadassah (better known as Esther) in the deliverance of the Jews should be noted, as she belongs to that group of women prominent in the Bible who saved the Jewish communities by various methods of assault on the enemy (see also Deborah, Jael, and Judith). According to the Bible, stealth and cunning can be very effective weapons of war when deployed by women!

The Book of Daniel, chapter 11, depicts the undoing of various kings and warriors by war, which ushers in a time of trouble for the Jewish people. The background to this conflict seems to be the Maccabean period (the second century B.C.E.), when a *Kulturkampf* developed among the Judean Jews over things Greek. This story is told in the Books of Maccabees. Unlike the story of Esther, when Jews escaped destruction by means of intrigue and massacre, the Maccabean war developed as a response to the imposition of Greek cultural practices on the Jews and the banning of vital religious customs, like circumcision. Many Jews went along with such cultural innovations, but some refused to conform, and their refusal led to armed opposition. Mattathias and his son Judas (Maccabeus) were the heroes of this resistance to foreign interference with Jewish culture (1 Macc. 1-4). Ironically, in order to defend Jewish culture, Mattathias was forced to break the sabbath, when pious Jews could not fight, instituting a rule that allowed fighting on the traditional Jewish "day of rest" (1 Macc. 2:29-41). The success of the Maccabean resistance to Greek enculturation and the rededication of the polluted Temple became the basis of the Jewish festival of Hanukkah. Part of the tactics of the resistance movement reflected approval of political assassination derived from the story of Phinehas in Numbers 25:6-13 (1 Macc. 2:23-26, 54). However, the story of the Maccabean war against Greek oppression is not told without ambivalent feelings by the biblical writers. The second Book of Maccabees tells the story from a rather different perspective, playing down the element of armed resistance in favor of pious suffering and martyrdom (see 2 Macc. 6-7).

Other wars and strategies for fighting them have an indirect bearing on the biblical witness to war. They include the theoretical and somewhat apocalyptic war prepared for in the Qumran War Scroll (one of the Dead Sea Scrolls), which raises all the interpretive problems of texts about war being theoretical or practical, and the Jewish War against the Roman imperial power in 66-70 C.E., which led to the destruction of Jerusalem and the second Temple. We know about this war from Josephus and as dim background to some of the New Testament texts, as well as from later rabbinic sources. The Bar Kochba war of 132-135 C.E. brought Jewish militarism to an end for many centuries and may be regarded as a nonbiblical event. But it, along with the resistance to Rome at Masada in 74 C.E., yielded many inspiring stories of armed resistance to oppression and much information about military strategies of the biblical period.

YAHWEH THE WARRIOR

The loosely chronological approach I have used until now needs to give way to a more thematic analysis in order to consider a number of important aspects of war in the Bible. Here, the religious dimension of political ideology in the ancient world is significant. Many of the gods cultivated by ancient cultures were militant figures believed to fight for—

and, on occasion, *against*—their own devotees. Religion in the Bible is no different. Yahweh, the personal name given to the main god worshiped by the writers of the Bible (the role of other gods is played down very much in the Hebrew Bible), is a god of battles, rejoicing in warlike activities and praised for military achievements—hence the reference to the "Book of the Wars of Yahweh" in Numbers 21:14. The Song of the Sea declares:

> Yahweh is a man of war;
> Yahweh is his name.
> (Exod. 15:3)

And in the cult, he enters the city as a mighty warrior returning from triumphant war-making:

> Who is the king of glory?
> Yahweh, strong and mighty,
> Yahweh, mighty in battle!
> (Ps. 24:8)

In the cult-influenced hymns of the Second Isaiah, his warrior qualities are celebrated:

> Yahweh goes forth as a warrior,
>   as a man of war he stirs up his fury;
> he cries out, he shouts aloud,
>   he shows himself mighty against his foes.
> (Isa. 42:13)

When the Israelites went to war, they believed that their warrior god led them into battle and gave them victory (or defeat, if his mood was bad). In some stories, the ark of Yahweh—believed by some scholars to be a kind of palanquin for the deity—is taken into battle (cf. Num. 10:35-36; 1 Sam. 4-6), but the results of such a ploy are ambiguous in the extreme. It does not appear to have been a regular tactic in time of war, though our ignorance here may be due to the lack of stories in the Bible about the ark. The warrior-god motif is, however, indisputable, and it appears in many different strands of the book.

A concomitant feature of the warrior-god belief is the equation of Israel's with Yahweh's enemies. Those peoples, nations, and groups that opposed Israel were viewed as being enemies of Yahweh; they therefore warranted the most extreme treatment possible. The conclusion to Deborah's Song makes this belief very clear:

> So perish all your enemies, O Yahweh!
> But your friends be like the sun as he rises in his might.
> (Judg. 5:31)

Yahweh's friends are those who have fought (or will fight) against Yahweh's enemies. David's gift to the elders of Judah acknowledges this belief: "Here is a present for you from the spoil of the enemies of Yahweh" (1 Sam. 30:26). Those Israelites who were exiled to Babylon after the fall of Jerusalem in 587 B.C.E. are addressed in a way that presupposes this very close link between Yahweh and the people: "For thus says Yahweh of hosts, after his glory sent me to the nations who plundered you, for he who touches you touches the apple of his eye" (Zech. 2:8).

If the conviction that Israel's enemies were therefore the enemies of Yahweh fueled utter hostility toward all things foreign, there was another side to the belief in the warrior god. When defeated in battle or frustrated in military strategy, Israel believed that the warrior Yahweh was fighting against them. David may boast against Goliath that he has come out against "Yahweh of hosts, the god of the armies of Israel" (1 Sam. 17:26, 36, 45), but the cultic community also knew a different experience:

> Yet you have cast us off and abased us,
> and have not gone out with our armies.
> (Ps. 44:9; cf. Ps. 60:10)

This failure of divine activity on Israel's behalf is one kind of explanation of defeat. There is a stronger expression of it in the prophetic books, where Yahweh is seen to be on the side of the invading armies of the imperial forces arrayed against Jerusalem (see Isa. 10:5-6; Jer. 25:9-11, 27:4-7). According to the prophets, the rebellion of the people against Yahweh is answered by Yahweh supporting their enemies. For the prophets, Yahweh becomes the real enemy, the invading nations merely the means used to implement that enmity: "But they rebelled and grieved his holy spirit; therefore, he turned to be their enemy, and himself fought against them" (Isa. 63:10). The beliefs about the warrior god who fights for *and* against his own people are common among the peoples of the

ancient Near East and belong very much to the cult of the warrior god
of ancient mythology.

TOTAL WAR

War being what it is—violent conflict—it has always entailed atrocities,
especially against civilians and other noncombatants. Sieges of cities lead
to death by hunger and disease, as well as to executions after the success
of the siege. Because stories of wars and battles are such a key feature
of the Bible, inevitably there are texts that afford a glimpse of the sufferings
caused by such fighting. The Book of Lamentations offers various images
of the devastation caused by a city's defeat (Lam. 2:11-12, 19-21; 4:4-
10; 5:1-18), and Amos 1:3-15 describes some of the atrocities common
in war (cf. Deut. 28:47-57 for some of the depredations that resulted
from sieges). The extreme cruelties of war may be read in the Assyrian
annals and observed in the art describing the conquests of the great
empires.

Genocide makes its appearance in biblical texts that portray the
Canaanite peoples; cursed by Yahweh, they are assigned to the Israelites
for total slaughter. Seven nations are listed in Deuteronomy 7:1 (the
number varies in other texts) as people who are to be annihilated without
mercy. Various texts depict the successful massacres of men, women,
and children (see Deut. 2:26-35; Josh 6:15-21, 8:18-29, 10:6-43, 11:1-22).
This kind of wholesale slaughter is now often called "holy war," though
the term itself is not used in the Bible. The phenomenon of religious
killing described by such a term is known from Assyrian sources in
the ancient world, and it occasionally survives in modern states. It stems
from a religious worldview that sees enemies of the community as enemies of God—and as therefore destined for slaughter. In the Hebrew
Bible, the slaughter of all the Canaanites is presented as an ideological
war against enemies who would corrupt the purity of the holy people
by miscegenation or cultural influence (see Deut. 7:2-5, 20:16-18).

Permanent war rather than genocide (if this can be regarded as
a valid distinction) was directed against the Amalekites (Exod. 17:8-16;
1 Sam. 15:1-3). This hostility was caused by Amalekite opposition in
the past, not fears of cultural assimilation. In the story of Saul's slaughter of the Amalekites (1 Sam. 15), the recurring motif of their annihilation is mainly used to attack Saul for failing to *fully* carry out the
killing (he spared one Amalekite, the king, and the best animals for

sacrifice!). Samuel's subsequent hacking to pieces of the Amalekite king Agag (vv. 32-33) makes good Saul's defective action and indicates the nature of this kind of permanent hostility. Amalek is included in the genocide program in Deuteronomy 25:17-19. An echo of the conflict between Israel and Amalek appears in the story of Esther, where the chief enemy of the Jews is identified as Haman the Agagite (Esther 3:1). Apparently, the Amalekites were never completely wiped out, no matter how often they were slaughtered!

Whereas war is still regarded as a normal, if unhappy, state of affairs in the political life of nations, genocide is reckoned these days to be a heinous offense and a war crime. Disquiet in the Bible about blood-thirsty acts *is* occasionally expressed (see Hos. 1:4; Amos 1:3-15; Hab. 2:12, 15-17), though never about the treatment of the Canaanites. Clearly, total war can make sense from a strategic point of view, but it raises serious moral problems; and the genocidal war against the Canaanites in the Bible has bothered sensitive readers of a book often thought to express perfect, divinely ordained morality. It is not my intention to defend the Bible or to acquit it of charges of moral insensitivity and even immorality—neither activity would be successful—but this question of genocide *does* reveal some of the moral difficulties of treating the Bible as normative for religion, ethics, and the conduct of war. This approval of genocide in some biblical texts makes for a dangerous doctrine in cultures where the Bible is granted a privileged status. Indeed, on occasion the Bible has encouraged militarism in religious matters. Oliver Cromwell's Joshua-like campaign against the Catholics of Ireland in the seventeenth century, which led to bloody massacres of civilians, was inspired by the Bible. A more intelligent and carefully selective reading of the Bible, however, might help to avoid atrocities of a Cromwellian nature.

ORACLES AGAINST THE NATIONS

War is necessarily a xenophobic activity, though the quest for territorial gains need not entail a hatred of any particular people. The Hebrew Bible contains much nationalistic writing and is therefore often very xenophobic in its outlook. Foreigners may be tolerated under certain conditions, but generally they are despised. The New Testament, which mostly addresses like-minded people, harshly criticizes Jews and gentiles who will not join the Christian churches. One set of texts that exemplifies the antiforeigner outlook of much of the Hebrew Bible (the Wisdom literature typified by Job, Ecclesiastes, and Proverbs is international rather than nationalistic in outlook) is that genre in the prophetic literature known as "oracles against the nations." These appear in the larger collections of prophetic material (Isa. 13-23; Jer. 46-51; Ezek. 25-32) and in some of the smaller books (Amos 1:3-2:3; Joel 3; Obad; Nah.; Zeph. 2). Their precise meaning and function in these books is not clear, nor is it known what their origins and purposes may have been. All that *is* clear about them is that they speak out against the foreign nations and threaten them with dire destruction from various sources directed by Yahweh, the God of Israel. To some extent, these oracles balance the anti-Israel/Judah sentiments collected in the prophetic books, and they often have an implicit, where not explicit, note of salvation for the oppressed Judeans who have suffered at the hands of the foreign tyrant (see Isa. 47:5-7; Jer. 50:1-10, 51:1-5; Zeph. 2:8; Nah. 1:15).

One view is that they are *war oracles*. Some of them certainly reflect conditions of war and belong to the period when the Babylonians, under Nebuchadnezzar, were invading Palestine and campaigning against Egypt (see Jer. 46-51; Ezek. 26-32). Why Judaean sources should produce oracles delighting in the Babylonian destruction of Egypt is not easy to explain, but such oracles may have been traditional expressions of xenophobic policy; the attribution of the power behind Assyria and Babylon to Yahweh incorporated international politics into Judaean ideology. The concomitant destruction of the smaller nations surrounding Judah by the Babylonians allowed for *Schadenfreude* and furthered the hopes of Judaean nationalists—a case of "my enemy's enemy is my friend." If we knew the sources of these oracles, it might be easier to understand how they related to the sweeping victories of the empires (cf. the incorporation of the Persian conquest of Babylon into the hymnic celebrations of the Jerusalem cult in Isaiah 40-48). The production of such war oracles may have been the function of Judah's cult prophets, whose duties included the maintenance of national fervor and chauvinistic hopes. Ironically, they are now included in collections of texts that bear testimony to the Babylonian devastation of Judah and Jerusalem! But that irony may have been lost on the collectors of such oracles because they believed in Yahweh's ultimate defeat of the Babylonian power.

Speculations about the origins of the genre include the notion that they were originally intended to give advice to the national king on going to war (cf. Christiansen, *Transformations*). Thus, they belong to any treatment of war in the Bible. Perhaps they were magical utterances (typical of prophets) accompanying ritual practices (cf. Num. 22:41-24:24) designed to defeat the enemy. Uttered as curses against the enemy in time of war, they may have functioned as magical incantations intended to encourage the armies of the king and to aid the destruction of the nation's foes (cf. Isa. 8:9-10). Curses and blessings in a war context may have had stronger force than mere expressions of wishes and hopes; and the invocation of the deity, accompanied by the appropriate ritual gestures performed by cult prophets (cf. 1 Kings 18:20-40; 2 Kings 13:14-25), might have been part of the national manipulation of power in a world greatly controlled by faith in magical procedures. On other occasions, the appeal to the deity was all that was left to a defeated people:

> Remember, O Yahweh, against the Edomites
>   the day of Jerusalem,
> how they said "Raze it, raze it!
>   Down to its foundations!"
> O daughter of Babylon, you devastator!
>   Happy shall he be who requites you
>   with what you have done to us!
> Happy shall he be who takes your little ones
>   and dashes them against the rock!
> (Ps. 137:7-9)

The warrior god who fought for his people against the enemy— and who, on occasion, turned against his own people and defeated them— is depicted in Isaiah 63:1-6 as a blood-spattered fighter who has waded through the blood of the defeated nations. Behind the imagery is a mythological reading of the experience of slaughter at the hands of the empire (unnamed, but Babylon, Persia, or any of the imperial powers will fit) in which the local deity is credited with having the executive power in battle. In such poems, which are to be found in many of the prophetic books, the nations are seen as the victims of Yahweh's wrath on a grand scale. Some of the poems depict an international conspiracy against Jerusalem in which the nations attack the city and are annihilated by Yahweh (cf. Joel 3; Zech. 14; Obad. 15-21). These fragments of war poetry may be pieced together to form the background to later apocalyptic visions of war in the heavens and ultimate battles on the earth (cf. Ezek. 38), battles and wars now called "Armageddon" (cf. Rev. 12-16; the name *Armageddon* appears in Rev. 16:16). Thus, whatever the origins and functions of the "oracle against the nations" genre, the poetry of xenophobic gesture and sentiment came to have a shaping influence in later biblical thought—not to mention subsequent European political history and American religious thought.

RULES AND TECHNIQUES OF WAR

Deuteronomy 20 and 21:10-14 set out some regulations that can be regarded as embryonic rules of war, though they are by no means comprehensive. They are so dominated by a deuteronomistic ideology of cultural contamination that it is arguable that they are more ideal than real—that is, these rules illustrate the ideological concerns of the writer more than they reflect the actual practice of ancient Israelites. Like the War Scroll in the writings of the Qumran community, the rulings may envisage the conditions under which ideal battles should be fought rather than be constructed from knowledge or experience of real fighting.

The war oracle spoken by the priest to encourage the people in battle (Deut. 20:2-4) presents war as *Yahweh's* fight, so the rules that follow are essentially religious rather than military. Proscribed from taking part in battle are men who have more important things to do, such as dedicating a new house or having intercourse with a newly married wife. Cowards and the "fearful of heart" are also dismissed from war service. Behind these proscriptions may be notions of bad luck involved in interrupting important tasks; they might also reflect more common-sense ideas, like not using people who have other things on their mind.

The conquest of cities is divided into those far away and those nearby (Deut. 20:15-16). Cities are to be offered the opportunity of surrendering and enslavement or resistance followed by slaughter of the men and spoliation of women, children, and goods. But the cities of the Canaanites are to be totally destroyed. Here, the ideology of the writer becomes apparent. The reason offered for the wholesale slaughter of Canaanite men, women, and children (v. 18) is a rationalizing of this ideological attitude, because there is no reason to think that Canaanite propaganda and culture were somehow more powerful, insidious, and attractive to the Israelites than those of the people of cities "very far" from Israel (cf. Deut.: 21:10-14, where such foreign wives are permitted!). A further rule for the siege of cities prohibits the use of food-yielding trees in the making of siegeworks (Deut. 20:19-20). It is difficult to judge whether

2 Kings 3:25 should be regarded as a breach of this rule, because the attack against the Moabites is not technically a siege. The rule about shaving the head of a beautiful woman taken captive in war (Deut. 21:10-14), setting out the limits of her treatment, is connected to the rules of war only because of the source of such captives. Orthodox Judaism many centuries later developed the regulation into a ruling about how married women in general should behave.

In spite of the amount of material on war in the Bible, no text provides a *general* account of how war was fought in ancient times. Strategies and tactics on particular occasions may be detected in various stories (see Josh. 8; Judg. 4; 1 Sam 14:1-15, 17), but these do not constitute a comprehensive presentation of how the Israelites fought. The standard weapons of the period are all mentioned in the Bible: swords, knives, javelins, spears, bows and arrows, chariots, and siegeworks. These can all be found illustrated in the iconography of the larger empires, and it can be presumed that Israelite weaponry was not significantly different. War was fought "at the turn of the year" (2 Sam. 11:1) and could continue until the winter rains made fighting impossible. Between the city-states the techniques of siege were important, and the circumvallation of cities was an important means of defending them against invading armies. Places such as Megiddo and Lachish were powerful centers dominating the entrances to the central plains, and taking them was a necessary strategy for attacking cities like Jerusalem. The stories in the Books of Samuel and Kings give glimpses of battles fought and individual deeds of bravery or cowardice, but they cannot be used with certitude as guides to how actual wars were fought, The hand-to-hand individual combat of David's killing of Goliath (1 Sam. 17) is very uncharacteristic of the biblical world.

Ancient society made little distinction between religion and politics (these are very much modern categories), and the Bible is characteristically ancient in this sense. War was not only politics continued by other means, it was also religion in practice. What little we can discern of the pursuit of war in the Bible indicates its religious nature. The priestly formal assurance of victory to the warriors in Deuteronomy 20:2-4 has been noted already. Reference has also been made to the occasional use of the sacred ark in battle (Num. 10:35-36; 1 Sam. 4-6). And, of course, the many references to the warrior god Yahweh identify deity and the battle formation of Israel as an interconnected unity. Depending on the context, the women who normally greet the returning warriors after battle (see Exod. 15:19-21; 1 Sam. 18:6-8; Judg. 5:28-30) may celebrate the victory with a hymn of praise to Yahweh (Exod. 15:21). The ritual preparation for war—involving seers, omens, curses, and sacrifices (Num. 22:40, 23:1-6, 13-17, 27-24:2)—may reflect an ancient practice of offering sacrifices when commencing wars (in Jer. 6:4, the phrase translated as "prepare war" uses *qdv,* a word with strong cultic overtones, meaning "make holy, sanctify," or, in this context, "make ready [for war].") Echoes of priestly ritual parades are used to describe the military penetration of the land of Palestine in the Joshua story of the conquest of Jericho (Josh. 6:3, 6, 8-9, 13, 16). The effect of a sacrifice to end a battle can be seen in 2 Kings 3:27, where the king of Moab sacrifices his eldest son in order to overcome the resistance of the Israelites, thereby succeeding in getting them to withdraw from battle. However, this is an extraordinary act and cannot be regarded as typical. It represents a desperate king's ultimate deterrent against a formidable enemy, who cannot be defeated by the standard tactics of war. He therefore invokes the god Chemosh in this most awe-inspiring act of piety. Small wonder that the Israelites abandoned the successful campaign and returned to their own land!

SHALOM

The practice of war for the pursuit of territory, wealth, slaves, and power is a normal feature of human communities, and the Bible reflects a wide variety of stories about such activities. Some biblical literature speaks out of the experience of defeat and oppression brought about by war and so looks forward to a period in the future when war will either be successfully engaged in or avoided altogether. Jerusalem, the inviolable city of Yahweh (Pss. 46, 48), had experienced numerous defeats in the Assyrian and Babylonian period and had been the target of many sieges by foreign powers. Hence, the vision of a future in which nations would go up to Jerusalem and submit themselves to the instruction of Yahweh:

> He shall judge between the nations,
>   and shall decide for many peoples;
> and they shall beat their swords into ploughshares,
>   and their spears into pruning hooks;
> nation shall not lift up sword against nation,
>   neither shall they learn war any more.
>   (Isa. 2:4; Mich. 4:3)

Whatever the origin of this dream may have been, the prospect of the warriors turning into farmers may reflect a technique of how ancient wars were fought. In Joel 3:9-10 (Hebrew 4:9-10), the nations are commanded:

> Prepare war,
>> stir up the mighty men.
> Let all the men of war draw near,
>> let them come up.
> Beat your ploughshares into swords,
>> and your pruning hooks into spears. . . .

Taken together, these statements cover the transformation of warriors into farmers and the reversal of that process. So it may be fair to infer from these texts that when farmers were called to war, they simply took up their agricultural implements and went off to fight. After the (successful) prosecution of war, the survivors would return home and take up farming again. The vision in Joel is somewhat different from that in Isaiah and Micah, but both visions cover the range of options for farming people.

After battle comes the division of the spoils among the victors—an image of great joy in Isaiah 9:3. The burning of the bloodied garments and the accession to the throne of the new, victorious king herald the emergence of peace after a grim time of war (Isa. 9:2-7, cf. 8:21-9:1 [Hebrew 8:21-23]). Among the titles for the new king was "prince of peace." These images perhaps reflect a more urban approach to postwar experiences, but the sense of relief from oppression is palpable in the text (more pastoral images appear in Jeremiah 31:2-14 and Micah 4:4). Different images of peace and security also apply to Jerusalem after the Babylonian devastations of the city, most notably this wish:

> Old men and old women shall again sit in the streets of Jerusalem, each with staff in hand for very age. And the streets of the city shall be full of boys and girls playing in its streets. (Zech. 8:4-5)

The force of such a delightful picture of the future derives from the bitter experiences of the past, when the young and the elderly were particularly hard-hit victims of invasive war.

Yahweh the warrior is also known as the god who "breaks the bow of the enemy" (cf. Jer. 49:35, 51:56; Hos. 2:20; Ps. 76:4). This idiom belongs to the world of the ancient Near East and is used of gods and goddesses praised for their warrior qualities on behalf of their devotees. In the Bible, it is used in the same way, and it characterizes Yahweh as the warrior god who makes war cease:

> He makes wars to cease to the end of the earth;
>   he breaks the bow, and shatters the spear,
>   he burns the chariots with fire!
>
> (Ps. 46:9)

This activity will particularly benefit Jerusalem and its king:

> Rejoice greatly, O daughter of Zion!
>   Shout aloud, O daughter of Jerusalem!
> Lo, your king comes to you;
>   triumphant and victorious is he,
> humble and riding on an ass,
>   on a colt the foal of an ass,
> I will cut off the chariot from Ephraim
>   and the war horse from Jerusalem;
> and the battle bow shall be cut off,
>   and he shall command peace to the nations;
> his dominion shall be from sea to sea,
>   and from the River to the ends of the earth.
>
> (Zech. 9:9-10)

The great emphasis on peace in many of the prophetic hopes for the future should not be read in isolation from an equally great emphasis on the defeat of the enemy, the dividing of the spoils, and the centrality of Jerusalem in the rule of the nations (see Zech. 14:12-21; Isa. 11:11-16). No one line of thought can be said to predominate in the Bible. Different settings, occasions, and purposes determine the outlook of the writers, and neither war nor peace is advocated as a good in itself. Dreams of a time when the king will rule over land, and when nature will be in harmony with small children (as in Isa. 11:1-9) should not be read as if they outranked triumph over the enemy in time of war. The foreigners who flow to Jerusalem in one text should be balanced with other texts that see a holy Jerusalem without any strangers at all (eg., Isa. 2:2-4; Joel 4:17). A cultic ruling like "thou shalt not kill" (Exod. 20:13; Deut. 5:17) is at no point in the Bible understood to be some sort of

absolute principle ruling out war, judicial execution, the defense of home
or land, animal sacrifices, or killing animals for food.

THE NEW TESTAMENT

*Whoever takes up the sword shall perish by the sword, And whoever
does not take up the sword (or lets it go) shall perish on the cross.*
—Simone Weil, in *Gravity and Grace*

Stories of war and peace do not dominate the New Testament, but they
do provide a necessary background. Rome's domination of Palestine
is reflected throughout the text, much of which was produced between
the Roman war against Jerusalem in 66-70 C.E. and the Bar Kochba
revolt in 132-135 C.E. The phrase "wars and rumors of wars" (Matt.
24:6) is an apt description of the period of the New Testament's
composition. Having neither homeland to defend nor political interests
to advance at a communal level, the early Christian churches had little
need for war strategy. Those Jewish groups that constituted some of
the early churches were presumably not aligned to the "fourth philosophy" movement of Jewish patriots, who believed that Rome should
be opposed by force of arms. Apart from whatever traditions inspired
the group behind the Book of Revelation, there is little of a warrior
spirit in the New Testament.

Images of war can nonetheless be detected in the New Testament.
Metaphors of violence pervade Ephesians 6:10-17, for example. Sayings
attributed to Jesus include a few that hint of battle preparation:

He said to them, "But now, let him who has a purse take it, and
likewise a bag. And let him who has no sword sell his mantle and
buy one. . . ." And they said, "Look, Lord, here are two swords."
And he said to them, "It is enough." (Luke 22:36, 38)

The saying "Do not think that I have come to bring peace on earth;
I have not come to bring peace, but a sword" (Matt. 10:34) is given
a metaphorical interpretation in the verses that follow it (Luke 12:49-
53; cf. Mic. 7:6); but in another context, it might well sustain armed
revolt. The incident in Gethsemane, where one of Jesus' companions
draws a sword and lops off the ear of the high priest's slave (Matt.

26:51-52; Mark 14:47; Luke 22:50-51; the sword-bearer is identified as Peter in John 18:10-11), gives rise to the oft-quoted saying "Put your sword back in its place; for all who take the sword will perish by the sword" (only in Matt. 26:52; only in Luke is the slave healed). Little or much may be drawn from this incident, depending on the context of discussion. Under the circumstances of Roman occupation, passive resistance may have been favored by the Gospel writers. But within the story of the seizure of Jesus, armed resistance might well have frustrated the execution of Jesus! Hence, the tendency here to soft-pedal the possibility of an armed response in the Gospels. Time alone would change context and circumstances.

For many Christians, living in the Roman Empire curtailed the possibilities of violence and war-making, hence a conformity to political and civil authority is therefore enjoined on believers:

> Let every person be subject to the governing authorities. For there is no authority except from God, and those that exist have been instituted by God. Therefore he who resists the authorities resists what God has appointed, and those who resist will incur judgment. . . . Would you have no fear of him who is in authority? Then do what is good . . . for he is God's servant for your good. But if you do wrong, be afraid, for he does not bear the sword in vain; he is the servant of God to execute his wrath on the wrongdoer. (Rom. 13:1-4)

> Maintain good conduct among the Gentiles. . . . Be subject for the Lord's sake to every human institution, whether it be to the emperor as supreme, or to governors as sent by him to punish those who do wrong and to praise those who do right. For it is God's will that by doing right you should put to silence the ignorance of foolish men. (1 Pet. 2:12-15)

Such concern for living a quiet life in conformity to the prevailing social mores of the empire and for paying taxes (Rom. 13:6-7) hardly permits preparation for armed resistance against the empire. Thus, many early Christian communities were quietist and conformist. War and weaponry belong to their vocabulary as metaphors of spiritual struggle, not as a part of any political program.

> Put on the whole armour of God. . . . For we are . . . contending against the principalities, against the powers, against the world rulers of this present darkness, against the spiritual hosts of wickedness in

the heavenly places. . . . put on the breastplate of righteousness . . .
with the equipment of the gospel of peace . . . the shield of faith . . .
the helmet of salvation . . . the sword of the spirit which is the word
of God. . . . (Eph. 6:11-17)

And in Hebrews 4:12-13 the Word of God is described as being "sharper than any two-edged sword."

A somewhat more violent world appears in the Book of Revelation, where sword imagery abounds (Rev. 1:16; 2:12, 16; 6:4, 8; 13:14; 19:15, 21). Much of this language is taken over from the Hebrew Bible, especially from the "oracles against the nations." The rhetoric of the visions is full of violent images, falling empires, and cosmic warfare. This apocalypse (so described in Rev. 1:1) envisages the triumph of the Christian communities over all their enemies, but the fighting appears to be done by heavenly beings rather than by armed Christians.

Centuries would pass and the Roman Empire would fall before various churches would discover the need for taking up arms in order to spread or defend the gospel. The interim ethics ("interim" in the sense that early church leaders believed that the end of the world was at hand!) of the "Sermon on the Mount"—with its "blessed are the peacemakers, for they shall be called the sons of God" (Matt. 5:9; cf. Luke 6:27-31)—would always provide an alternative to fighting wars. But in the writings of the New Testament, elements of war and peace provide the backdrop to a spiritual struggle for survival in a violent world.

Viewing the Bible from the perspective of the twentieth century and in the light of modern warfare and the struggle for peace, it is difficult to discern any principles that might be usefully applied today. The Bible reflects the changing cultures of its times and offers a multiplicity of viewpoints. It favorably portrays strength in battle. It applauds the cunning of the gifted tactician that allows the weaker side to win against heavy odds. And the Bible also recounts human expressions of bitter loss and mourning after defeat, especially over dead children (Jer. 9:20-21). David's lament for the slain Saul and Jonathan (2 Sam. 1:17-27) can still move the modern reader to tears. Thus, Ecclesiastes' balanced view of the "seasons" of human activity would appear to be the only reasonable summation of the Bible's stance toward war: "To everything there is a season, and a time for every matter under heaven . . . a time of war, and a time of peace" (Eccles. 3:1, 8).

FOR FURTHER READING

D. Christiansen. *Transformations of the War Oracle in Old Testament Prophecy.* Harvard Dissertations in Religion 3. Missoula, Montana, 1975.

P. Hanson. "War and Peace in the Hebrew Bible." *Interpretation* 38(1984) 341-362.

P. Miller. *The Divine Warrior in Early Israel.* Harvard Semitic Monographs 3. Cambridge, Mass., 1973.

R. de Vaux. "Military Institutions." *Ancient Israel: Its Life and Institutions.* Translated by J. McHugh. London, 1965, 213-267.

WEALTH
R. Joseph Hoffmann

There is no uniform biblical view of wealth. The various biblical writers differ markedly in their opinions of money, financial gain, investment, human acquisitiveness, and ownership just as they do on their opposite: *poverty.* This lack of uniformity is hardly surprising. The Bible is the product of a millennium of writing, revising, and shifting cultural and political fortunes. Despite these variations, however, we can trace the history of certain customary opinions of material prosperity. In this brief essay I should like to synopsize these opinions under three headings: (1) Attitudes toward the "morality" of wealth in early Hebrew literature, which out of habit rather than preference I shall refer to as the "Old Testament." Special attention will be paid to the pentateuchal and historical books. (2) Revisionist opinions of wealth in the sayings attributed to the Prophets in the so-called "wisdom books" and in Old Testament apocryphal and pseudepigraphic (extracanonical) writings. (3) The views of the New Testament writers, especially those thought to represent the opinions of Jesus of Nazareth.

This system of classifying a diffusion of attitudes has, I think, more to recommend it than not. In the end, however, we must recognize that such schemes can do as much to obscure details and significant exceptions to a pattern as to define historical realities. What can be said in preface is that the older writings, composed during a period of relative prosperity in Israel, tend to present a generally favorable view of wealth. The prophetic, apocryphal, and extracanonical books, however, reflect a rather more provisional view of wealth, owing in large part to the changed political circumstances of the writers who lived between the eighth and the first centuries B.C.E.. In these texts, wealth is often seen as a false source of comfort, one often associated with idolatry, although the hope for political restoration is still represented in economic terms. Finally, the writings of the New Testament represent an inversion of what I will call throughout these pages the *economic theology* of the Hebrew Bible. Due chiefly to an increasingly tenuous relationship with the synagogues of Palestine and the Jewish diaspora, the early Christians developed an ethic of poverty that, in effect, indicted wealth as a source of sinfulness and blamed the wealthy for impeding the spread of the Christian gospel of repentance and judgment.

THE OLD TESTAMENT:
PENTATEUCH AND HISTORICAL WRITINGS

The Old Testament has a great deal to say about wealth as a sign of divine favor and source of human happiness. It is arguable that no single aspect of ancient Israelite religion stands in such obvious contrast to ancient Greek speculation concerning the *immaterial* nature of the good as the insistence of the Hebrew writers that the things of this world, being "God's possession and man's ward," are a source of delight, contentment, and blessing.

The theme is recurrent. We meet it on a literary level first in the Book of Genesis, where God is depicted as a creator and provider who desires the material well-being of his creatures. There is a noticeable emphasis on the raw numerical increase of this bounty (Gen. 1:14f.). In the second account of humankind's creation (Gen. 2:7ff.), we have the story of the leasing of a heavenly "Garden of God" (cf. Gen. 13:10; Isa. 51:3)—itself an idea imported from Babylon—which is thought to supply every material want—provided the terms of the lease are kept. As thematically central to the Book of Genesis as the stories of creation is the belief that prelapsarian happiness is defined in *material* terms: The man (Adam) without sin is a creature whose needs are met. Not only does God provide water, foodstuffs, and a companion to ease man's loneliness (cf. Gen. 2:22), but he gives him gold, onyx, and various resins (the benefit of which in a mercantile economy has been retrojected into a story of a man without pockets). Despite the use made of this story by Christian writers as far removed as St. Paul and St. Augustine, the theology of Genesis is not a lesson in metaphysics. Rather, it is the mythological embodiment of a fundamentally this-worldly, economic theology: To be cut off from God is, materially speaking, to be cut off by God. In its original Near Eastern context, the story of the fall of Adam is a fable designed to explain why people have to work for a living. God's penalty is not to infect every soul anew with the stain of Adam's transgression—as Augustine believed—but to substitute thorns, thistles, and sweat for fruit, gold, and aromatic resins. In its ancient form, moreover, the creation story reflects its tellers' concern to explain occasional economic and physical hardship (Gen. 3:16f.) and agricultural setbacks (Gen. 3:18) as owing to God's curse on the land. Nevertheless, this curse is understood to be provisional. Material prosperity remains the ideal and standard; only its attainment has become more difficult.

The account of Yahweh's covenant with Abraham (Gen. 15) is likewise told in terms of this-wordly reward and material blessing (Gen. 22:17). Those who accept Yahweh as God participate in the benefits of a "chosen" family; hence, it becomes important to establish the lines of descent, to know one's family history, and to confirm by legal means the rights of inheritance and land-claim (e.g., Gen. 23:17-20). Like the story of Adam, the saga of Abraham belongs to the economic theology of the "divided kingdoms" (c. 927-722 B.C.E.) and reflects a belief that those who obey God—more precisely, who submit to the worship of Yahweh alone—are entitled to a reward for their efforts. The Abraham saga is unlike the story of Adam in that Abraham's fidelity (Gen. 22:18) earns him the right to a covenant—a title—to his property, whereas Adam's faithlessness gets him thrown out of paradise. Abraham's obedience will become normative in Hebrew and (to a degree) in early Jewish theology. He acts as the god of the nation wishes him to act and so can expect to get a reward for his loyalty to his God—the quintessential link in the tribal confederation: "The Lord has blessed [Abraham] abundantly and he has become wealthy. He has given him silver and gold, menservants and maidservants, and camels and donkeys" (Gen. 24:34ff.).

The same doctrine of conspicuous reward for obedience is seen in the story of Joseph's settlement of his family in Egypt (Gen. 47-48). The legend itself reflects a growing need to supply theological warrants for the history of Jacob's descendants, who apparently did not retain possession of the land promised to Abraham, returning instead to nomadic ways, owing to the vicissitudes of seasonal pasturage, the need to find food, and an interest in trading. According to the biblical account (Gen. 47:11-27), these tribes filtered into Egypt by invitation and were among the more prosperous inhabitants of the country. That their success as herdsmen was a source of digruntlement and hostility among the native inhabitants of the region almost certainly explains the expropriation of Hebrew landholdings mentioned in Exodus 1:8-11, and the subsequent degradation of Hebrew families and family associations in the form of slavery. We know from the tomb paintings at Beni-Hasan that a number of Pharoahs forcibly removed segments of the Canaanite population, Hebrews among them, to Egypt.

With the exodus from Egypt and the handing down of the convenant to Moses, we reach a kind of climax in the pentateuchal narrative. The sojourn in Egypt is presented as a thwarting of God's plan to reward Abraham and his heirs; God responds forcefully to that interruption with a series of attacks ("plagues") on the source of Egyptian economic life— the Nile—and Egyptian property (Exod. 9-10) and inheritance (Exod. 10). With these curses God also orders the consecration of the Israelites' first-born males to himself in exchange for his smiting the Egyptians' first-born sons. Dependent as this story is on ancient Near Eastern notions of barter, vengeance, and exchange, one may be disposed to miss the economic implications of the Passover instruction. Here God is the purveyor of a service—or, more exactly, one party to a contract—the execution of which entitles him to a portion of the goods and chattels entailed in its performance. Thus God "swears an oath" to provide the land (Exod. 13:11; cf. Gen 9:13-20); and, as a contractual binder, the family elders (Exod. 13:14) are enjoined to keep their end of the bargain. On a practical level, this ritual sanctifies property law and explains the primogeniturial character of the tribal inheritance system, startling abberrations of which are at issue in such fables as the story of Esau and Jacob (Gen. 27).

At the center of the pentateuchal history is the Sinai/Horeb covenant, which legitimates the acquisition of wealth and the holding of property, including slaves. What is generally true of the Pentateuch, where the benefits of property-ownership and landholding by right loom large, is particularly true of Exodus, chapters 20-23, the part of the covenant-book having to do with the rights and duties of owners. The book is filled with advice useful to the agriculturally *nouveau riche,* who are told, sometimes redundantly (Exod. 22:21; Exod. 23:9), to remember what it was like to live as nomads. In the property laws of the Book of the Covenant (Exod. 22), a balance is struck between the requirements of protecting one's property and one's social responsibilities toward the needy: "Do not take advantage of a widow or orphan"; "If you lend money [to one of your own] . . . do not charge interest" (Exodus 22:22, 25, etc.). But the penalties for thievery are severe, even for accidental destruction of a trust (22:6, 7). The code serves ultimately to sanction the acquistion and protection of wealth as a sign of God's fulfilling his oath. This God, "before whom let no one come emptyhanded" (Exod. 23:15b), shows that he owns the world by applying the sabbath law (six years of sowing followed by one year of fallow) to farmers and in ordering one inheritance festival and two "prosperity" festivals a year (Exod. 23:13-15). The God of the nation himself stands behind the laws as guarantor of their morality.

The economic theology of the Pentateuch also dominates the historical books, which describe events from the twelfth through the eighth centuries (B.C.E.). In the period described in 1 Kings (c. 971 to the death of Ahaziah in the eighth century B.C.E.), Solomon is represented as praying for discernment and honesty in governing the commonwealth of Israel and Judah. In return for this request, God announces that he will also give Solomon what he did not ask for: "riches and honor, so that you will have no equal among kings. And if you walk in my ways and obey my statutes and commandments as David your father did, I will give you a long life" (1 Kings 3:12-14). The legendary wealth of Solomon is hence linked to faithful keeping of the law. His reign is the realization of the promise to Abraham—soon to be undercut, however, by the division of the kingdoms and fall of Israel (722 B.C.E.): "The people of Judah and Israel were as numerous as the sand on the seashore; they ate, they drank, and they were happy. . . . During Solomon's lifetime, Judah and Israel, from Dan to Beersheba, lived in safety, each man under his own vine and fig tree. Solomon had four thousand stalls for chariot horses and twelve thousand horses" (1 Kings 4:20, 24-26).

The subsequent history of the monarchy (cf. 2 Kings 8-17) in Israel and Judah is the rather hateful narrative of rulers who capitulated to the religious customs of the Assyrians and Canaanites, including the erection of sacred poles to the fertility goddess Asherah (2 Kings 13:4-6; cf. Judg. 3:7; Exod. 34:13) and the practice (under Ahaz at least) of child sacrifice and nature worship (2 Kings 16:3f.). The price paid for this betrayal of the covenant was both political and economic: an increase in pillaging and raids, intermarriage, and an inevitable confusion of the inheritance laws, followed by the "desolation" of Israel and— notwithstanding the interlude of the good Hezekiah and the "recovery" of the law under Josiah—the fall of Judah to the Babylonians (2 Kings 25:8-12). The specific message of the historical books centers on a decline in prosperity caused by a decline in fidelity to the law of God: With the fall of the southern kingdom, gone is the time when "Solomon made silver and gold as common in Jerusalem as stones" (2 Chronicles 1:15). By the same token, however, the desirablity of wealth and the morality of prosperity go largely unquestioned.

THE WISDOM TRADITION, THE PROPHETS, AND APOCRYPHAL WRITINGS

The writings that go under the names of various prophets and the so-called "wisdom" literature, which is closely related to the prophetic tradition, sharply criticize the tendency to see material abundance as the mark of divine favor. Political precariousness has given way to a more sober outlook on life, not unlike that occasioned in the Middle Ages by the persistence of plague and early death. To trust in wealth is folly; people do not live long enough to enjoy it: "Do not be overawed when a man grows rich, when the splendor of his house increases, for he will take nothing with him when he dies; his splendor will not descend with him. . . . A man who has riches without understanding is like the beasts that perish" (Ps. 49:16, 17, 20).

The collection of prayers and poems known as the Book of Psalms describes the way of the world—gain and loss doled out by a God whose ways are difficult to scan and not always possible to accept. In times of trouble, God is distant, and "the wicked hotly pursue the poor" (Ps. 10:2). This indifference accounts for a certain vituperative tendency in some of the Psalmist's prayers: "Break the arm of the wicked and evildoer"—the rich who prey on the poor—"and do justice to the father-less and the oppressed." Money and the abuse of power are commonly equated (Ps. 17:14, 14:4). While the idealistic strain, centering on the belief that Yahweh is a God who deals fairly with those who keep his laws, exalts the poor, and casts down the mighty from their seats of power (Ps. 18:27) is never entirely out of view, the Psalmist nonetheless sees *wealth* and *wickedness* as identical terms. (cf. Ps. 26:5; 34:20f., 37:1ff., etc.). By the same token, the "righteous" are generally considered to be the righteous *poor,* the afflicted (Ps. 34:19) who will reappear in the Sermon on the Mount as those who "hunger and thirst for jus-tice." It is to the Psalms more than to any other book of the Old Testa-ment that the early Christians looked for an explanation of their materially perilous and socially downcast situation. What they found was a book brimming with resentment against the inherited privileges and arrogance of the materially well-off, and religious expression of the need for vengeance on the part of a disinherited people. For in general (as Max Weber long ago recognized, and Nietzsche before him), the Psalms teach that the unequal distribution of mundane goods is caused by the cheating and sinfulness of the privileged.

The aphoristic wisdom of the Book of Proverbs (falsely attributed to Solomon) is contrived (after a foreign model, probably Egyptian and Babylonian) to teach common sense to the young. The *hakamin,* or sages, responsible for conveying this tradition stress the moral excellence of humaneness, patience, care for the poor, and decency to enemies. They are on the whole concerned with the affairs of daily life and certainly not with the wealth of kings; they are thus suspicious of the way in which fortunes are amassed (through plunder) and of the effect of money on the immature: "Ill-gotten gain takes away the lives of those who get it" (Prov. 1:19). Prudence, knowledge, and wisdom—the perquisites of maturity—are more valuable than gold and silver (Prov. 8:10f), whereas those who are wealthy are commonly arrogant and evil (Prov. 8:12-21). Indeed, the Proverbist anticipates later biblical reflection, especially that of the New Testament period, by equating the rich with the dishonest (Prov. 10-11) and predicting destruction for those whose money-values have clouded their judgment: "The wealth of the rich is their fortified city, and poverty is the ruin of the poor; the wages of the righteous bring them life, but the income of the wicked brings them punishment" (Prov. 10:15-16). The theme of ill-placed confidence in wealth breeds its correlate: Those who pride themselves on what they possess lead anxious care-filled lives, while the poor are free of such anxiety (Prov. 13:8; cf. Luke 12:22-31). While there is no actual polemic against being wealthy (cf. Prov. 14:20, 24), there *is* a strong suggestion that wealth is an inducement to sin and negligence (14:31) and a source for what the scholastics of another day would call *concupiscentia vitae*—"pride of life" (Prov. 17:1).

The tradition of instructional wisdom is given a pessimistic turn in Ecclesiastes, probably written toward the middle of the third century B.C.E. Strongly influenced by Hellenistic philosophy, the book is pervaded by a sense that the things of this world are not a sufficient end for human achievement. According to the Preacher (by report an educated, upper-class Jew who is nonetheless detached from the political aspirations of his people), time and chance are the true eternals of human existence, and death snatches us in the end "like a bird taken in a snare." With the author of Job, he worries that the good suffer and the wicked prosper. And in view of this injustice, the wise man is entitled to wonder where all his wealth, striving, and material success have got him: "When I surveyed all that my hands had done and what I had toiled to achieve, everything was meaningless, a chasing after the wind" (Eccles. 2:11f.). Here, as in the Book of Job (probably written two centuries prior to Ecclesiastes, but after the fall of Judah), the message is not that wealth is inherently sinful, but that in the grand scheme of things wealth cannot serve as an indicator of the justice of God.

Although the Book of Job is something of an editorial patchwork, its challenge to the received theology is clear: No longer is it possible to see submission to God's law as an entitlement to his justice, defined in the old economic theology as material reward. Job's victory, if it is that, is his purely technical refusal to "curse God and die." As a player on stage, he is actually a spokesman for the economic theology of the earlier period, in terms of which he has been denied justice in being deprived of property (Job 27:2f.). It is characteristic of the widsom literature to be ambivalent on the subject: thus the editorial addition to the Book of Job, in which God gives him twice as much as he had before (Job 42) and the optimist's revision of the Preacher's words in Ecclesiastes to the effect that "money is the answer for everything" (Eccles. 10:19).

The Prophets—especially Jeremiah, Ezekiel, and Zephaniah—were critics of an established order and hence of the economic theology also scrutinized in the wisdom books. In fact, those oracles displaying the greatest contempt for the privileges of the monied classes are exactly those showing the closest parallel to themes developed in the wisdom literature—hence Jeremiah's advice that a wise man should not boast of his wisdom, nor a rich man of his riches (Jer. 9:23). Knowledge of God is more important than either. Like Job, Jeremiah raises the question of justice—"Why do wicked men prosper and the faithless live well?" (Jer. 12:1)—while still insisting on the righteousness of God in essentially economic terms (Jer 32:15f.)

The inscrutability of God's justice has the potential to lead to several explanations for the material success of the wicked (i.e., those who do not keep the law, or those neighboring people who have come to wealth by plundering the Hebrew kingdoms). One such explanation is provided by the Book of Job, which vividly contrasts human ignorance with divine power—a view foreshadowed in the Book of Jeremiah (31:37f.). Another view, and one with considerable appeal for the early Christian teachers, belonged to those prophets who argued that the old covenantal theology, with its doctrine of material reward and punishment, was being phased out by a turnabout in God's plan for salvation: " 'The time is coming,'

declares the Lord, 'when I will make a new covenant with the house
of Israel and with the house of Judah . . . ; all of them, high and low
alike shall know me . . . for I shall remember their sin no more' " (Jer.
31:31, 34b). Nor does the prophetic literature lack the more cynical view
of wealth, elsewhere found in Proverbs and in Ecclesiastes. In his vision
of the desolation of Israel, Ezekiel blames the pride of possession for
the wantonness of the people, "Their silver and gold will not be able
to save them in the day of the Lord's wrath" (Ezek. 7:19). This message
has in turn been assimilated by the author of the Book of Zephaniah
(1:18) and by the apocalyptic writers of the Hellenistic period.

The apocryphal Old Testament writings, composed in the midst of
the political destitution of Judaism under Ptolemaic and Seleucid rule
(c. 323-142 B.C.E.), amplify the wisdom and prophetic attitudes toward
wealth without discernibly rehabilitating anything of the ancient economic
theology. In other words, the political events of the fourth through the
first century B.C.E.—wherein Judaism struggled, unsuccessfully, to retain
a geopolitical identity—led to a profound restructuring of attitudes toward
economic questions like wage-earning and tax-paying. The prophetic
writers had, albeit unsystematically, laid the ground for such a restructuring. Under the reign of Josiah (639-609 B.C.E.) or Jehoaiakim (608-
598 B.C.E.), the prophet Zephaniah had graphically forecast a "day of
the Lord" when the blood would be poured out like dust and the wealth
of men would not be able to save them (Zeph. 1:18). The memory of
the destruction of Judah in 587 B.C.E. (a scene added to the book attributed
to Zephaniah by a later editor of his oracles) served as a model for
what later generations believed would indeed be the scene when the Day
of the Lord—the judgment of the world—came to pass.

Building thus on the leitmotives of the prophets, the apocryphal
writers emphasized the severity of God's judgment on those who put
their faith in material possessions, a theme doubtlessly occasioned by
a growing cynicism toward the priestly elite and the Hellenized aristocracy
of Judaea and the Jewish diaspora. Orthodoxy in the centuries prior
to the birth of Jesus of Nazareth defined itself chiefly against the merchant-
economy and ritual laxity of "Hellenizers"—the "sinners" of the Gospels.
The so-called "pathetic history" of 2 Maccabees (5-7), written around
124 B.C.E., makes the point: "The Lord did not see fit to deal with us
[Jews] as he deals with the other nations; with them he patiently holds
his hand until they have reached the full extent of their sins, but upon
us he inflicted retribution [through the Syrians] before our sins reached
their height." (2 Macc. 6:14f).

Jewish piety just prior to the birth of Christianity sought ways to explain the political and religious impoverishment of the Maccabean state. It did this retrospectively in the form of tales—customarily set in the past—tailored to show how God works his designs in history. The story of blind Tobit, a pious Jew who suffers a number of calamaties in Nineveh, holds out the prophetic hope for a faithful remnant who will be saved from political oppression and live to enjoy the bounty God has in store for those who observe the law. Its moralistic stance includes Tobit's fulsome advice to his son Tobias: Poverty is God's way of disciplining his people, and great wealth lies in store for those who avoid wickedness (Tob. 5:21). Later additions to the book (cf. 5:11-14) endorse alms-giving as a way of being saved from (spiritual) death and condemn waste and infrugality as "the mother of starvation." Along with this advice comes the encouragement to "pay workmen their wages on the same day" and not to hold back money from a laborer (5:12), themes that resurface in Jesus' parable of the laborers in the vineyard (Matt. 20:1-16).

From around 180 B.C.E., equivalent sentiments ("Trust the Lord, stick to your job, and do not envy a fool his money") are expressed by the authors of the book sometimes known as Ecclesiasticus (Sirach 11:21): "A man may grow rich by stinting and sparing, but what does he get for his pains? When he says, 'I have earned my rest, now I can live on my savings,' he does not know how long it will be before he must die and leave his wealth to others. . . . Hardship is forgotten in times of success and success in times of hardship" (Sir. 11:18-19, 25). The same moralizing tone can be observed in the apocryphal wisdom book pseudonymously assigned to Solomon but probably written in Alexandria very close to the birth of Christianity. More pessimistic than the author of Tobit, the writer laments the mistakes of the past, in particular the acquisitiveness of his people: "What good has our pride done us? What can we show for our wealth and arrogance? All those things have passed by like a shadow, like a messenger galloping by, like a ship that runs through a surging sea, and when she has passed, not a trace is to be found, not a track of her keel among the waves." (Wisd. of Sol. 5:8-10). The pride in past glory and riches—the symbols of political autonomy—had by the first century B.C.E. led to a reappraisal of what we would call "priorities." This soul-searching stance intensified the hope for a deliverer or "messiah" anointed for the purpose of restoring the inheritance of the past—an inheritance that is often enfigured in crassly opulent ways (cf. Tob. 13:16-17). Not surprisingly, the messianic hope—bolstered by visions of a new David, a new Moses, and a new Israel—carried with it the hope for renewed prosperity.

Yoked with this political hope, however, is a more rigorous strain of thought, usually referred to as "apocalyptic," which emphasized the judgment of God upon the world—or more precisely, a verdict upon those who had put their faith in the wrong place. Thus the Sibylline Oracles (4:173): "Fire shall come upon the whole world. . . . The whole world shall hear a rumbling and a mighty roar. And [God] shall burn the whole earth, and consume the whole race of men, and all the rivers and cities, and the sea. He shall burn everything out and there shall be [only] soot and dust." Comparably grotesque predictions can be found throughout books written during the period (cf. Daniel 7:10); *Assumption of Moses* 10:1-10; *Psalms of Solomon* 15; *1 Enoch;* "The Song of the Three," 25; Mark 13, etc.), without prejudice to their canonical status. Political instability, the loss of home-rule, religious factionalism, and the scandals surrounding the temple cult and its leaders, militant opposition to the Romans by the zealots, capitulatory tendencies among the intelligentsia—this complicated picture is the basis for wideningly disparate opinions of gain, wealth, and property. The apocalyptic genre at its most cyncial despairs of mundane solutions and projects a return to primordial chaos as God's only way of restoring material blessing—if at all—in the indefinite future: "Thus lawlessness will make the whole world desolate, and active wickedness will overturn the thrones of princes" (Wis. of Sol. 5:23).

EARLY CHRISTIAN LITERATURE: THE NEW TESTAMENT

Christianity builds its understanding of wealth on the foundation of Jewish messianic, wisdom, and apocalyptic thought. Only indirectly does it represent a reaction to the economic theologies of the ancient writers. The reason for the rather different understanding of the morality of wealth in the earliest Christian literature has largely to do with the view of history that the writers of the Gospels and the missionary literature derived from their changed relationship to Judaism. That relationship had, in the middle decades of the first century, been largely informed by the view of the Jewish apocalyptic writers, a view that was contemptuous of any suggested correlation between wealth and divine favor. The Christian writers transformed this theoretical contempt into an active polemical thrust against the wealthy and wise of this world—against the power structure of Judaism and the wider Hellenistic world in which they had been set adrift. At the end of the transformation stands both the Psalmist's contempt for the rich and the enthronement of poverty as the mark of God's blessing. Even in the more radical critiques of economic theology offered by the prophets and the wisdom writers, this inversion would have been unthinkable, unthinkable because the messianic hope in "orthodox" Judaism remained primarily political, tied to the tangible accoutrements of power and prosperity. Poverty, to quote Tevye (the Milkman), was no sin—but it was no great honor either.

While it is mattter of considerable uncertainty how much of this polemic against the wealthy can be traced to the teaching of Jesus himself, it is at least plausible that his preaching of the judgment or "kingdom" of God, like that of John the Baptist before him, contained a polemicizing strain (cf. Luke 3:10-14; Mark 1:15). This strain, it would seem, has been amplified by writers whose own religious situation, representing that of their communities, led to a general rejection of money-values and property ownership as impediments to the preaching of the kingdom.

At the same time, one must be careful to distinguish views occasioned by resentment of the wealthy and difficult-to-convert classes of Jewish society and the general Christian expectation of future rewards and prosperity in the kingdom of God. Glum financial prospects produce both responses, of course: Those who "have" will be the "have-nots" of the coming kingdom; those who labor in the vineyards of the gospel and wait patiently for the Day of the Lord will be first instead of last at the great banquet table of God. The poor will be assigned thrones and will reign as judges over their earthly persecutors. Drawing on a theme already fully fledged in the vituperative sections of the Psalms, Luke suggests (22:24-30) that humility and hardship in the present is the price one has to pay for reward in the future. The point can further be illustrated from Matthew's and Luke's different versions of the "first beatitude": Where Matthew represents Jesus as quoting Isaiah 66:2 ("The man that is humble and poor in spirit, to him will I look"), Luke makes poverty itself ("Blessed are the poor") the entitlement to future bounty in the kingdom of God. Hence the poverty ethic is not an endorsement of being poor for its own sake, but of poverty as the *discipline* that prepares the Christian for his future inheritance— a mark of God's blessing (Luke 21:1-4).

A brief survey of the New Testament literature suggests that the writers possessed an abundance of aphoristic wisdom describing the Christian's proper duty toward the poor and proclaiming that wealth and power are hindrances to salvation from God's judgment (Matt. 11:12b). The two themes are inseparably linked in a source common to the authors of the Books of Matthew and Luke. In the latter's version of a discourse to his disciples, Jesus is given to appraise wealth in the language of a sage: "Do not worry about your life, what you will eat, or about your body, what you will wear. Life is more than food and the body more than clothes. . . . Sell your possessions and give to the poor. Provide purses for yourself that will not wear out, a treasure in heaven that will not be exhausted, where no thief comes near and no moth destroys" (Luke 12:22, 23:33). What is remarkable in this assessment is that poverty is praised as an adjunct of learning to do without worldly goods. Ceasing to care about material prosperity contributes to caring about "inexhaustible" treasure—that which cannot be material because it cannot be stolen. Hence: "Where your treasure is, there also is your heart" (Luke 12:34; cf. Matt. 6:19-21).

Luke in particular presents the poverty ethic as a central Christian requirement. In the legend of Jesus' temptation in the wilderness, for example, he is seen rejecting an offer of "authority" and "splendor"— the tangible symbols of kingship—as being contrary to the worship of God (Luke 4:6). In the sayings usually called "beatitudes," Jesus is shown heaping praises on the poor, the hungry, and the outcast (Luke 6:20-22), while cursing those who are rich and well-fed (6:24-35). Indeed, in a saying offered by Matthew (6:1-4), even those Christians who can afford to give alms are told to do so secretly lest their alms-giving become a source of pride to them.

The poverty ethic also pervades the moralistic teaching ascribed to Jesus by Luke and, to a large degree, by Matthew. In the story of "the unjust steward" (Luke 16:1-13), Jesus appears to endorse wastefulness as a way of coming more quickly to repentance: The sooner one realizes that money does not last, the sooner one will know what is of ultimate importance (16:9). Coupled with this is a suspicion of the "shrewdness" of the Pharisees (described soon after [16:14] as money-lovers) and a general division—possibly shaped by the apocalyptic views of the Christians themselves—between serving God and serving money (Luke 16:13). The Christian doctrine of salvation itself (cf. Luke 15) is calculated in economic terms as the finding of a lost sheep, a coin, or a wayward son. So, too, the rewards of the faithful, as in the "parable of the pounds" (Matt. 25:14-30; Luke 19:11-27), or the story in Luke of Zacchaeus— whose wealth the writer equates (19:6) with sinfulness and whose salvation, like that of the "rich young man" of Mark's gospel—depends on selling property and giving the proceeds to the poor (Luke 19:8; cf. Mark 10:21).

As prototypes of this vision of faithfulness to the gospel, the apostles are characterized as men who have left their families and homes behind. They are vagabonds who depend on the charity of listeners and sympathizers (Matt. 10:10; cf. 2 Cor. 11:9). Although the Gospels can be inconsistent on the point, the antimaterialism of a sizable part of the early tradition is such that even conventional notions about the visible "signs of the last days" are challenged (Mark 8:12; Luke 27:20f), if not overturned (Mark 13; Matt. 25:31-46).

The marginality of the new faith vis-à-vis Judaism and the Hellenistic cults bears on early Christian resentment of authority, structure, and "title," resentment that has reasserted itself in nearly every purifying movement from the early monastics to the Reformation. Thus Jesus is shown by Mark to have cautioned his disciples against struggles for leadership (doubtless a response to existing struggles in Mark's Roman community); by Luke to have commended humility and poverty as ways to be "exalted" by God (Luke 14:9-11; cf. John 13:2-16); and by Matthew as someone who "does not regard the position of men" (22:16) and who denies the title "teacher" ("rabbi") to his followers (Matt. 23:8). In short, there is clear contempt for persons of power, money, and influence who flaunt their wealth as proof of their righteousness: "You blind fools! Which is greater: the gold or the temple which makes the gold sacred?" (Matt. 23:17).

This contempt is sometimes extreme—not a condemnation of money as something that induces people to sin or distracts them from the things of ultimate value, but of wealth *as* sin. The parable of the rich fool (Luke 12:13-21) illustrates the sort of attitude fostered by the poverty ethic; the nature of possession is self-indulgent, and it lessens one's "richness" toward God. The tale of the rich man and Lazarus (Luke 16:19-31) is also contrived to illustrate the hopelessness of the rich with regard to salvation. The tale itself, with its imputation of punishment for the wealthy in Hades, and of reward for the poor in a place of refreshment and comfort, seems to reflect Christian perturbance over the failure or refusal of the wealthier classes to heed the gospel-message of judgment for the unrepentant. The *rejection* of wealth in such passages is tantamount to being repentant: The sins occasioned by wealth are not distinguished from the condition of being wealthy. Thus the well-to-do are condemned for their material advantage over the poor, and, as the logic of the community would have it, the poor must have *ultimate* advantage over the rich (Luke 16:8). Only in this connection can we explain the counsels of Jesus to the "rich young man" (Mark 10:17) and the rationale following this advice: "It is easier for a camel to go through the eye of a needle than for a rich man to enter the kingdom of God" (Mark 10:25). This "saying" of Jesus is stated to cause astonishment among his followers, who remind him that they have forsaken family and sold property to be his disciples (Mark 10:28f.). Paradigmatically, to be a "true" follower is to be poor. The general poverty of the little communities has, by the example of other apostles, become the very mark of their discipleship (cf. 1 Cor. 1:26).

The writings of other New Testament writers are essentially in harmony with the viewpoint of the Gospels. A few points are worth noting, however. In his romantic account of the church's early missionary activity, Luke tells us in the Acts of the Apostles that the church operated as a communalistic and charismatic fellowship; members sold all their possessions and goods and contributed the proceeds to a common fund. Out of this, monies were apportioned according to need (Acts 2:45). The legend of Ananias and Sapphira (Acts 5)—in which a married couple sells their property but keeps some of the profit for themselves and are smitten by God as punishment—was evidently a kind of morality tale intended to impress upon new believers the importance of the common life and the value of personal poverty. It is all but certain that Luke's account preserves some memory of the economic organization of the early Christian churches and the value apparently placed by these communities on equal distribution of financial resources. That the communalistic ideal of wealth-sharing was subject to the vagaries of church membership and ethnic factionalism is shown by the story of quarreling between Greek-and Aramaic-speaking Jews in Acts 6. The story also seeks to explain the origins of hierarchy or administration as a measure designed to ensure the continued equal distribution of goods (Acts 6:3). The explanation, however, suggests that by Luke's day—the nineties of the first century—the contempt for authority reflected in the Gospels had diminished and that the social structure he describes is based on hearsay rather than observation (cf. Acts 15:19f.).

The letters of Paul, written prior to the Gospels and Acts, contain fugitive references to wealth and the fate of the wealthy. In those sections in which Paul describes the coming of the final days of the world, he advises Christians that any and all material concerns are misplaced: Those who are contemplating marriage may as well remain single; those who are about to buy property should understand that it is not theirs to keep; and those who are engrossed in worldly things should learn they are of no account, as "the world in its present form is passing away" (1 Cor. 7:29-31). Paul believes that the resurrection of Jesus has thrown the epicurean philosophy of life (1 Cor. 15:32) into doubt: Material possessions will not do for the newly formed spiritual creation, and so one must learn to live without them. "What is seen is temporary; what is unseen is eternal "(2 Cor. 4:18).

Letters written in Paul's name in the early decades of the second century lack the original hortatory motive for Paul's view of wealth, but they nonetheless preserve what had become a central theme of Christian social philosophy: Be content with food and clothing, admonishes the author of 1 Timothy, as we brought nothing into the world and will take nothing with us when we go. Rich people are more easily tempted and entrap others with money-making schemes: "To be in love with money is the root of all kinds of evil" (1 Tim. 6:6-10). One observes, however, a departure from both the Gospels and authentically Pauline context in such admonitions. By the early second century, when perhaps a third of the twenty-seven books of the New Testament remained to be composed or redacted into final form, money was seen as an endangerment to a faith now perceived to have a future and not as an encumbrance to salvation from a world with no time left (1 Tim 6:17ff.). Where the older theme does resurface (e.g., James 5:1-5), it bears all the marks of nostalgia for the days when God's judgment was expected to be swift and sure and when luxury and self-indulgence were inherently offensive to the preachers of imminent tribulation. More typical of a church obliged to make its peace with the world, following the failure of the early eschatological prophecies, is the trend of thought that runs from around the year 95 or so through the mid-second century. That trend marks the end of a view of wealth and possession informed chiefly by a pessimistic philosophy of history and offers the love of God as an alternative to loving the things of the world. Clarions for a return to the older expectations and the old view of the world (Jude 18; 2 Peter 3:3-10) were loud, but they finally failed to make the view of the Gospels programmatic for the further development of the Christian church.

WISDOM
John T. Townsend

The biblical concept of wisdom includes a wide range of meanings, far wider than any modern definition. In the oldest parts of the Bible, "wisdom" generally means technical skills, knowledge, or general intelligence. In sections written later, though, the word acquires new, more specific meanings. Indeed, in some books "wisdom" even takes on personal qualities, until in some passages it appears as a separate entity that acts as the divine agent of creation. Within Judaism, this personified wisdom also came to be identified with the Torah, i.e., the Jewish Law; within Christianity, it came to be identified with Jesus Christ. Still, the earlier meanings of wisdom continued alongside these later ones.

Within the Bible the distribution of words meaning "wisdom" is uneven. Well over half of the total are found in the "Wisdom Books": Job, Proverbs, Ecclesiastes, The Wisdom of Solomon, and the Wisdom of Jesus, the Son of Sirach (also called Ecclesiasticus). There are forty-one biblical books where the Hebrew and Greek words for "wisdom" or "wise" never appear.[1]

The biblical meaning of "wisdom" varies, not only from book to book, but even within a given work. In a majority of cases, however, biblical wisdom represents a concept that is not unlike the way we think of wisdom today. Indeed, as synonyms for "wisdom," the Hebrew Bible uses words commonly translated as "knowledge," "understanding," "insight," "instruction," "justice," "counsel," "reasoning," and "truth."[2] To these the Greek Bible adds words translated as "thought," "intelligence," and "education," etc.[3] The adjective "wise" is most often coupled with words meaning "understanding," "discerning," and even "wily."[4] But in certain contexts, it is associated with old age and justice. Thus "old" and "righteous" sometimes occur as equivalent of "wise."[5] One can also interpret biblical "wisdom" in terms of the word's opposites. The Bible contrasts "wisdom" with "folly" and "madness," for example, while "wise" is contrasted with "stupid" and "foolish."[6]

Another way the Bible uses the word "wisdom" is less familiar to modern readers. This usage denotes a mastery of merely *technical* skills. Apart from Deuternomony 4:6 and 34:9, this is the *only* sense of the word found in the Pentateuch. Such skills are of all sorts, from spinning to military strategy, from house-building to snake-charming, and even to the way one weeps at funerals.[7] Moreover, as the nature of these skills suggests, those possessing them included both men and women.[8] Though such a definition of "wisdom" sounds somewhat strange to modern ears, it was not unusual for the ancient world; a similar notion of wisdom is found in Homer's *Iliad,* 15:410-12. Both the Bible and the Greek classics traced this kind of wisdom to divine origins.[9] Among the technical skills that made one wise was the ability to rule or judge, and this ability to make wise decisions and judgments was, of course, a necessity for any king.[10] Throughout the Bible there was one above all others who exhibited this wisdom of the ruler, and that was King Solomon. In fact, Solomon became the biblical epitome of all wisdom, royal and otherwise (1 Kings 3, 5, 10, etc).

Sometimes the Bible depicts the wisdom of a royal court more as a sly cunning than legal brilliance or statecraft.[11] More commonly, however, court wisdom was associated with the ability to compose proverbs and songs, so that 1 Kings 5:12 can illustrate the greatness of Solomon's wisdom simply by stating, "He uttered three thousand proverbs *[mashal],* and his songs numbered a thousand and five." This description of wisdom sounds more restrictive in English than it does in Hebrew. *Mashal* has a far broader meaning than the English noun "proverb." It includes parables, allegories, fables, riddles, and songs, and it is in this broad sense that "wisdom" is often used in the Bible. Two books (The Wisdom of Solomon and the Wisdom of Jesus, the Son of Sirach) use "wisdom" in their titles; others (Ecclesiastes and much of Proverbs) are attributed to Solomon, the embodiment of biblical wisdom; and Proverbs 1:1 uses the plural of *mashal* as a descriptive title.

Along with royalty went royal courts. If the king was paramount in wisdom, those whom he gathered around him also needed to possess wisdom. Some of these wise courtiers were masters in technical skills (1 Kings 7:13-14). More important were those who advised the ruler on political and personal matters (Isa. 19:11, etc.). Their position as advisers to the king would have been like that of Joseph in the court of Pharaoh; Ahithophel, who advised first David and then Absalom; Daniel in Babylon; or the wise men who advised King Ahasuerus in Susa (Esther 1:13). Nor were such royal advisers limited to males. From early biblical times, the royal women of a court might have had the advice of their own wise women, like those who gave the wrong advice to the mother of Sisera (Judges 5:29).

Sometimes biblical wisdom could take on a supernatural cast. The Bible regards such supernaturalism either as magic or a divine gift. The difference depended largely upon whether a particular biblical writer saw the power of the wise sage as stemming from the God of Israel or from some unfriendly source. Enemies who practiced this kind of wisdom were deemed "magicians." Thus Exodus 7:11, for example, declares the wise men of Pharaoh's court to be "sorcerers" and "magicians," and Isaiah 44:25 lumps together those who practice false wisdom with lying diviners (cf. Isa. 19:1-15, 47:10-13; Jer. 50:35-36). By contrast, although Daniel is lumped with the wise advisers of Babylon (Dan. 2:18, 48), his supernatural power is declared to come from God, not demons (Dan. 2:20-45).

The "wise" were not limited to the royal courts. Wise men and women were found throughout the land, where they enjoyed respect for their ability in political, social, and ethical decisions (2 Sam. 14:2, etc.). In time the wise became a learned class, who transmitted their teaching through schools (Sirach 51:23). Nor do Israel's representatives of wisdom appear very different from their counterparts in Egypt and Mesopotamia. These counterparts produced similar kinds of literature and played a role in their societies that seems akin to the role of Israel's wise sages.[12]

The literature the Bible has attributed to those known for their wisdom tends to represent upper and middle class values. Sirach said that one should not be ashamed "of making the side of a bad domestic slave bloody," presumably through beating (42:5).[13] Indeed, while the biblical wisdom books in general present moral rules for personal conduct, they show little concern for general social injustice. It is therefore not surprising that those prophets who *do* express concern for social injustice speak out *against* the wise and their teaching.[14]

In spite of this lack of concern for social injustice, some biblical views of wisdom came to have a religious element, distinguishing false wisdom, which leads to temporary prosperity, from true wisdom, which is in accord with the will of God.[15] "The mouth of a just person will speak wisdom . . . [because] the law of his God is in his heart, and [therefore] his steps will not slip" (Ps. 37:30-31). The only parts of the Bible that seem to question this joining of righteousness to wisdom are the books of Job and Ecclesiastes. Job's wisdom leads to a savage attack on God's righteousness, and Ecclesiastes declares that "wisdom is vanity."[16] Yet even here, wisdom and righteousness are made to agree. God comes in a thunderstorm and frightens Job into repenting "in dust and ashes" (42:6), while Ecclesiastes concludes with the following: "The end of the matter, when all has been heard: Fear God and observe his commandments."[17]

This coupling of wisdom with the fear of God is significant, and it is found throughout the Bible. Most commonly, the concept appears this way: "The fear of the Lord is the beginning of wisdom." This assertion, or some close variant, appears in Job, Psalms, Proverbs, and Sirach.[18] For an educational system that made much use of whipping, such a maxim had clear utility. One of the best-known lines from Proverbs is, "Whoever spares the rod hates his child" (13:24). Sirach maintains that "whippings and education are always wisdom" (1:27, 22:6; cf: Prov. 29:15). However, one should not always equate such fear of the Lord merely with being "terrified of God." This "fear," which was regarded as the proper attitude of mortals before God, sometimes seems more akin to *reverence* than to terror. To be sure, this "fear of the Lord was not necessarily even an unpleasant emotion; it could bring *joy*. According to Sirach 1:11-13,

> The fear of the Lord is glory and exaltation, also gladness and a crown
> of rejoicing. The fear of the Lord delights the heart; it also gives gladness,
> joy, and long life. Whoever fears the Lord will have things go well
> at the last, and on the day of his death he will find favor.

In fact, "whoever fears the Lord shall not be afraid, nor shall he lose courage, because [the Lord] is his hope. Happy is the soul of the one who fears the Lord" (Sirach 34:14-15).[19]

"All wisdom comes from the Lord," as Sirach proclaims at the beginning of his book.[20] Furthermore, since the Lord is righteous, one who is wise must live righteously. In time, this relation between wisdom and righteousness resulted in the identification of wisdom with God's

Law, i.e., the Torah, the five books "of Moses." For Sirach and Baruch, wisdom and the Torah were one. Typical is Sirach's statement in 19:20: "All wisdom is the fear of the Lord and in all wisdom there is the fulfillment of the Law."[21] Moreover, Sirach was quite specific about what he meant by the Law that gives wisdom; it was "the book of the covenant of God Most High" (24:23). Similarly, Baruch 4:1 proclaims that wisdom "is the book of the commandments of God, even the Law that endures forever."[22]

Throughout the biblical Wisdom Books, there are certain passages that speak of wisdom in personal terms—so much is certain. But what is far from certain is whether these passages are claiming to depict an actual supernatural being—perhaps even some deity—or are merely using metaphorical language. Commentators have doggedly argued both positions. An exegete who believes that Jews could never revere any deity besides the Lord God is unlikely to accept the biblical personification of Wisdom in a literal sense. Exegetes who believe otherwise understand the personification of wisdom literally and even suggest that biblical writers borrowed mythic material associated with foreign goddesses like the Egyptian Maat or Isis.[23] The latter position is strengthened by the frequency with which wisdom was personified in later Jewish and Christian texts.

The passages which speak of wisdom as a personified entity include Proverbs 1:20-21 and 8:1-9:6, Sirach 1:4-9 and 24:1-34, and The Wisdom of Solomon 6:12-11:1. Some would also add the poem of Job 28 to this group, but Job 28 does not clearly represent wisdom as a personified power of God or as some entity apart from God. What the poem does affirm is that while we cannot locate wisdom in any part of the world, "God understands the way to [wisdom] and knows its place. For he looks to the ends of the earth, and sees everything under the heavens. . . . And he said to humanity: 'See! The fear of the Lord, that is wisdom; and to depart from evil is understanding' " (28:23-24, 28).

Proverbs 8 clearly depicts wisdom, whether metaphorically or literally, as God's agent in creation. That wisdom is presented speaking in the first person perhaps argues for the view that the author regarded wisdom as an actual entity. First God created wisdom (Prov. 8:22), and then wisdom became the divine *amon* (translated by *RSV* as "master worker") for the rest of creation (Prov. 8:30). Although the meaning of *amon* is uncertain,[24] the context demands that as *amon* wisdom somehow was associated with God in creation.

Sirach examines the subject further. Not only does 24:23 identify this wisdom with the Law of Moses, but verses 2-4 maintain that this Torah-Wisdom "came forth from the mouth of the most high, covered the earth like a mist," and now sits in the assembly of the most high on a throne in a pillar of cloud. Then verse 9 has Wisdom say, "From the beginning before eternity [God] created me, and throughout eternity I shall not pass away." Sirach also develops the concept of Wisdom as the object of love. Those who would possess her must pursue her like a lover (14:22-27, 51:13-30); indeed, she is both bride and mother (4:11-12, 15:2). Furthermore, Torah-Wisdom has a special relation to Israel, in that the Creator has commanded her to make her dwelling in Jacob (24:8). Therefore, according to verse 10, "In the Holy Tabernacle I [wisdom] ministered before him, and so I was established in Zion." Still, wisdom is not for Israel alone, since God "poured out [wisdom] on all his works," an assertion suggesting that wisdom permeates creation (1:9). The verb "pour out" might suggest that this wisdom is more fluid than personality, but personality and fluidity need not be entirely exclusive. After all, in Romans 8:26-27 Paul describes the Holy Spirit in personal terms, even though he speaks of "drinking the spirit" in 1 Corinthians 12:13.[25]

According to The Wisdom of Solomon, wisdom is a creature of God (6:22) subject to divine guidance (7:15), intimately related to God but still separate, "remaining in herself" (7:25-27). Because of this relation with God, she is an agent of creation (7:22, 8:4, 9:9), but is also fully knowable, at least to the one who takes her for his bride (8:2, 8-9). In fact, as a spirit who dwells with God (8:2) and comes forth from God in answer to prayer (7:7, 8:21), wisdom is also able to *reveal* God. The quest of wisdom begins with the most sincere desire for education, a beginnning that leads to the keeping of her laws. For those who follow her ways, wisdom brings all good things, including innumerable riches (7:11) and immortality in a kingdom with God (6:17-20; 8:17). Since The Wisdom of Solomon does not hesitate to use several Greek philosophical terms in describing wisdom,[26] it is not surprising that the work treats wisdom as equivalent to the Word *(Logos)* of God (9:1-2). Both are instruments in creation (9:1-2, 9); both punish the enemies of the righteous (10:19, 18:15); both can bring salvation from what is evil (9:18-10:1 and 16:12); both are all-powerful (7:23, 18:15); and both sit by the throne of God (9:4, 18:15). Finally, in addition to being equivalent to God's Word, wisdom is also the equivalent of the Holy Spirit (9:17) and, as such, responsible for prophecy (7:27).

Like the Hebrew Scriptures and the Apocrypha, the New Testament understands the concept of wisdom in more than one sense. In one case (1 Cor. 3:10), the concept alludes to technical skill. In Revelation 13:18 and 17:9, wisdom is esoteric knowledge. In general, New Testament allusions to wisdom correspond to one or another type of modern usage. As in the Hebrew Bible, they often suggest that it is not a matter of learning or skill but primarily a moral attitude towards God's will.[27] Allusions to wisdom that do not satisfy such a moral imperative generally portray it as false or at least insufficient.[28]

Just as certain parts of the Hebrew Scriptures and the Apocrypha depict wisdom as a distinct personality separate from God, so do the writers of the New Testament. Like The Wisdom of Solomon 9:17, Acts 6, verses 3 and 10, links wisdom with the Holy Spirit as that which empowers the followers of Jesus. More significantly, a few passages in the New Testament suggest an equivalence between personified wisdom and Jesus Christ. This view finds clear expression in 1 Corinthians 1:24, 30, which maintain that God had made Christ Jesus our wisdom.[29] It is necessary to recognize, however, that throughout the first four chapters of 1 Corinthians, Paul is speaking *against* those who would claim to possess what he calls "the wisdom of this world" (1:20). This is how he answers such claims:

> Where is the wise one? Where is the scribe? Where is the debater of this age? Has not God made foolish the wisdom of the world? For since, in the wisdom of God, the world did not know God through wisdom, it pleased God through the folly of what we preach to save those who believe. For Jews demand signs and Greeks seek wisdom, but we preach Christ crucified, a stumbling-block to Jews and folly to Gentiles, but to those who are called, both Jews and Greeks, Christ the power of God and the wisdom of God. For the foolishness of God is wiser than humans, and the weakness of God is stronger than humans (1:20-25).

Clearly by naming Christ as the wisdom of God, Paul is opposing those who have other views about wisdom. In 1 Corinthians 2:6-16, Paul seems to be using the very language of his opponents. He maintains that he imparts wisdom among those mature enough to comprehend it, wisdom that is "not of this age nor of the rulers of this age," but wisdom that "God decreed before the ages" (2:6-7). Perhaps Paul's opponents were speculating about some kind of personified, divine wisdom in addition to Christ, with Paul responding that the only true personal wisdom figure is Christ Jesus himself.

Two other examples that suggest some relationship between personal wisdom and Jesus appear in Matthew and Luke. In the first example, Luke 11:49-51 attributes a saying to "wisdom" that Matthew 23:34-36 puts on the lips of Jesus. If Luke represents the earlier tradition, Matthew must have understood the "wisdom" of his source to be Jesus. If Matthew represents the earlier tradition, however, the fact that Luke attributed a saying to wisdom in the midst of a series of Jesus' sayings suggests that Luke considered Jesus and wisdom to be interchangeable.[30] The second example, Matthew 11:16-19 and Luke 7:31-35, compares John the Baptist and Jesus. Luke's version concludes: "Wisdom is justified by her children." Here wisdom is again personified, but it is not identified with Jesus. Rather, Jesus and John are both seen as wisdom's children. Matthew's conclusion is somewhat different: "Wisdom is justified by her works," i.e., Jesus and John show their relation to wisdom by producing her good works. Both versions agree on this point: Jesus' relation to wisdom is one of witness rather than identification.

NOTES

1. The Books of Leviticus, Numbers, Joshua, Ruth, 1 Samuel, 2 Kings, Nehemiah, the Song of Solomon, Lamentations, Hosea, Joel, Amos, Jonah, Micah, Nahum, Habakkak, Zephaniah, Haggai, Zechariah, Malachi, Tobit, The Song of the Three Holy Children, Susan, Bel and the Dragon, Prayer of Manasses, 1 Maccabees, John, Galations, Philippians, 1 and 2 Thessalonians, 1 and 2 Timothy, Titus, Philemon, Hebrews, 1-3 John, and Jude.

2. Prov. 2:6; Job 38:36; Ps. 49:4; Prov. 2:2, 6; 3:13; Prov. 1:2, 3; Ps. 37:30; Jer. 49:7; see also Job 26:3; Eccl. 7:25; Ps. 51:8.

3. Deut. 4:6; Prov. 1:7; Prov 8:33; Prov 2:3, 3:5; 1 Kings 5:11; Prov 18:2; Exod. 35:33; 1 Chron. 22:12; Wisd. of Sol. 7:7; Jth. 8:29; Wisd. of Sol. 3:11; Sirach prologue, 1:43, 4:24, 18:22, 39:66; cf. 22:6.

4. 1 Kings 3:12; Hos. 14:10; Isa. 5:21.

5. Ezek. 27:8-9; Deut. 16:19; Prov 9:9, 23:24; Eccl. 9:1.

6. Prov. 2:12, 14:1; Sir. 20:31, 41:15; Eccl. 1:17; 2:12-16, 7:25; 1 Cor. 1:21-25; further uses are found in Prov. 10:1; 13:20; 14:24; 15:2, 20; 21:20; 26:5, 12; 29:11; Eccl. 2:19, 4:13, 6:8, 10:2, 12; Ps. 49:11; etc.; also Prov. 10:8, 14; 12:15; 14:3; 17:28; Jer. 4:22; Sir. 27:11. "Wise" and "wise person" are the same word in Hebrew. So also "foolish" and "foolish person" or "fool," etc.

7. Exod. 28:3-6, 31:3-6, 35:10-36:8; 1 Kings 7:14; Ps. 58:6; Prov. 24:3; Jer. 9:16; Ezek. 27:8-9; Judith 11:8; Wisd. of Sol. 7:15-16, 14:2.

8. Exod. 35:25.

9. Wisd. of Sol. 7:15-17. Greeks ascribed such wisdom to Athene (Homer, *Iliad* 15:412) and to other deities and heroes.

10. Deut. 34:9; 2 Sam. 14:20; Isa. 11:2; cf. Isa. 10:12, 47:10; Ezek. 28:2-19; Sir. 45:26; Acts 7:10; 2 Chron. 1:10, etc. Cf. Plato, *Protagoras* 321d.

11. 1 Kings 2:6, 3:16-28, 10:1-5. See also the "cunning" of Daniel.

12. For biblical examples of such foreign sages, see Esther 1:13 concerning the court of King Ahasuerus; Daniel 1:3-2:48, 4:1-18, and 5:7-16 concerning the court at Babylon; and Esther 6:13 for a wise counselor to someone less than a king, namely Haman. A good example of Mesopotamian "wisdom" is the legend of Ahigar, in J. B. Pritchard, *Ancient Near Eastern Texts,* Princeton, 1950, 427-430.

13. The Hebrew versions, even when complete, omit this verse. English translations of the Greek usually soften it. Thus the *Revised Standard Version* translates, "of whipping a wicked servant severely." Cf. Sir. 33:24-31.

14. Isa. 29:14; Jer. 8:8-9, 9:22-23; cf. Isa. 47:10-11 on the wisdom of Babylon.

15. See Isaiah 10:13-19 (re the Assyrian king); 47:10-15 (re Babylon); Ezek. 28:1-10 (re the prince of Tyre).

16. Job 12-19; Eccl. 2:15-26; see 1:16-18; etc.

17. Eccl. 12:13. Critical interpreters generally regard the last chapters of Job and the last verses of Ecclesiastes as additions by later editors; but this is what the Bible says now.

18. Job 28:28; Ps. 111:10; Prov. 1:7, 2:2-6, 9:10, 15:33; Sir. 1:20, 27; 15:1; 19:20; 21:11; 25:10; cf. Ps. 90:11-12; Prov. 8:12-13; Isa. 33:6.

19. Note also the joyful context where the "fear of the Lord" appears in Ps. 19:9 and Jer. 32:40.

20. Similarly 1 Kings 4:29, 5:12; Ezra 7:25; Prov. 2:6; Eccl. 2:26; Isa. 11:2; Dan. 2:20-21; 1 Esd. 4:59-60; 8:23; Wisd. of Sol. 7:15ff.; Sir. 1:1, 9; Bar. 3:12-13; Luke 21:15; Rom. 11:33; 1 Cor. 1:30; Eph. 1:9-10, 17; James 1:5.

21. Similarly Sir. 15:1; 21:11; 33:2-3; 34:8; 39:1. See also Wisd. of Sol. 6:18; Sir. 2:16; 6:37; 9:14-15; 17:11; 19:17-24; 32:14-16. Cf. Col. 2:23.

22. See also Wisd. of Sol. 6:18 and Bar. 3:9, 4:1 for the Torah as the content of wisdom. Cf. 2. Pet. 3:15, where wisdom begins to be equated with Church teaching.

23. Cf. R. Scott, *Proverbs, Ecclesiastes,* Garden City, 1965 (*Anchor Bible* 18) pp. 39, 69, with E. Schussler Fiorenza, "Wisdom Mythology" in *Aspects of Wisdom,* ed. R. Wilken, Notre Dame, 1975, 26-33. For further discussion of the problem, see R. E. Murphy, "Wisdom—Theses and Hypotheses," in *Israelite Wisdom,* ed. J. Hamme et al., Missoula, 1978, 35-42 (S. Terrien volume).

24. For various possibilities, see R. Scott, "Wisdom in Creation," *Vetus Testamentum* 10 (1960) 213-23.

25. In a similar vein, Acts 2:17 mentions the pouring out of God's spirit (part of a citation from Joel 3:1).

26. Wis. of Sol. 7:22-24 applies twenty-one epithets to wisdom, mostly from Greek philosophy. For details, see D. Winston, *Wisdom of Solomon,* Garden City, 1979 (Anchor Bible 43), 178-83.

27. For example, see Matt. 23:34; Luke 2:40, 52; Rom. 16:19, 27; Eph. 1:17-18, 5:15; Col. 1:9-10, 28; 3:16-17; James 3:13-17. For some possible exceptions, see the parallels among Matt. 12:42; Luke 11:31 and 21:15; and Acts 7:10; but even here a moral aspect to wisdom cannot be ruled out. At least the wisdom alluded to in these verses had a practical application.

28. For references to insufficient wisdom or to those who possess such wisdom, see the parallels among Matt. 11:25; Luke 10:21; and 1 Cor. 1:17-2:16, 3:18-20.

29. See also 1 Cor. 2:7, where Paul maintains that God's wisdom is the content of his own preaching, a content that he has already identified as Christ crucified (in 1 Cor. 1:23). See also Col. 2:3.

30. It is possible that Luke represents Jesus here as citing a passage from a wisdom book, but no ancient Christian mentioned the source, and no modern scholar has found it.

FOR FURTHER READING

R. L. Wilken, editor. *Aspects of Wisdom in Judaism and Early Christianity.* Notre Dame, 1975.

J. L. Crenshaw, editor. *Studies in Ancient Israelite Wisdom.* New York, 1976.

———. *Old Testament Wisdom.* Atlanta, 1981.

J. M. Sasson, editor. *Oriental Wisdom: Six Essays on the Sapiental Traditions of Eastern Civilizations.* A special issue of the *Journal of the American Oriental Society* 101:1 (1981) 1-131. R. E. Murphy's article, "Hebrew Wisdom" (pp. 21-34), is of particular interest.

G. Von Rad. *Wisdom in Israel.* Translated by J. D. Martin. London, 1972.

R. B. Y. Scott. *The Way of Wisdom in the Old Testament.* London, 1971.

WOMEN IN THE OLD TESTAMENT
Mary Chilton Callaway

The Bible speaks about women in many different ways, sometimes explicitly, but more usually indirectly. Our purpose in this and the following essay is to collect the most important texts that refer to women and to set forth their plain sense, noting problems of interpretation where the sense is not clear. The Old Testament will be treated in its three traditional parts: the Torah, Prophets, and Writings.

THE TORAH

The Narratives

The two creation stories in Genesis (1:1-2:4a and 2:4b-3:24) give differing accounts of the creation of woman. Genesis 1:26 describes God creating the male and the female simultaneously, while Genesis 2 tells how the Lord, having formed man from the dust of the ground, thought his work incomplete. Trying to provide man a helper, the Lord formed all the animals; when none was adequate, he took one of the man's ribs and built it into a woman. The man recognized her as "bone of my bones and flesh of my flesh." (All translations, unless otherwise noted, are taken from the Revised Standard Version of the Bible.) The woman became his wife, a relation the text says would then take precedence over a man's relation to his father and mother.

The story in Genesis 3 tells how the serpent approached the woman to discuss the prohibition against eating from the "tree of knowledge of good and evil." The serpent explains the consequences of eating from the tree. She will not die, but her eyes will be opened and she will be "like God." Drawn by her desire for the good and beautiful food, and for the wisdom that it will confer, the woman eats, and she gives some to her unquestioning husband. A large part of Genesis 3 is given over to the punishments meted out by the Lord. While the serpent is cursed, the man and the woman are both given *itzbon,* toil or anguish. Anguish will characterize the woman's role as mother and wife, and the man's role as tiller of the accursed ground. The woman's life will be made difficult by childbearing and by the conflict between her desire for her husband and being ruled by him. The original sense of these words is not clear, but they do indicate that the relation between the man and the woman intended by God at creation has been disrupted.

The rest of the book of Genesis tells the story of God's promise to Abraham: He would become the father of a great nation, whose descendants would be as countless as the stars. The four wives of Abraham, Isaac, and Jacob—Sarah, Rebecca, and Rachel and Leah—are prominent in the story, in part because the promise cannot be fulfilled without them, and their barrenness presents an obstacle to its fulfillment. Further, they are active in the affairs of their families, petitioning, persuading, and even circumventing their husbands to achieve what they want. When Sarah cannot conceive, she gives her maid Hagar to Abraham to bear a child for her. But when Hagar conceives and looks on her mistress with contempt, Sarah treats her so harshly that Hagar flees to the desert (Gen. 16). Later, Sarah asks Abraham to cast out Hagar with her young son Ishmael so her own son Isaac can receive the full inheritance of Abraham (Gen. 21:1-21). Rebecca wants her favorite son, Jacob, to receive the blessing that legally belonged to his older brother, Esau, so she devises a scheme by which Jacob disguises himself as Esau and tricks his blind and aged father into blessing him (Gen. 27:1-45). It is Rebecca who sends Jacob away to her brother Laban's house, where he marries Rachel and Leah. Rachel tries a variety of schemes to overcome her barrenness, including giving Jacob her maid to bear sons for her. Leah, although she does bear sons, also sends in her maid as a substitute, to keep ahead of Rachel (Gen. 29).

Genesis 38 tells the intriguing story of Tamar, the childless widow who disguises herself as a harlot to entice her father-in-law, Judah, to comply with the law and provide her an heir. Judah pronounces that, far from being a harlot, "She is more righteous than I, inasmuch as I did not give her to my son Shelah" to provide the heir (Gen 38:26). One of Tamar's twins conceived through Judah is in the lineage of David and is named in Matthew's genealogy of Jesus (Matt. 1:2-6). Taken together, the stories in Genesis show that women played an important role in God's plan for Israel.

The beginning of the Book of Exodus shows women outwitting Pharaoh in several ways. First, the Hebrew midwives Shiphrah and Puah defy Pharaoh's decree to kill the male babies whose births they attend; then they deceive him by saying the Hebrew women gave birth before they could arrive. When Moses is born, his mother first hides him, then sets him afloat in an ark on the Nile. When Pharaoh's daughter finds him, his sister offers to procure the services of a wet-nurse. Moses' own mother nurses him at the expense of the princess until he is old enough to be raised in the Egyptian court. While these stories were surely told to disparage the Egyptians (Hebrew women were able to circumvent the Pharaoh's rulings), they are also part of a biblical tradition of clever women who are important in the fulfillment of God's promise.

On the other hand, a number of women in the Torah are portrayed as deceitful and shameless, using their sexuality to exert power over men in an attempt to achieve their goals. Lot's daughters, fearing after the destruction of Sodom and Gomorrah that no man is left on earth but their father, get him drunk and lie with him to conceive sons for themselves (Gen. 19:30-38). The sons they bear, Moab and Benammi, are the ancestors of the Moabites and the Ammonites, two of Israel's most hated enemies.

The wife of Potiphar, Pharaoh's captain of the guard, presses Joseph daily to lie with her; her failure to seduce him incites her to accuse Joseph of rape and have him imprisoned (Gen. 39). Ironically, even her unseemly behavior is used by God in the fulfillment of his divine plan. It is while Joseph is in prison that he begins to interpret dreams, thereby coming to the attention of the Pharaoh. During the Hebrews' forty years of travelling through the wilderness toward the Promised Land, foreign women were perceived as a particular danger. The women of Moab lure the Israelite men to worship the god Baal, and a Midianite princess who is brought into the tent of an Israelite man brings on a divine plague (Num. 25). Significantly, all of these dangerous, seductive women are *foreigners,* who might seduce a man away from the Lord into idolatrous worship. The wives of Moses, however, present a more positive picture of foreign women. First his wife Zipporah, the daughter of a Midianite priest, saves his life when the Lord attacks him (Exod. 4:24-26). And when Aaron, his brother, and Miriam, his sister, complain about Moses' Cushite wife, the Lord reprimands them. Indeed, when Miriam the prophetess—who had led the women in a song of praise to the Lord after the Egyptians drowned in the sea (Exod. 15:21-22)— speaks against Moses' foreign wife, she becomes afflicted with leprosy.

The Legal Material

The legal material of the Old Testament indicates that women were in some ways seen as property—first the property of father or brother, then of husband. A man could sell his daughter as a slave (Exod. 21:7-11) or give her in marriage to whomever he chose. Marriage was a legal transaction between the bride's father and the prospective groom; there is no indication that the woman was consulted.

A man is said to "take a wife" or to marry, literally to become the *baal,* or master, of the woman. There is no ancient Hebrew verb meaning "to marry" of which "woman" can be the subject. Further, the groom paid the father a bride-price, not only because the bride was a "laborer," but also because the children she would bear would belong to her husband rather than her father. In a list of laws concerning property damage, Exodus 22:16 states that a man who seduces a virgin must pay her father the bride-price, even if the father refuses to give her to him in marriage. Seduction of a virgin is a form of property damage for which the offender must make restitution. A parallel law in Deuteronomy 22:28-29, however, occurs in the context of laws concerning divorce, adultery, and rape; here the man is required to pay the father of the violated virgin fifty shekels of silver and to marry the woman (subsequent divorce is not permitted). A man could have as many wives and concubines as he could support; Abraham (Gen. 22:24, 25:1-6), Jacob (Gen. 29:1-30:25, 35:22-26), David (2 Sam. 5:13, 11:27), and Solomon (2 Kings 11) all had a variety of wives and concubines.

The husband's claim on his wife could extend beyond the grave; if he died before she bore him a son, the law of the Levirate marriage forbade her from marrying outside the family; indeed, the law required her husband's brother to take her as his wife. The first son born of such a marriage would bear the name of her dead husband, "so that his name might not be blotted out of Israel" (Deut. 25:5-10).

This legal subordination of women to father and husband is reflected in the narratives of the Old Testament. A father could offer his daughter in marriage as a prize for the successful completion of a dangerous task. Caleb, for example, offers his daughter Achsah to whoever takes the city of Debir (Josh. 15:16-19). Saul offers his eldest daughter, Merab, to the Israelite who can defeat Goliath (1 Sam. 17:25), and his younger daughter, Michal, to David for one hundred Philistine foreskins (1 Sam. 18:17-27). In Genesis 12:10-20 and 20:1-18, Abraham allows his wife to be taken by the king in order to save his own life. In Genesis 19:8, when the men of Sodom demand that Lot hand over his guests for their sexual pleasure, Lot tries to save his guests by offering his two virgin daughters instead. A similar tale is told in Judges 19: A man protects his male guest by giving his concubine to base men, who rape and murder her.

The laws governing adultery and divorce protected the man's rights, but the woman had few rights to be protected. Adultery was defined as "lying with another man's wife"; the act was defined from the male perspective only. A married man who commited adultery did not legally transgress against his own wife, but against the husband of his illicit partner (Lev. 20:10). The tenth commandment—an injunction against coveting another man's house, wife, servants, or animals—again indicated that a man's wife was protected by the laws governing property rights (Exod. 20:17). However, a later version of the tenth commandment (Deut. 5:21) forbids *coveting* a neighbor's wife and *desiring* his property.

The penalty for adultery was death for both men and women. However, if a husband suspected his wife of adultery but had no witness, and "if the spirit of jealousy [came] upon him," he could bring her to the priest, who would test her by ordeal (Num. 5:11-31). The ordeal relied on magic. If the woman was guilty, her thigh would be made to swell by a potion she was given to drink. If she was proclaimed innocent, her husband was not liable for damages because he brought charges against her. The description of the procedure ends with the ruling: "The man shall be free from iniquity, but the woman shall bear her iniquity" (Num. 5:31).

Since marriage gave the man rights over the woman, it is not surprising that divorce proceedings could be initiated by the husband only. The grounds for divorce were simply "if she finds no favor in his eyes because he has found some indecency [literally, "nakedness"] in her." Since a woman found guilty of adultery was not divorced by her husband but put to death by the community (Deut. 24:1-4), it is not clear what "indecency" provided grounds for divorce. According to Ezra 10, the men who had returned to Jerusalem after the Exile had defiled themselves by marrying foreign women, so Ezra asks them to divorce their wives and send their children away.

Other laws regarding women indicate that their place in society was carefully circumscribed. Their lack of authority over their own affairs is evident in the ruling on women's vows. The vows of an unmarried woman, for instance, could be nullified by her father on the day she made them; the vows of a married woman could be nullified by her husband if he expressed his disapproval on the day she made the vow (Num. 30). The children she bears are not hers but her husband's. According to Exodus 21:22, if two men are fighting and they hurt a pregnant woman, causing a miscarriage, the woman's husband sets the damages to be paid by the one who hurt her—because it is he who has been deprived of offspring.

Inheritance rights of women are discussed in Numbers 27 and 36. When Zelophehad dies without a son, his five daughters petition Moses for the inheritance. The Lord rules that, "If a man dies, and has no son, then you shall cause his inheritance to pass to his daughter" (Num. 27:8). Later, the male members of the daughters' tribe press Moses to rule that the women must marry within their tribe or forfeit their father's land (Num. 36). The rights of the family as a whole, as well as the individual members of the family, must be protected.

The laws regarding the purification of women after menstruation (Lev. 15:19-24) are part of a larger section of laws governing purification after diseases and "bodily discharges" (Lev. 12-15). Both men and women are ritually impure for seven days after a bodily discharge, but on the eighth day only the man must bring an offering to the priest. The birth of a child, causing a discharge of blood, makes a woman ritually impure. After the birth of a male child, a woman is ritually impure for seven days, and she must continue her purification for thirty-three days; after the birth of a female child, she is impure for fourteen days and continues her purification for sixty-six days (Lev. 12:1-8). (Perhaps the potential impurity of the female child doubles the mother's.) When the days of purification are complete, the woman brings a "burnt offering" and a "sin offering" to the priest, and "she is clean."

THE PROPHETS

The Former Prophets

The Books of Joshua, Judges, 1 and 2 Samuel, and 1 and 2 Kings, called "the Former Prophets" in the Hebrew canon, tell the story of the Hebrews' entry into and conquest of the land of Canaan, and of life there until the Babylonian Exile. The period covered is about six hundred years, from about 1200 B.C.E. to sometime after 586 B.C.E. The history is mainly told in stories, and among these are tales of numerous women, many of whom helped rescue men from disaster, spoke with wisdom, or trusted the Lord.

The first of the wise women is the judge Deborah, who advises an Israelite commander Barak against Sisera, the commander of the Canaanite army. When Barak refuses to go to war unless Deborah accompanies him, she prophesies that he will not have glory, because his enemy will be given into the hand of a woman. Her prophecy is fulfilled when Sisera flees from battle to the tent of Jael, a Kenite woman who kills him with a hammer and tent peg while he sleeps (Judg. 4-5). Another female adviser is an Israelite girl captured in war by the Syrians and given as maid to the wife of Naaman, commander of the Syrian army. Naaman is afflicted with leprosy, and the Israelite girl tells her Syrian mistress of the prophet Elisha's power to heal (2 Kings 5:1-19). Another story tells about a wise woman at Endor who has the power to call up spirits from the dead. Although King Saul has outlawed such activities, he goes to the woman at Endor by night in disguise, desperately seeking a word from the spirit of Samuel. When Samuel's prophecy—that Saul will die in battle the next day—leaves Saul weak and filled with fear, the woman prepares a meal for him and strengthens him to go on his way (1 Sam. 28). The story of King David includes accounts of half a dozen women, two of whom are among David's numerous wives. In 1 Samuel 25, a wise and beautiful woman named Abigail speaks eloquently to David, staying his hand when his anger impels him to murder. During her speech, she recognizes David as the chosen of the Lord, and she pledges her loyalty to him; later, when her husband dies, she becomes his wife. Another wife of David, Bathsheba, appears first in a passive role, taken in adultery by David; when she becomes pregnant, he arranges for the death of her husband and marries her. Later, however, she actively involves herself in his affairs, persuading him to name her son Solomon as his successor.

Tamar (2 Sam. 13), David's daughter, is raped by her half-brother Amnon. Her wise and poignant words stand in stark contrast to her brother's deceptive and crude actions. To avenge her, Tamar's brother Absalom kills Amnon and flees from Jerusalem. When David's general sees that the king longs to bring Absalom back but is unable to act, he summons a wise woman from Tekoa (2 Sam. 14) to persuade the king. Later in the story, a wise woman in the city of Beth-Maacah (2 Sam. 20:14-22) approaches David's general, about to destroy the city, and negotiates with him to save her city. In 1 Kings 10, Solomon's wisdom is challenged by the Queen of Sheba, who comes from Arabia "to test him with hard questions."

Three women save the lives of men by quick-witted action, hiding them from their enemies, then misleading the pursuers while the men escape. Rahab the Canaanite prostitute hides the Hebrews whom Joshua sends to spy out the city of Jericho, then lowers them through her window to escape over the city wall (Josh. 2). She subsequently marries a Hebrew man and becomes the mother of Boaz, who marries Ruth. The great-great-grandmother of King David, named in Matthew's genealogy of Jesus (Matt. 1:5), Rahab the harlot is praised in Hebrews 11:31 and James 2:25. A similar story is told of David's first wife, Michal. When King Saul sends soldiers to kill David, she deceives them by putting a dummy into David's bed and lowering him through the window to safety (1 Sam. 19:11-17). In 2 Samuel 19:11-17, a maidservant serves as go-between for the pro-Davidic priests in Jerusalem and their sons, who are hiding outside the city. When Absalom gets wind of this and sends his men to pursue them, a woman at Bahurim hides them in a well and conceals its mouth. She misdirects Absalom's men so the boys can escape and bring their warning to David; this warning saves David's life and his throne.

A third group of women in the narratives of Samuel and Kings are those whose faith brings blessing in Israel. Hannah, who is barren and vexed by her rival wife, shows trust in the Lord's power, not only to give her a son but to raise up the lowly (1 Sam. 1-2). The widow of Zarephath (1 Kings 17) and the wealthy woman of Shunem (2 Kings 4) both recognize the true prophet of the Lord and extend hospitality to him, and both have sons who die and are raised from the dead by the prophet living in their houses.

Not all women in this part of the Bible are saintly, though. Two deceitful women, for example, cause their husbands' destruction. (Both are foreign.) Delilah (Judg. 16), a Philistine woman and the second wife of Samson, accepts a bribe from the Philistine lords to seduce Samson and learn the secret of his great strength. She wears him down with her persistent requests and finally succeeds in delivering him to the Philistines, which results in his death and theirs. Unlike Samson's first wife (also a Philistine), who wheedles a secret from him in order to save the life of her father's family, Delilah deceives him solely for money. Her treachery, however, is used by God for the good of Israel: Samson brings more Philistines down with his death than he does in his life.

Jezebel, a Phoenician princess taken in marriage by Ahab, king of Israel (1 Kings 16:31), is a devoted worshiper of Baal, and she has a large temple built for him, maintained by hundreds of prophets and priests. Her ruthless ways are shown in the stories of her pursuit of the prophet Elijah, who had murdered 450 of her prophets (1 Kings 18:20-19:3) and in her cold-blooded arrangements for the murder of her neighbor Naboth (1 Kings 21). Elijah prophesies that she will be devoured by dogs. The gruesome fulfillment of his words is told in 2 Kings 9:30-37, which begins by picturing her as a whore ("she painted her eyes and adorned her head, and looked out of the window") and ends by describing her corpse as "dung upon the face of the field."

The stories of Delilah and Jezebel portray the dangerous sexuality of foreign women, a motif that persists throughout the Old Testament. Solomon's seven hundred wives and three hundred concubines, many of them foreign (1 Kings 11), are named as the cause of his downfall and of the division of the kingdom of Israel (1 Kings 11:4). This association of foreign women with sex also appears in the curious image of "the woman looking out the window," the conventional act by which the professional prostitute advertised her attractions. (The image was probably borrowed from the literature of Israel's neighbors.) In the Old Testament, it is a derogatory description of a woman, the biblical equivalent of calling a woman a whore. Jezebel is described in this way. And the mother of the Canaanite commander Sisera, waiting in vain for her son to return from battle with Israel, is pictured peering out the window and gazing through the lattice (Judg. 5:28). Sirach 12:3, bemoaning the ravages of old age, describes the eyes poetically as aged harlots—"those that look through the window are dimmed."

The Queen Mothers

The history of the kingdoms of Israel and Judah in 1 and 2 Kings includes the names of twenty-one women with title of "Queen Mother."

The formula by which each king is introduced includes the year his reign began, the length of his reign, the name of his mother, and whether he "walked in the ways of the Lord." That "Queen Mother" was a position of power and not simply the name of the king's mother is clear from 1 Kings 15:11-13, which tells how King Asa removes Maacah, his mother, as Queen Mother after she makes some adornment for an image of the Canaanite goddess Ashera. More striking is the story of Athaliah, daughter of Ahab, king of Israel and mother of Ahaziah, king of Judah (2 Kings 11). When Ahaziah is killed in battle, she destroys the royal family (but for one infant son, hidden by Ahaziah's sister) and seizes the throne. She rules Judah for six years, during which she strengthens the worship of Baal in Judah—until she is murdered in a coup led by Jehoiada the priest. The power of the Queen Mother is apparent in Jeremiah 13:18 and 22:26, in which she is condemned along with the king.

The Later Prophets

The prophetic Books of Hosea, Jeremiah, Isaiah, and Ezekiel portray Israel as a woman, and they take the bold step of using the metaphor of marriage to describe the covenant between God and Israel. Semitic grammar and the traditions of Canaan provided the basis for the prophetic imagery. The land is feminine—notice the earth "bringing forth" vegetation and animals in Genesis 1:12 and 1:24 and the reference to "mother earth" in Job 1:21. Cities and nations are also feminine in Hebrew and its cognate languages. That Israel is called "she" is to be expected, but the use that the prophets make of this tradition is startling.

It is Hosea, the eighth-century prophet from the northern kingdom, who first describes the unhappy marriage between God and his people, Israel. Rather than avoid the sexual language of the Baal cults, which were drawing Israel away from the Lord, Hosea took it over and used it to define Israel's apostasy. The story of Israel as the adulterous wife of the Lord was not simply a poetic metaphor for Hosea, for his own painful marriage to a faithless woman seems to have provided a model for him. While the lewdness of Israel's involvement in the religion of Baal is conveyed in the description of the faithless wife seeking her lovers (Hos. 2:1-13), God's willingness to take Israel back shows the depth of his love (Hos. 2:14-23).

In the seventh century B.C.E., Jeremiah applied Hosea's language of marriage and sexuality to Jerusalem, describing her with indelicately graphic language as a faithless wife who, like a camel in heat, shamelessly and indiscriminately sought lovers to satisfy her sexual desires (Jer. 2). The most lurid picture of Jerusalem as the beautiful but depraved and sexually insatiable woman is painted by Ezekiel (Ezek. 16), who says that God's punishment of Israel is fitting. Ezekiel 23 develops this image in an allegory of the two sisters Oholah and Oholibah (Samaria and Jerusalem), who outdo each other in their harlotry.

While both men and women in Israel seem to have participated extensively in the worship of the deities of the neighboring states, women are sometimes singled out for biting criticism by the prophets. Amos likens them to the cows of Bashan (Amos 4:1-3); Isaiah mocks the mincing walk and wanton glance of the ladies of Jerusalem (Isa. 3:16-17); Jeremiah blames the women who bake cakes and pour out drink offerings to the Queen of Heaven (Jer. 7:18; 44:15-19); and Ezekiel castigates the abominations committed in the temple by women (Ezek. 8:16-17, 13:17-19).

In the sixth-century writings of Second Isaiah (Isaiah 40-55), the picture of Jerusalem is different. Writing after the fall of Jerusalem to the Babylonians in 586 B.C.E., this prophet presents Jerusalem as a formerly barren woman who suddenly finds herself needing to enlarge her tent because of all her children (Isa. 54:1-3). She is like a wife cast off by her husband who is taken back with a love even greater than at first (Isa. 54:4-8). Isaiah here artfully combines the traditions of the barren matriarchs from Genesis with the prophetic image of Jerusalem as the wife of the Lord. In Isaiah 66:7-14, Jerusalem is portrayed almost as a mother goddess, with breasts that nourish an entire people, and a lap big enough to hold them all. So wonderful is the comfort of Mother Jerusalem that the deepest comfort that God brings is likened to it (Isa. 66:12-14).

The themes of female sexuality—including desire, conception, birth, and maternal love—are used often in the prophetic books. These themes form the central metaphor for the relation between God and Israel, and Israel's deepest experiences with her God, in both apostasy and grace, are expressed in the language of woman's love.

THE WRITINGS

The Book of Proverbs

One of the themes central to Proverbs is the recurring contrast between two kinds of women: the wise woman and the foolish woman, the wife of one's youth and the adulteress, the good wife and the ruinous wife. The descriptions of human women are interwoven with pictures of Wisdom and Folly, personified as contrasting feminine figures.

Wisdom is portrayed as a goddess throughout the Ancient Near East. While it is not surprising that the divine Wisdom *(Hochma)* is feminine in Israel, it is noteworthy that Proverbs 8 portrays Lady Wisdom as God's helper at creation: "When he established the heavens, I was there, when he drew a circle on the face of the deep . . . when he marked out the foundations of the earth, then I was beside him, like an *amon,* and I was daily his delight" (Prov. 8:27, 30). Unfortunately, the meaning of the Hebrew word *amon* is uncertain; it may mean either "architect" or "darling." In any case, Wisdom is feminine and has a unique relation to the Lord.

Wisdom is repeatedly named in Proverbs 1-9 as the proper female companion for young men. She is to be loved and not forsaken (4:6), prized and embraced (4:8), desired (3:15), and called "my sister" and "my intimate," terms of endearment used of a wife or lover (7:4). Like the good wife in Proverbs 31, Wisdom is worth more than jewels (3:15, 8:11). She brings blessing and life to the man who walks with her.

Descriptions of human women in Proverbs echo the language of Wisdom. The good wife brings favor from the Lord (18:22); indeed, she is a gift from the Lord (19:14). The good wife in Proverbs 31:10-31 describes her as bringing prosperity and honor to her husband. She energetically cares for her household, participates successfully in real estate and commerce, and is praised for the independent judgment she uses in directing the affairs of her family.

Wisdom's contrast seems to be a non-Israelite woman and a devotée of the cult of Ishtar. "Her house sinks down to death, and her paths to the shades; none who go to her come back, nor do they regain the paths of life" (2:18-19). Proverbs 7 paints a lurid picture of her snare and of the foolish young man who falls into it. With her sexuality, the foreign woman is able to entice the young Israelite to idolatry and destruction. Here, as in the narratives from Genesis through Kings, the warnings against foreign women are graphic and strongly worded.

A particularly loathsome feminine trait in Proverbs is *contentiousness.* A man is better living in the desert (21:19) or on the corner of the roof (25:24) than with a contentious and fretful wife. Like a continual dripping on a rainy day, she cannot be restrained by her husband (27:15-16). Women were socially and legally subordinated to men in ancient Israel, but Proverbs shows how they could bring blessing or destruction to men. The good wife "is the crown of her husband, while she who brings shame is like rottenness in his bones" (Prov. 12:4).

The portrait of divine Wisdom as a feminine beauty present with God at creation is elaborated in the deutero-canonical books. In The Wisdom of Solomon 6:1-9:18, Lady Wisdom is praised as an associate of all God's works, and in 10:1-12:27 Wisdom actually *replaces* the Lord as the one who protects and delivers Israel throughout her history. In Sirach 24 and 51, Wisdom is portrayed as a gracious and lovely woman, receiving those who seek and desire her, and feeding those who come to her; her words are echoed by Jesus' invitation in Matthew 11:28-30.

> Come to me, all who labor and are heavy-laden, and I will give you rest. Take my yoke upon you, and learn from me; for I am gentle and lowly in heart, and you will find rest for your souls. For my yoke is easy, and my burden is light.

Four books of the Bible—Ruth, Esther, Judith, and Susanna—bear the name of a woman. Ruth is one of the rare exceptions to the unfavorable view of foreign women in the Old Testament. Originally from the land of Moab, Ruth marries a man from Bethlehem. When she is widowed, she does not stay in Moab to find another husband but returns to Bethlehem with Naomi, her mother-in-law. She is given in marriage to Naomi's kinsman Boaz, and she bears a son who becomes King David's grandfather. Esther and Judith are tales of women who outwit evil men bent on destroying the Jewish people; Susanna is the tale of a righteous woman whose honor is saved by Daniel's wisdom. The stories of these women besting powerful enemies were models for Israel herself, God's small but beloved people, triumphing over her persecutors.

While women in the Old Testament are described and judged largely for their *actions,* their physical appearance is sometimes of interest to biblical authors. The Old Testament texts about women suggest that feminine beauty was prized and was often understood as a sign of divine favor. Sarah (Gen. 12:11, 14), Rebecca (Gen. 24:16, 26:7), and Rachel (Gen. 29:17) are called "beautiful," although no comparable description is given of their husbands, Abraham, Isaac, and Jacob. Abigail (1 Sam. 25:3) is of "good understanding" and "beautiful," in contrast to her husband Nabal, called churlish and ill-behaved, but not "ugly." The story of Esther depends on her beauty and wisdom; because of her beauty she is chosen from all the virgins of the land to be queen to the Persian king Ahasuerus, and by her wisdom she saves her people from destruction by the wicked Haman. The end of the book of Job tells how God restores Job's fortunes by giving him seven sons, of whom nothing is said, and three daughters, whose names mean Dove, Cinammon Fragrance, and Horn of Eye-Liner. "In all the land there were no women so fair as Job's daughters" (Job 42:15). The link between beauty and divine favor is made explicit in Ezekiel's description of Jerusalem. Because God chose and nurtured her, Jerusalem grew beautiful and "your renown went forth among the nations because of your beauty, for it was perfect through the splendor which I had bestowed upon you, says the Lord God" (Ezek. 16:14). Only the wives of the Patriarchs and women of good character are described as beautiful in the Old Testament; none of the seductive or deceitful women (Potiphar's wife, Delilah, Jezebel, etc.) is called beautiful. In contrast, even men who are not to be trusted are sometimes described as "handsome" (Saul in 1 Samuel 9:1-3; Eliab in 1 Samuel 16:6-7; Absalom in 1 Samuel 14:25-26; and Adonijah in 1 Kings 1:5-8.) Indeed, the wicked king of Tyre was "perfect in beauty" (Ezek. 28:11).

The most extensive paean to beauty in the Old Testament is the Song of Solomon. In this collection of love songs, the lovers describe each other by evoking images of the exquisite flowers, animals, and landscape of Israel. In light of the prophetic tradition of Israel as the beloved of the Lord, it is not surprising that these descriptions of lovers' longings were understood to refer to the love between God and Israel. This interpretation of the Song of Solomon was established by the end of the first century C.E., and it may have helped ensure that the book was included in the canon.

While beauty was highly prized in Israel, it was also a potential source of trouble. Beauty led to arrogance and destruction of primal man (Ezek. 28:12-19), Queen Vashti (Esther 1), and Jerusalem (Ezek. 16:15-29; Jer. 4:29-31). Two proverbs express distrust of beauty:

> Like a gold ring in a swine's snout
> is a beautiful woman without discretion.
> (Prov. 11:22)
> Charm is deceitful, and beauty is vain,
> but a woman who fears the Lord is to be praised.
> (Prov. 31:30)

A careful reading of the texts reveals that the subject of women in the Old Testament is complex. While the laws show that they are legally subordinated to men, the narratives portray them as powerful forces in Israel's history. Women are seen as weak in battle, and it is shameful to be killed by the hand of a woman (Judg. 4:9, 9:53-54; Jer. 50:37, 51:30); yet the stories of Deborah and Jael show women important in war. Women's sexuality can bring life or lead to death. Foreign women are to be avoided, yet both of Moses' wives were foreigners, as were three women in the ancestry of David (and hence of Jesus). Women are full members of the community when the people are called to enter the covenant with God (Exod. 19; Deut. 29, 31:9-13; 2 Kings 23:1-3; Neh. 8), yet only males are required to appear before the Lord for the annual festivals (Exod. 23:17, 34:23: Deut. 16:16). No single passage can accurately represent what the Old Testament says about women. Only when all the texts are read together and allowed to illuminate each other can the truth of the Bible be heard.

FOR FURTHER READING

See the list at the end of "Women in the New Testament."

WOMEN IN THE NEW TESTAMENT
Judith L. Kovacs

This survey is divided into three parts: The first examines the four gospels and Acts, where there are no explicit discussions of women, but where there are many female characters; then we look at the epistles, both Pauline and later, for their very definite pronouncements on women and for indications of the actual status of women in the church; our final section treats female imagery in the Book of Revelation.

THE GOSPELS

Women appear in the gospel narratives as recipients of Jesus' healing and forgiveness, as family, followers, and friends of Jesus, and as witnesses to Jesus' crucifixion and resurrection. Women healed by Jesus are Peter's mother-in-law (Mark 1:29-31 and parallels), a woman crippled for eighteen years (Luke 13:10-17), and a woman suffering from a hemorrhage (Mark 5:24-34). The Gospels also report that Jesus raised the twelve-year-old daughter of Jairus from the dead (Mark 5:21-24, 35-43, and parallels); that he raised the son of a widow from Nain out of pity for his widowed mother (Luke 7:11-17); that, in response to the "great faith" of a Canaanite woman, Jesus cast a demon out of her daughter (Matt. 15:21-28 and parallels); and that he responded to the "faith" of Martha and Mary by raising their brother Lazarus from the dead (John

11:1-44). ("Faith" might also be translated "trust." The Greek term does not in itself imply theological belief.) Two stories that picture Jesus pronouncing forgiveness on sinful women are Luke 7:36-50 and the account of the woman caught in adultery, which is found in some manuscripts of the Gospel of John (John 7:53-8:11). Several of these narratives call attention to the "faith" of the women involved (Mark 5:34 and Matt. 15:28). In the story of the raising of Lazarus, his sisters' theologically specific faith is particularly emphasized (John 11:3, 21-32).

Other narratives picture women as followers and friends of Jesus. Luke 10:38-42 describes a visit of Jesus to Mary and Martha, during which Mary "sat at the Lord's feet and listened to his teaching." Another story portrays an unnamed woman who interrupts a dinner party to anoint Jesus' head with oil (Mark 14:3-9 and parallels; John 12:1-8 identifies this woman as Mary, the sister of Lazarus). In John 4:1-30, Jesus has a long dialogue with a Samaritan woman, in which he reveals his identity as the Christ. Although Jesus' disciples "marveled that he was talking with a woman" (4:29), the Evangelist goes on to report that many Samaritans believed in Jesus "because of the woman's testimony" (4:39). (But see also 4:42, in which the Samaritans say to the woman, after Jesus has stayed with them for "two days," that "It is no longer because of your words that we believe, for we have heard for ourselves, and we know that this is indeed the Savior of the world.").

Luke 8:1-3 names several women who assisted Jesus in his missionary journeys:

> Soon afterward he went on preaching and bringing the good news of the kingdom of God. And the twelve were with him, and also some women who had been healed of evil spirits and infirmities: Mary, called Magdalene, from whom seven demons had gone out, and Joanna, the wife of Chuza, Herod's steward, and Susanna, and many others, who provided for them out of their means.

Women are particularly evident in the narratives of Jesus' crucifixion and resurrection. Certain unnamed women accompany Jesus on the road to Golgotha, bewailing his death (Luke 23:27-28). All four gospels mention the presence of women at the crucifixion:

> There were also many women there, looking on from afar, who had followed Jesus from Galilee, ministering to him; among whom were Mary Magdalene, and Mary, the mother of James and Joseph, and

the mother of the sons of Zebedee (Matt. 27:55-56; see also Mark 15:40-41 and Luke 23:49).

In John's account, Jesus' mother, Mary, together with Mary, the wife of Clopas, and Mary Magdalene, stands at the foot of cross (John 19:24-27), from which Jesus entrusts his mother into the care of his "beloved disciple."

All the Gospels also agree that women were the first to discover the empty tomb (Matt. 28:1-8; Mark 16:1-8; Luke 23:55-24:12; John 20:1). While Mary Magdalene is mentioned in all the accounts, the names of the other women vary. In the Synoptic stories, these women are the first to receive the message that Jesus has been raised from the dead (from angels in the tomb), and they are commanded to bear witness to the disciples. In John, Mary Magdalene is the first to see the resurrected Christ (20:11-18).

Other sections of the Gospels in which women are prominent are the birth and infancy narratives of Matthew 1-2 and especially Luke 1-2. While the genealogy in Matt. 1:1-17 traces Jesus' descent through his father, Joseph, its inclusion of the names of four women (the Old Testament figures Rahab, Tamar, Ruth, and "the wife of Uriah" [Bathsheba]) is unusual, the more so since all four were women whose premarital or marital careers were irregular. In addition to Mary, other women who figure in Luke 1-2 are John the Baptist's mother, Elisabeth (1:5-6), described as "righteous before God, walking in all the command-ments and ordinances of the Lord blameless" (1:6), and Anna, who prophesies about the baby Jesus when he is first brought to the temple in Jerusalem (1:36-38).

While Matthew's story of Jesus' birth focuses on Joseph, Luke's narrative makes Mary the central character. It is she who receives the angel's promise of Jesus' birth (Luke 1:26-38), to which she responds with belief (1:38,45), singing a song of praise, the "Magnificat" (Luke 1:46-55). Luke reports not only her giving birth (2:6-7), but her inner thoughts as well (2:19, 35, 51). Mark contains no account of Jesus' birth but refers to Mary twice, in 6:3 (see also Matt. 13:55-56) and in 3:33-35 (see also Matt. 12:46-50; Luke 8:19-21).

In John's account, Mary figures prominently in the wedding feast at Cana (2:1-11). It is she who tells Jesus that the wine has run out:

And Jesus said to her, "O woman, what have you to do with me? My hour has not yet come." His mother said to the servants, "Do whatever he tells you." (2:4-5)

The Gospels also contain a few references to women outside Jesus' circle, including Herodias, the wife of King Herod Antipas, and her daughter, who were responsible for John the Baptist's beheading (Mark 6:17-29; Matt. 14:3-12; Luke 3:19) and a servant girl who questioned Peter in the high priest's courtyard (Mark 14:66-70; Luke 22:56-57; Matt. 26:69-72 mentions two female servants). Matthew tells of the wife of the Roman governor Pilate, who warns her husband not to get involved in Jesus' case (Matt. 27:19).

In Jesus' teachings, women appear as characters in parables, as examples, and in his discussions of marriage and divorce. The following parables have women as their main character:

The kingdom of heaven is like leaven which a woman took and hid in three measures of flour, till it was all leavened. (Matt. 13:33; see also Luke 13:20-21)

Or what woman, having ten silver coins, if she loses one coin, does not light a lamp and sweep the house and seek diligently until she finds it? And when she has found it, she calls together her friends and neighbors, saying, "Rejoice with me, for I have found the coin which I had lost." Just so, I tell you, there is joy before the angels of God over one sinner who repents. (Luke 15:8-10)

The second parable is placed between the parable of the lost sheep (Luke 15:1-8) and that of the prodigal son (Luke 15:8-10). All three illustrate God's love for sinners. It is noteworthy that Jesus uses both male and female images to speak of God.

Two other parables with female characters are the story of the five wise and five foolish virgins who await the arrival of the bridegroom for his wedding feast (Matt. 25:1-13) and the story of the widow who, through persistent pleadings, gets justice from an unwilling and "unjust" judge (Luke 18:1-8).

Jesus also uses women as examples. The wife of Lot serves as a bad example (Luke 17:32; see also Gen. 19:26), while a poor widow who gives "her whole living" to the temple treasury is a good example (Mark 12:41-44; Luke 21:1-4). Jesus reminds his hearers in Capernaum that the prophet Elijah was sent to help a non-Israelite widow (Luke 4:26-27).

Several of the sayings of Jesus examine marriage and motherhood. When the Sadducees ask Jesus about levirate marriage and its consequences in the future resurrection (levirate marriage was a custom of the ancient Jews by which a dead man's brother was obliged to marry the widow if she had no sons), Jesus says that in the resurrection there is no marriage (Mark 12:18-27 and parallels). Jesus' prohibition of divorce has been handed down in different forms by Matthew and Mark. In Mark 10 the Pharisees question Jesus about divorce. Jesus replies:

"What did Moses command you?" They said, "Moses allowed a man to write a certificate of divorce, and to put her away" [Deut. 24:1-4]. But Jesus said to them, "For your hardness of heart he wrote you this commandment. But from the beginning of creation, 'God made them male and female' [Gen. 1:27]. 'For this reason a man shall leave his father and mother and be joined to his wife, and the two shall become one' [Gen 2:24]. What therefore God has joined together, let not man put asunder." (Mark 10:3-9; see also Luke 16:18 and Matt. 5:31-32, 19:3-9)

There is some tension between the discussions of divorce and other sayings in the Gospels that contrast family loyalty to the demands of discipleship. Luke 18:29b, for instance, speaks of leaving wife and family for the sake of the kingdom (see also Matt. 19:29 and Mark 10:29), while Luke 14:26 says a disciple must "hate" his family, and even his own life (see Matt 10:37-38).

Jesus also uses images of pregnancy, birth, and motherhood. In John 16:21-22, he compares the sorrow of his disciples at his death to the sorrow of a woman in labor, and their later joy to the joy of a woman who has delivered a child. The hardship of pregnancy and nursing is reflected in the discourse on the end of the world in Luke 21. Jesus says: "Alas for those who are with child and for those who give suck in those days" (21:33). On the road to Golgotha he predicts, "The days are coming when they will say, 'Blessed are the barren, and the wombs that never bore, and the breasts that never gave suck' " (Luke 23:28-29).

In sum, the Gospels tell us that Jesus healed women, that he used female figures and imagery in his teaching, and that he prohibited divorce. They portray Jesus teaching women and having female followers.

On the other hand, the Gospels speak repeatedly of Jesus' closest disciples—"the twelve"—as an all-male group (see the lists in Mark 3:13-19, Matt. 10:1-4, and Luke 6:13-16). The reader may wonder what exact roles women had, but the Evangelists do not spell these out.

THE ACTS OF THE APOSTLES

Luke's second work, the Acts of the Apostles, raises similar questions. Here, too, the twelve who lead the first church in Jerusalem, and the seven deacons chosen to help them (7:1-6), are male, as are Philip, Peter, Paul, most of their travelling companions, and leading figures of the churches they establish. But several women characters appear: Sapphira, a member of the Jerusalem church who with her husband sold property without giving all the proceeds to the church (5:1-12); the "disciple" Tabitha, "full of good works and acts of charity," whom Peter raised from the dead (9:36-41); a slavegirl possessed by a spirit of divination, who testified about Paul and was exorcized by him (16:16-18). Other women mentioned are the Jewish mother of Timothy in 16:22, Paul's sister in 23:16, and Drusilla, the wife of the Roman prefect Felix, in 24:24.

Two characters who take an active role in the spread of the gospel (the main theme of the book of Acts) are Priscilla and Lydia. Priscilla, together with her husband Aquila, houses Paul in Corinth, accompanies him to Ephesus, and teaches there (18:1-26). References to Priscilla in two of Paul's letters indicate her importance in the early church (1 Cor. 16:19; Rom. 16:3).

Paul's first convert in Europe is a woman: the businesswoman Lydia. Arriving in Philippi, Paul sought a "place of prayer" and found a group of women, to whom he preached. Lydia believed and was baptized "with her household," and she served as his host during his stay in the city (16:13-15, 40). Acts 21:8-9 mentions female prophets—the four daughters of Philip "the Evangelist." Several of Luke's summarizing remarks also refer to women in the Christian movement. In Jerusalem after Jesus' ascension, the eleven apostles (the twelve minus Judas) were "together with the women and Mary the mother of Jesus, and with his brothers" (1:12-14). Before his conversion, Paul was intent on imprisoning both "men and women" (8:3, 9:1, 22:4). It is noted that "both men and women responded to Philip's preaching in Samaria and were baptised" (8:12). Reports of Paul's mission in Greek cities often mention women:

Some were persuaded, and joined Paul and Silas as did a great many of the devout Greeks and not a few of the leading women. (17:4)

Many therefore believed, and not a few Greek women of high standing as well as men. (17:12)

But some men joined him and believed . . . and a woman named Damaris and others with them. (17:34)

Similar is the reference to "wives and children" from the church in Tyre in Acts 21:5. In 13:50 "devout women of high standing" figure in the opposition to Paul in Psidian Antioch. The relative prominence of women in Luke through Acts suggests that the author had a special interest in women—even if he does not spell out their exact role in the early church.

THE LETTERS OF PAUL

Unlike the narratives surveyed thus far, the New Testament epistles contain explicit directives about women. In the seven letters of Paul that most scholars accept as genuine—1 Thessalonians, Galatians, 1 and 2 Corinthians, Philippians, Romans, and Philemon—there are two texts that give instructions about women's conduct:

But I want you to understand that the head of every man is Christ, the head of a woman is her husband, and the head of Christ is God. Any man who prays or prophesies with his head covered dishonors his head, but any women who prays or prophesies with uncovered head dishonors her head—it is the same as if her head were shaven. . . . For a man ought not to cover his head, since he is the image and glory of God [Gen. 1:27]; but woman is the glory of man. For man was not made from woman but woman from man. Neither was man created for woman, but woman for man [Gen. 2:18ff.]. That is why a woman ought to have a (sign of) authority on her head, because of the angels. (Nevertheless, in the Lord, woman is not independent of man nor man of woman; for as woman was made from man, so man is now born of woman. And all things are from God.) Judge for yourselves; is it proper for a woman to pray to God with her head uncovered? Does not nature itself teach you that for a man to wear long hair is degrading to him, but if a woman has long hair, it is her pride? For her hair is given to her for a covering. If anyone is disposed to be contentious, we recognize no other practice, nor do the churches of God. (1 Cor. 11:3-16—Revised Standard Version modified)

As in all the churches of the saints, the women should keep silence in the churches. For they are not permitted to speak, but should be subordinate, as even the law says. If there is anything they desire to know, let them ask their husbands at home. For it is shameful for a woman to speak in church. (1 Cor. 14:33-36)

On first glance these texts seem to give a clear picture of Paul as a consistent advocate of patriarchy in the home and in the church. The main point of the first text is that women, when they pray or prophesy, must cover their heads—a point Paul argues by asserting that man is the "head" of the woman and by appealing to Scripture, custom, and "nature." The second text forbids women to speak in church assemblies and commands them to be subordinate, again with an appeal to Scripture ("the law," perhaps an allusion to Genesis 3:16). How Paul would have reconciled the general command to silence in the second text with the permission, implicit in the first, to prophesy and pray, is an open question. By itself, 1 Corinthians 11 is unclear on several points, notably the role of "the angels," the nature of the problem in Corinth, and whether the statement about the interdependence of man and woman is intended to qualify other arguments in the passage.

While these two passages are the only explicit directives about women, several other Pauline texts relate to women. One is the discussion of marriage and sex in 1 Corinthians 7. Paul counsels against marriage in view of the impending end of the world (7:8, 29), but recommends regular sexual relations to couples already married (7:2-7). Paul takes care—even to the point of stylistic awkwardness—to address husband and wife equally, and he gives both the same advice: Each should "rule over" the other's body, and neither should separate, divorce, or deny the other conjugal rights (7:3-34).

In Galatians 3:28, Paul describes the unity of Christians as follows:

For as many of you as were baptized into Christ have put on Christ. There is neither Jew nor Greek, there is neither slave nor free, there is neither male nor female; for you are all one in Christ Jesus.

Interpreters who think Paul advocates the equality of women with men place particular emphasis on this text, but there is no mention of equality in the text itself, which speaks of "unity in Christ" and the absence of distinctions.

Other evidence is found in the greetings which close Paul's letters. In Romans 16, for example, the list of esteemed coworkers begins:

> I commend to you our sister Phoebe, a deacon [or "helper"—the word is ambiguous] of the church at Cenchreae, that you may receive her in the Lord as befits the saints, and help her in whatever she may require from you, for she has been a helper [or "protector"—another ambiguous term] of many and of myself as well. (Rom. 16:1-2)

Paul goes on to mention five other women who have worked with him, including the same Prisca Luke calls "Priscilla" in Acts:

> Greet Prisca and Aquila, my fellow workers in Christ Jesus, who risked their necks for my life, to whom not only I but also all the churches of the Gentiles give thanks; greet also the church in their house. (Rom. 16:3-5; see also 1 Cor. 16:19)

In Philippians 4:2-3, Paul names two women who "have labored side by side with me in the gospel," and in Philemon 2 he addresses "Apphia, our sister," together with two men, as leaders of a house church. Paul does not make a distinction between the religious work performed by males and females, though in 16:7 he does call two men "apostles," a term he never applies to a woman.

LATER EPISTLES

In the three Pastoral epistles (1 and 2 Timothy and Titus), which were probably written several decades after Paul to adapt his teaching to a new era in the young Christian Church, we find an unambiguous statement of the principle of female subordination. The conduct of women is a matter of particular concern to the author of 1 Timothy:

> I desire then that in every place the men should pray, lifting holy hands without anger or quarreling; also that women should adorn themselves modestly and sensibly in seemly apparel, not with braided

> hair or gold or pearls or costly attire but by good deeds, as befits
> women who profess religion. Let a woman learn in silence with all
> submissiveness. I permit no woman to teach or to have authority over
> men; she is to keep silent. For Adam was formed first, then Eve;
> and Adam was not deceived, but the woman was deceived and became
> a transgressor. Yet woman will be saved through bearing children,
> if she continues in faith and love and holiness. (1 Tim 2:8-15)

This exhortation shares with 1 Corinthians 14:33ff. the ideas that women
should subordinate themselves to men and that they should remain "silent." Indeed, 1 Timothy goes even further, forbidding women to teach
or to exercise any authority. Like Paul, the author appeals to the Old
Testament, using the story of Eve's creation out of Adam (Gen. 2) to
justify differences in the status of men and women. He interprets the
story of the Fall in Genesis 2-3 to mean that *only* the woman "was
deceived and became a transgressor." (Contrast Paul's exegesis of this
same passage in Romans 5:12ff., which focuses on Adam, but compare
1 Cor. 11:3.) The remark that women will be saved "through child-
birth" is difficult to interpret, though there is evidently a connection
with the curse on Eve in Genesis 3:16.

The differentiation between men's and women's roles is even clearer
in the instructions that church officers follow. In contrast to the seven
genuine letters of Paul, which suggest an informal system of leadership
in which women pray, prophesy, serve, and work together with male
missionaries, the Pastorals prescribe a more patriarchal leadership.
Bishops (probably leaders of local churches) and deacons are to be "the
husband of one wife" (3:2, 12). The author interrupts his discussion of
deacons (3:8-13) with one sentence on women: "The women likewise
[i.e. like the male deacons] must be serious, no slanderers, but temperate,
faithful in all things" (3:11). With this brief ruling he returns to the
men. Were the woman also officials?

The exhortation to honor and support "real widows" in 5:3-16 also
leaves us with questions:

> Let a widow be enrolled if she is not less than sixty years of age,
> having been the wife of one husband; and she must be well attested
> for her good deeds, as one who has brought up children, shown hos-
> pitality, washed the feet of the saints, relieved the afflicted, and devoted
> herself to doing good in every way. But refuse to enroll younger widows;
> for when they grow wanton against Christ they desire to marry, and

so they incur condemnation for having violated their first pledge. Besides that, they learn to be idlers, gadding about from house to house, and not only idlers but gossips and busybodies, saying what they should not. So I would have younger widows marry, bear children, rule their households, and give the enemy no occasion to revile us. For some have already strayed after Satan.

This passage, like many texts in the Bible (e.g. Deut. 14:29; Acts 6:1), expresses a special concern for the support of widows, whose social and financial position was often quite precarious (see Luke 21:1-4, 18:1-8). 1 Timothy seems to indicate that the writer's church kept a list of "real" widows, who were to be supported, and that enrollment in this list of perpetual beneficiaries was a privilege limited to widows over sixty, who had had only one husband, had been hospitable and charitable, and would make some pledge. What they may have pledged and what services or functions they may have performed in the church, we should like to know.

Throughout the letter the author of 1 Timothy expresses a concern for the reputation of the church among non-Christians. In our passage, he mentions this as a motivation for women to exhibit proper behavior (prayer, raising children, hospitality, and other good deeds) and to avoid improper behavior (self-indulgence, idling, gossiping). In contrast to Paul (1 Cor. 7), he takes a distinctly favorable view of marriage; in 4:3 he combats Christian teachers who forbid marriage.

In the other two Pastoral epistles, similar themes appear. The letter to Titus requires that an elder or bishop (the terms are used interchangeably) be "the husband of one wife" (Tit. 1:6). 2 Timothy opens with a commendation of the faith of the recipient's mother, Eunice, and of his grandmother, Lois (1:5), and the author includes two women—Prisca and Claudia—in the greetings that conclude the letter (4:19-21). One text, however, portrays women as weak and particularly susceptible to false teaching (3:1-7).

The letter to Titus 2:2-5 gives a precis of proper conduct for older and younger members of each sex (see 1 Tim. 5:1-2). Older women are to be reverent and moderate and to be "teachers of what is good." Their teaching trains younger women in the virtues of submission, chastity, domesticity, and love of husbands and children. This suggests quite a different kind of teaching from the sort forbidden to women in 1 Timothy 2:12.

The ethic of submission set forth in Titus 2 and in 1 Timothy 2 is a prominent feature of the "household codes" found in three other post-Pauline epistles (Col. 3:18-4:1; Eph. 5:11-6:9; 1 Pet. 3:1-7). These codes list duties for different members of the household according to a patriarchal pattern. Three relationships (wife-husband, child-father, slave-master) are addressed, and in each case the socially inferior party is exhorted to be obedient to the socially superior. Colossians 3:18ff. tells wives to be subject to their husbands and exhorts husbands to love their wives and "not to be harsh with them." In 1 Peter 3:1-7, wives are told to follow the example of Sarah, who was submissive to her husband Abraham (see Gen. 18:12) and to be unostentatious in dress. The author expresses the hope that such behavior will lead the non-Christian husbands of some of the women to embrace the Word. Husbands, in turn, are urged to treat their wives with consideration, "bestowing honor on the woman as the weaker sex, since you are joint heirs of the grace of life."

In the third household code (Eph. 5:11-6:9), the exhoration to wives and husbands is expanded and given a christological basis:

> Be subject to one another out of reverence for Christ. Wives, be subject to your husbands, as to the Lord. For the husband is the head of the wife as Christ is the head of the church, his body, and is himself its Savior. As the church is subject to Christ, so let wives also be subject in everything to their husbands. Husbands, love your wives, as Christ loved the church and gave himself up for her, that he might sanctify her, having cleansed her by the washing of water with the word, that he might present the church to himself in splendor, without spot or wrinkle or any such thing, that she might be holy and without blemish. Even so husbands should love their wives as their own bodies. He who loves his wife loves himself. For no man ever hates his own flesh, but nourishes and cherishes it, as Christ does the church, because we are members of his body. "For this reason a man shall leave his father and mother and be joined to his wife, and the two shall become one flesh" [Gen. 2:24]. This mystery is a profound one, and I am saying that it refers to Christ and the church; however, let each one of you love his wife as himself, and let the wife see that she respects her husband. (Eph. 5:21-33)

This text both accentuates and qualifies the patriarchal pattern in marriage. On the one hand, it justifies patriarchal marriage by giving it a theological warrant: Just as Christ is head of the Church, so the husband is head of the wife. The author interprets the command to marry and become "one flesh" (Gen 2:24) as a symbol of Christ's relation to the church. On the other hand, the comparison with Christ is used to underscore the husband's obligation to love his wife: "Even so husbands should love their wives as their own bodies."

The six post-pauline epistles discussed here, taken together, provide a clear statement of patriarchy as the ideal in the church and in the household. Women are to be subordinate and obedient to their husbands; they are not to teach in church; their proper virtues are obedience, modest dress, domesticity, child-rearing, and the performance of good works. These views are supported by scriptural and christological arguments, and by stressing the need to make a favorable impression on pagans (1 Tim.; 1 Pet.). The ideal of male dominance in marriage, however, is counterbalanced by exhortations to husbands to love and honor their wives. Again, how far these desiderata reflect the role women actually played in the churches is uncertain.

THE REVELATION TO JOHN

The Revelation to John makes no pronouncements about women, but its vivid imagery includes several symbolic females. John does once refer to a real woman—a prophetess and teacher he calls "Jezebel" (after the idolatrous wife of King Ahab; see 1 Kings 16:33)—whom he denounces for causing Christians at Thyatira to "commit adultery" and leading them to eat food sacrificed to idols (Rev. 2:20-23). While it is possible that the prophetess encouraged irregular sexual relations, the Bible's frequent use of the term "adultery" to describe reprobated religious practices (see, for example, Jer. 2) makes a symbolic meaning also possible.

Similar imagery appears in Revelation 17-18 in the visions of Babylon "the whore" (a symbol of the city of Rome, as 17:9, 18 makes clear). Seated on a scarlet beast, the "whore" is dressed luxuriously. The "wine of her fornication" has made people drunk. She herself is "drunk with the blood of the . . . martyrs of Jesus" (17:6). Here John is clearly drawing on the Old Testament (and earlier) tradition of portraying cities as harlots (see Jeremiah 2; Ezekiel 16, 23; Isaiah 23:17-18; Nahum 3:4).

Two other female images, the "woman clothed with the sun and stars" of Revelation 12:1ff. and the Bride of the Lamb (Rev. 19:7; 21:2, 9-10), have quite different characters. Revelation 12:1, 5-6 depicts:

> A great portent appeared in heaven, a woman clothed with the sun, with the moon under her feet, and on her head a crown of twelve stars. . . . and a great red dragon (attacked her, but) . . . she brought forth a male child, one who is to rule all the nations with a rod of iron, but her child was caught up to God and to his throne, and the woman fled to the wilderness, in which to be nourished for one thousand two hundred and sixty days.

The mother of this text is probably a multivalent image. One possible reference is to the church (see 12:17).

The image of the Bride of the Lamb (Christ) appears in Revelation 21:2-11 and 19:7-8:

> Let us rejoice and exult and give him the glory, for the marriage of the Lamb has come, and his Bride has made herself ready; it was granted her to be clothed with fine linen, bright and pure—for the fine linen is the righteous deeds of the saints. (Rev. 19:7-8)

The last sentence suggests that the Bride symbolizes the church (or part of the church; see also Eph. 5:23ff). In 21:2ff., she is portrayed as "the new Jerusalem" (see Gal. 4:26-27, where Paul says that the "Jerusalem above" is "our mother"). The bride of the Lamb is set over against the whore Babylon, just as the Lamb is opposed to the dragon (Satan). These texts exemplify the reinterpretation of ancient symbols and myths characteristic of the Book of Revelation.

These surveys of Old and New Testament texts about women have touched on a great number of passages, including many whose original intentions are no longer clear, or whose antiquity make interpretation difficult. Clearly, what the Bible says about women cannot be gleaned from selecting a few favorite passages; many diverse voices speak in the Bible. Only the texts taken together in all their diversity constitute "what the Bible really says."

FOR FURTHER READING

Raymond E. Brown. *The Critical Meaning of the Bible*. Paulist, 1981.
Mary C. Callaway. *Sing, O Barren One*. Scholars Press, 1986.

Elisabeth S. Fiorenza. *In Memory of Her: A Feminist Theological Reconstruction of Christian Origins.* Crossroads, 1984.

Letty Russell, editor. *Feminist Interpretation of the Bible.* Westminster, 1985.

B. Witherington. *Women in the Ministry of Jesus.* Cambridge, 1984.

————. *Women in the Earliest Churches,* Cambridge, 1988.

THE WORLD
Thomas Podella and Paolo Xella

The books of the Bible are primarily concerned with the relationship between humanity and God. They say relatively little of the world; indeed, they do not even have a term denoting it. Neither as a single entity nor as the totality of physical objects does the world become a literary subject in Old Testament Hebrew. The writers of the New Testament do sometimes speak of the *cosmos,* but this word (*'olam*) designates a long period of time, not the physical universe.

Phrases like "heaven and earth" and "heaven, earth, and the waters under the earth" do appear in the Hebrew Bible (Exod. 20:4; Deut. 5:8; etc.), but in the main these refer to the experienced environment: mountains, hills, rivers, as well as nations and their inhabitants. For the most part, heavenly phenomena like the stars are commonly taken as experienced—lights in the sky—not as gods, as they were in other ancient cultures. (There are exceptions: In Judges 5:20 the stars fight against Sisera, and, according to Job 38:7, "the morning stars sang together" when the Earth was created.) Legally, however, they are only signs for counting days, years, and for determining the time for festivals.

The process of the creation of the world is commonly described, if at all, by analogies. Most of the terms for it are taken from human experience.[1] The making of the world was thought to be like human actions in building houses and shaping clay. Only the Hebrew verb *br',* "create," always has a divine subject in the Bible, but it does not describe *how* creation took place. Neither does the narrative form, "God said . . . and there was," used in Genesis 1.

Narrative, however, introduces a temporal phase into the account and implies a beginning of the process. "In the beginning God (*Elohim*) created the heavens and the earth" (Gen. 1:1). In other words, there must have been a time when heaven and earth did *not* yet exist.

As to the results of creation, the picture given by biblical texts is almost always geocentric. Earth is commonly described either as a flat disc or a flat square.[2] It has edges and corners: God "will gather the dispersed of Judah from the four corners of the earth" (Isa. 10:32 and elsewhere). The lower parts of the earth are supposed to be the realm of the dead and the regions of the sweet and bitter waters, the latter rising from the primeval abyss to help flood the earth (Gen. 6:11). (The Israelites had before their eyes the bitter waters of the Dead Sea as the lowest area of their land.) The insides of the earth housed the dead, and biblical texts often mention the gates or bolts of death (Job 38:17; Pss. 9:18, 107:18, etc.) Apart from these, however, the Near Eastern mythology of the underworld is generally omitted or transferred to Yahweh. In the Bible it is Yahweh "who sends a man down to *She'ol* [the underworld] and brings him up" (1 Sam. 2:6). Such human existence as there is in the underworld seems generally devoid of activity.[3]

Another view of the world is expressed by the term *tebel*—translated as "globe" or "earth"[4]—which is particularly important in descriptions of the sun and its orbit (especially Ps. 19:3-7). (To judge from Mesopotamian analogues, the sun was expected to get back to his "bridal tent" by crossing the underworld at night.[5]) Like the celestial bodies, Yahweh was often supposed to be in the sky. The temple on earth is his footstool, where only his train is visible (1 Kings 8:10; Isa. 6:1ff.).

That Yahweh was thought to be the creator of the world is clear from Genesis, but nowhere in the cosmogonic passages of Genesis do we find stories about the battles he had to fight against other gods or the powers of chaos, battles common in the creation myths of other cultures. For references to these we must go to Second Isaiah and the Psalms.[6] "The abyss" (*tehom*)—in earlier legends a formidable and monstrous deity—*is* mentioned in Genesis (1:2, etc.), but it is not an active chaos. Works of both priestly and heroic writers are preserved in Genesis, and both modify one and the same picture: In the beginning the world was chaotic and empty; there were no humans, animals, or even vegetation (Gen. 1:2, 2:5). From this beginning the process of creation is described as one of *building,* not of combat. We read that Yahweh founded the earth on pillars, or foundations, that he stretched out the heavens, and that he divided the waters and set a vault between them.

The texts that refer to conflicts with powers of chaos—like Tehom, Rahab, Leviathan, and unnamed demons—do not allude to creation.[7] They appear in hymnic passages praising Yahweh by contrasting his might with what other gods or what men are able to do.

Instead of locating such battles in creation, the authors of the accounts of Yahweh's work try to show how the surface of the earth and visible phenomena developed. Genesis 2:4ff. presupposes that heaven and earth exist, but it also says that there was no life on earth. Genesis 2:5 gives the reason: "Yahweh had not given rain, and mankind did not exist to cultivate the earth." But then water (a mist?) came up from the earth and produced fertility. To provide for the cultivation of the earth, first Yahweh, like a "workman," formed a man from clay and dust and, like a magician, endowed his image with life by breathing his spirit into it. Then he "planted a garden in Eden, in the East, and put there the man whom he had formed." The garden in Eden is the place where the primordial river rises and is separated into four branches, the Tigris, the Euphrates, and two now-unknown rivers named Gichon and Pison. All this is the world-view of a local agrarian culture. The world as a whole is referred to only by the words "heaven and earth." Geographic relations are indicated by referring to the lands of Assyria in the north and "Kush"—Ethiopia, Nubia, or Egypt—in the south.

Similarly, the priestly writer of Genesis 1:1-2:4a declares that in the very beginning "heaven and earth" were created. Earth was then chaotic and empty, but darkness and the divine spirit were hovering over the primeval waters (1:1-2). Here the primeval waters (*tehom*) have been added to heaven and earth. God's (Elohim's) command alone calls light into being, so that day and night become distinguished. Then God sets a vault in the upper water (*mayyim*) so that heavenly and earthly waters are separated. The vault separating them became visible as the firmament, and was called "heaven" (although the heavens had been created on the preceding day). Below heaven all was still flooded, so God ordered the lower waters to gather into one place, which made dry land appear. Next God goes on to call up vegetation, plants and trees, from the earth, and only after that does he create the luminaries—sun, moon, and stars— which thus are said to have come into being a day after the higher forms of vegetation. The two great luminaries—sun and moon—and the stars (as a minor afterthought) serve to give light, to rule their proper periods of time, to distinguish days, seasons, and years, and to give (prophetic) signs to men. Next came the creatures of the sea and the birds, and after these God called forth animals from the earth. Finally,

God raised the question of creating man (1:26) "in our image, according to our likeness; and let them rule over the fish of the sea and the birds of the air and over everything that walks the earth. . . . So God created mankind in his own image; he created them male and female, blessed them, and told them to procreate and be vegetarians (like all the other creatures). And he saw everything he had made was good, and on the seventh day he rested and was refreshed."

In this text the cosmic bodies, animals, and men appear to be in much the same category. All are creations; animals as well as men are told to eat vegetables and be fruitful and multiply; none of them gets a name; even the stars are not depicted as astral persons. Sun and moon are called "big light" and "little light," without any allusion to any other mythology than this. All the "lower" animals are clearly subjected to man. The only trace of polytheism appears when God says, "Let *us* make man in *our* image, according to *our* likeness" (1:26). To whom was he speaking? There is no indication in the text.

Cosmogonic motifs also occur in Psalms 104. The purpose of the psalm is to praise Yahweh by telling how he is related to the world. He wears light as a garment, he streches out the heavens like a tent, he builds his house above the waters—that is, in heaven. The clouds and wings of the storm are his vehicles, fire and winds his messengers and servants. He founded the earth on pillars/foundations, and dressed her with clothes of water. The waters were originally above the hills; but when Yahweh rebuked them and thundered at them, they fled to the valleys, to the places created for them, and Yahweh set borders around them to prevent their rising again. This cosmogonic part of Psalms 104— verses 1-9—has its cosmological counterpart in the following verses, 10-30: Rivers and streams provide animals, birds, and men with water, producing vegetation by which all are fed and housed. Even rocks and wild mountains serve to shelter animals (104:18). Moon and sun and night and day willingly set the temporal frame and sequence of human and animal life: "The sun knows when to set" (104:19). Wild animals willingly come out by night, men do their work by day, and all are creatures and proofs of the wisdom of Yahweh (104:24). The sea provides for fish, ships, and sea monsters (Leviathan). These and all creatures are fed by Yahweh, die when he takes away their breath, and are replaced by the action of his spirit, which brings forth new generations (104:27-30). When he looks at the earth, it trembles, and when he touches the mountains, they smoke—such phenomena anticipating the destined and desirable destruction of sinners.

Similar connections between the world and God's wisdom are the theme of Proverbs 8, where Wisdom is represented as a person and describes herself as the first created being, made prior to the beginning of the earth, the primeval waters, and the heavens. When Yahweh built the heavens and drew a circle on the sea, determined its springs and set its borders, and sketched out the vaults of the earth, Wisdom herself was with him and delighted in his creations, and especially in mankind.

A similar view appears in the book of Job (38:5ff.), which speaks of the earth as a building with foundations and pillars. The stars and the children of the gods rejoiced when it was begun. As before, borders, gates, and bolts shut in the sea (38:6-11). Dawn is rolled over the earth like a seal over clay (38:12f.). The "wide plains of the earth" in Job 18:18 accord with Proverbs' picture of the earth as flat. Yahweh "hangs" it "on nothing" (26:7) and completely controls and can instantly destroy the whole structure, including *she'ol* and the monsters Rahab and Leviathan (26:6-14).

For the author of Job 38:16-33, even the expanse of the earth is beyond comprehension, to say nothing of the depths of the sea, the underworld of the dead, the sources of light and darkness, the storehouses where snow and hail are kept (Yahweh's arsenals), the ways by which rain, thunder, and mist are distributed, and, of course, the movements of the stars. This sketch of necessary human ignorance is a puzzling contrast to the picture of a well-ordered world created by Yahweh with the help of Wisdom, the guide of the wise. Further contrasts are found in some critical remarks of the wisdom literature. Job's "friends" accuse him of having said, because God dwells on high, "What does he know? Can he [see and] judge [justly] through the dark clouds?" (22:13). Ecclesiastes goes even beyond this, to conceive of the world as a gigantic machine of which the pieces go on doing what they always do:

> A generation goes and a generation comes,
>   but the earth remains forever.
> The sun rises and the sun sets,
>   and goes right back where it rose.
> Going to the south and coming round to the north,
>   round and round goes the wind and returns on its circuit.
> All the rivers flow into the sea
>   and the sea is never full. . . .
> All things are weary,
>   inexpressibly.

> The eye is not satisfied with seeing,
>> and the ear is not filled with hearing.
> What has been is what will be
>> and what was done is what will be done,
>> and there's nothing new under the sun. (1:4-9)

Many brief references to the underworld appear in the Psalms and elsewhere in the Bible, but they are not specific. Muddy water, dust, and darkness are the general characteristics of existence after death.[8] By contrast to the underworld, Yahweh and the other gods have several holy mountains, but these are matters of cultic and/or literary diction, not cosmology. The height of mountains generally forms the opposite to the depths of the sea, and the two are sometimes rhetorically opposed (see Amos 9:2; Pss. 68:23, 139:8f.; Job 11:8). At the sea's edges the islands are situated. Around the corners or edges of the earth flow the sea and the cosmic streams (Ps. 72:8). Other allusions to the foundations or pillars of the earth, to the gates of the underworld, and the like, do not offer any coherent picture.

Cosmological ideas and depictions in the books of the prophets are even scantier. Survivals of the ancient myth of the morning star, called Hellel ben Shachar, are found in Isaiah 14:12ff. They mention a mountain in the north where the gods gather, presumably a remnant of Canaanite or Phoenician influences. More important for the biblical notion of the world is a group of texts concerned with "the day of Yahweh."[9] In these we find the notion that the nations Yahweh will call up for destruction are to come from the end of the heavens (Isa. 13:4ff.). Joel 2:2ff. pictures the coming of Yahweh as a cosmic event that will turn the land to chaos and desert. And Amos 5:8 states, "The day of Yahweh is darkness and not light." Cosmic disturbances, eclipses, earthquakes, famine, and war are closely related to this idea. Obviously, these prophecies of the day of Yahweh give no coherent account of the world, stressing as they do abnormal phenomena known, at least by rumor, to the authors. Does Amos's description of that day, "darkness and not light," reflect stories of a total eclipse?

The same picture of the relationship between heaven and earth that we have found in the Psalms can also be found in prophetic texts, though not so fully. The dualism of "heaven and earth," as well as the triad "heaven-earth-waters," are well attested.[10] Moreover, heaven is repeatedly contrasted to the depths of the earth (Isa. 44:23; Jer. 31:37). The heaven above is Yahweh's abode, the earth is relegated to mankind, and *She'ol* is for the dead. In Isaiah 2:2ff. the Jerusalem temple hill ("mountain") appears to be the center of the world, where the nations will meet to learn the Law of God. The main topic of verses 6ff. is the house of Jacob, situated within a world including the Lebanon, the Transjordan region of Bashan, and the sea traversed by the "ships of Tarshish" (2:16).

After the fall of Samaria in the eighth and of Jerusalem in the sixth centuries B.C.E., Assyrians and Mesopotamians deported most of Israel's leaders to Syria and Babylonia and the Assyrians briefly conquered Egypt. The consequently extended geograhic horizon is reflected by Isaiah 11:11ff., where Assyria, Elam, Kush, and Egypt are mentioned. However, the biblical authors show little interest in these newly relevant lands as such; they are mainly concerned with the Jewish diaspora in them. This is particularly true in the books of Ezekiel and Second Isaiah (Isa. 40-55).

Further changes came with the Macedonian conquests and the consequent influx of Greeks. The *dynamic* aspect of the world now begins to be stressed. Under the influence of hellenistic philosophy (see Sir. 42:15; Wisd. of Sol. 18:15), the notion of a cosmic order (*logos*) appears, and Greek notions of wisdom (*sophia*) begin to modify the old Hebrew "wisdom" (Wisd. of Sol. 7:22, 9:4ff.). Persian influence also now appears. Angels become much more numerous and active. (For ancient thought they were a part of the world order, but in the Bible their parts are usually peripheral. In Job, Tobit, and Revelation they have major roles, but elsewhere they are only factors in the increasing complexity of the hellenistic and Roman concepts of the world. The same is true of devils, who now make their appearance—Satan, in the Old Testament, is merely one of Yahweh's malicious servants. With these and the development of speculation about wisdom, the *logos,* the spirit of God, and the souls of men, a world was produced in which natural phenomena usually continued as before, but in a new environment of what we now call "the supernatural.")

There are few cosmogonic and cosmological allusions in the New Testament. The theory of creation from nothing is reiterated by Paul in Romans 4:17. The idea of a new creation of the world appears in 2 Peter 3:5ff., 12ff., where it is connected with the expectation of a destruction by fire of the present one, in contrast to the destruction by water, in the ancient flood, of the former heavens and earth, "formed out of water and by means of water." That the flood *completely* destroyed the earth is a novel idea, even more so the implication that the present heavens and earth were created by fire (a well-known Stoic doctrine unexpected here). After the coming universal conflagration (also a Stoic idea), the writer expects "a new heaven and a new earth in which righteousness dwells" (2 Peter 3:13).

In contrast to this philosophical-pietistic cosmology, the other books of the New Testament commonly carry on the cosmology we have already found in the Old Testament, though with much more emphasis on a coming destruction of the world and its replacement by a new one. There is general agreement that Yahweh made heavens and earth, or heavens, earth, and sea (Acts 4:24, 14:15; Phil. 2:10). He is therefore "Lord of heavens and earth" (Matt. 11:25; Luke 10:21; Acts 17:24), and Paul emphasizes particularly that "the earth is the Lord's and the fullness thereof" (1 Cor. 10:26, quoting Ps. 24:1), evidently in contrast to dissenting Christian opinion of which the sharp antithesis between "heavenly" and "earthly" things, prominent in John 3:31, may be an echo—though Paul, with his usual inconsistency, can use the same antithesis when it suits his purpose (see 1 Cor. 10:15, 17). Anyhow, even if the earth *is* Yahweh's, he is himself in heaven (Matt. 6:10), and the earth is merely his footstool (Matt 5:35; Acts 7:49). On the other hand, even the heavens are not spared in the end; heaven and earth alike will pass away (Matt 5:18; Mark 13:31; Luke 21:33). The author of Revelation, not content with this, predicts the resumption of the primordial battle against the monsters and the powers of chaos, who have now become the powers of moral evil. With their destruction the old heaven and the earth and the sea will be destroyed. This is how Revelation 21 puts it:

> Then I saw a new heaven and a new earth; for the first heaven and the first earth had passed away, and the sea was no more. And I saw the holy city, new Jerusalem, coming down out of heaven from God, prepared as a bride adorned for her husband; and I heard a great voice from the throne saying: Behold, the dwelling of God is with men . . . he will wipe away every tear from their eyes, and death shall be no more, neither shall there be mourning nor crying nor pain any more, for the former things have passed away" (21:1-4).

NOTES

1. Cf. "to make," "to build," "to found," and "to construct," in Gen. 1:7, 16, 26; 2:22; 14:19, 22; Ps. 139:13; Prov. 8:22.

2. Isa. 11:12, 40:22; Ezek. 7:2; Job 17:3; Prov. 8:27.

3. T. Podella, "Thematischer Vergleich zwischen Gen. 37:34-5 und *KTU* 5 VI 23-25," *SEL* 4 (1987) 67-78, 72.

4. 1 Sam. 2:8; 2 Sam. 22:16; Prov. 8:31.

5. Cf. W. Heimpel, "The Sun at Night and the Doors of Heaven," *JCS* 38 (1986) 127-51, *passim*.

6. Cf. C. Kloos, *Yhwh's Combat with the Sea,* Amsterdam, 1986, *passim*.

7. Job 3:8; Hab. 3:8; Pss. 74:13-14, 89:10f., 93; Isa. 27:1. The idea of the primordial combat, which took place before creation, was later used in eschatological predictions of the End before the creation of a new world.

8. For a collection of the terminology used to describe the underworld, see T. Podella, "L'Aldilà nelle concezioni vetero-testamentarie," in P. Xella (ed.), *Archeologia dell'Inferno,* Verona, 1987, 163-90.

9. Isa. 13:6, 9; Ezek. 13:5; Joel 1:15; 2:1, 11; 3:4; 4:4; Amos 5:18ff.; Obad. 15; Zeph. 1:7, 14f.; Mal. 3:23; cf. H. Barstad, *The Religious Polemics of Amos,* Leiden, 1984 (*SVT* 34).

10. Isa. 1:2, 50:2ff.; Ezek. 18:20; Amos 9:2f.

FOR FURTHER READING

C. Blacker and M. Loewe, editors. *Ancient Cosmologies.*London, 1975.

W. Burkert. *Greek Religion.* Cambridge, Mass., 1985.

M. Dresden. "Science." In *Interpreter's Dictionary of the Bible.* New York, 1962.

T. Gaster. "Cosmogony." In *Interpreter's Dictionary of the Bible.* New York, 1962.

W. Heimpel. "The Sun at Night and the Doors of Heaven." *Journal of Cuneiform Studies* 38 (1986) 127-51.

C. Kloos. *YHWH's Combat with the Sea.* Amsterdam, 1986.

AFTERWORD

The idea for the present volume was hatched by Professor Morton Smith and me at a 1985 conference on biblical ethics at the University of Richmond. Neither of us was sure that the plan would work; both of us were certain that a book entitled *What the Bible Really Says* would be thought presumptuous by those sage in "interpretation" and blasphemous by those who claim proprietorship of the word of God in its "literal" sense. It is not easy to hit upon a project that promises to offend liberal exegetes and conservative scholars alike; and it may be helpful to know that if that is indeed what we have done in choosing so wanton a title, it is not what we intended. Since we are trading in plain words in these pages, let me say more plainly what I mean.

Good scholars are not always good writers. Some would argue in fact that a really good scholar—a good biblical scholar, let us say— cannot write crisply and clearly because profound ideas and interpretations demand profound (read: turgid) expression. Simplicity of style and simplification are sometimes thought to be two names for the same thing.

The editors of this volume have watched with considerable dismay as the technical jargon of a dozen disciplines cognate to biblical studies has, by sheer weight of words, buried the "facts" of the text beneath the refinements of method and procedure. Just as for the fundamentalist Christian the biblical text exists without context, so for the contemporary biblical scholar context has largely displaced text. There is a wickedness in both extremes, and (to beg the question) the extremes exist because the "literalist" and the "scholar" understand their approaches, as it were, counteractively.

In the middle is the text itself—neither illuminated by the threadbare evangelical assurance that its meaning is as accessible to the pawn as to the bishop nor much helped by the notion that its truth (Albright and co.) or falseness (Guignebert) will be established by the careful pursuit of the "cognates."

Even before the current bout of obscurantism in dealing with the Bible, the art of interpretation was beset with the fustian of academic theology, largely German in origin and style and often betraying its source —especially among American scholars—in its reliance on long sentences —like this one—with lots of embedded profundities and tangents. American graduate students in the field of biblical studies (including biblical theology) were expected to write an English like unto Karl Barth's German, to end each sentence of a dissertation with a period and a footnote (declaring the ideas so noted unoriginal and often based on a reading of secondary interpretations rather than primary sources), and to follow with a reference twelve times longer than the sentence noted. British scholarship, owing to its traditional antipathy for all things German, had fared better prior to the entry of Britain into the European Community. Today, however, German "style" is as much on display in England as are German cheeses.

As we see it, there are many causes for concern: the art of biblical scholarship awash in the language of the social sciences, "new" literary criticism, a new historicism that delights in the compilation and "input" of raw data and finds process more intriguing than conclusions, and methods designed to "liberate" the text from its roots in ancient Near Eastern culture and society. We do not believe that the methods and vocabularies of the newer modes of interpretation are useless. We do not dismiss their value out of hand. We do not suppose for a minute that our view of what the text "really" says is uninformed by such methods. And we are not so naive as to think that what we have to say on these thirteen-odd topics is terribly different from what a good commentary might have to say on the same issues—if a good commentary could be found. In other words, we do not assume that we are not interpreting. What we assume—very deliberately—is that our interpretation of the text more faithfully conveys what the writers *said*—and does so, insofar as this is possible, without theological (or other) sleight-of-hand or any attempt to disguise the clear import of the text's meaning. We have not assayed to find universal "relevance" in a text whose cultural and geographical boundaries are circumscribed. We have not paved over contradictions or tried to find harmony or Big Themes. We have stuck to the principle (and encouraged contributors to do likewise) that meaning and influence are two different things and demand different treatment. Church history is, as Harnack once observed, the history of biblical interpretation. This is not a book about church history.

Any book on the Bible is a target sure to draw fire. Theologians of all persuasions are trained to find fault with any method that relies on the plain sense of words rather than on the ambiguities and implications of those words for the communities of faith. Lexica, concordances, and "frequency distributions" exist to make preaching possible. The Bible, we are assured, is "faith speaking to faith"; hence its interpretation as practiced in seminaries and divinity schools must be responsive to the life of faith. Too often, however, faithfulness to the text means fidelity not to its assertions but to its ambiguities—to what Jesus does not say (for example) about abortion or the status of women, or other issues of contemporary importance, or to what Paul might have meant by the Greek word *kyrios* if he did not mean what he plainly meant when he used it. In the last century, Matthew Arnold wrung his hands moodily over the trends in biblical scholarship and noted that the scholarly apologetic directed against the German critics bespoke a lack of "culture" in the British theological establishment. "Sweet religion," said Hamlet, "makes a rhapsody of words." Are we much enlightened to know where Shakespeare was sitting when he wrote that—or how many times in the same act (and in what connection) he refers to "words"?

If the writers here represented have anything in common, it is their rejection of the idea that the spectacles of faith render the text plain and accessible. We have chosen to read and report without the aid of spectacles because we believe that the text is, on the whole, clear, and our eyes—given proper training in what to look for and adequate knowledge of the languages required—pretty good. As biblical scholars and historians, we are also aware that unaided sight and clear meaning have had little part to play in the development of the art of biblical criticism. Only through a powerful magnification of self-interest—not to say distortion in vision—does St. Augustine make the ark of Noah the church of Christ, or Luther the church of Rome the whore of Babylon. "Eisogesis"—the skill of reading out of a text the interests we read into it—is a well-developed habit in theological circles: And in this habit the fundamentalist who sees the Bible as an inspired and inerrant document is no better off than the liberation theologian who must spend half his time apologizing for the crudities of biblical religion and the other half invoking its authority in support of his program. Both must do grave injustice to the text to do justice to their agendas.

It can be taken for granted that 75 percent of what the average Christian or Jew "thinks" about the Bible is interpretation and not scripture at all. My students, for instance, are usually appalled to find out not only that there is no biblical commandment against lying ("bearing false witness" is a different issue) but that in the culture from which the Bible sprang a good lie—like a good joke—was clearly valued (cf. Ezek. 14:9; 1 Kings 22:23, etc.). They are the stuff good stories are made of—and the Bible is full of good stories.

From the time of Philo Judaeus (first century C.E.) onward, the postulate of an inspired (read: God-breathed) text has necessitated picking and choosing what parts of these stories are essential in order to be a good Jew or a good Christian—or, derivatively, a good Muslim. The subject of how the biblical canon or short list of approved books came to be is a separate matter and one that can—with great relief—be avoided here. But picking and choosing is how the Bible came to be, and further picking—at the expense of whole mounds of literature already canonized—is how Judaism and Christianity—roughly at the same time—came to define their religious world-views.

Picking and choosing: It is to the likes of Philo and the Christian teacher Origen that we must trace our habits. For them, the plain sense of scripture was an embarrassment, especially as they were trying to make inroads into the philosophical middle class of the late Roman Empire. Thus whatever contradicted common sense (How, Origen wonders, can Jesus be taken to a mountaintop high enough to see all the kingdoms of the world?), popular morality, or later on, scientific knowledge and the dicta of the bishops, required the faithful reader to search for an interpretation that vindicated the text. So—given only the vicissitudes of changing needs—has the practice remained. Interpretation has always been the child of necessity and self-interest. Clarity and plain meaning are unfriendly not just to the doctrine of inspiration (hence not only to the fundamentalist form of exegesis) but to theology in general and often enough to those cognate disciplines that want to see the Bible as a subspecies of ancient Near Eastern and Hellenistic literature, important chiefly for the light it sheds on surrounding cultures.

If these approaches have anything in common, it is this: All assume that the Bible is not what it should be—perhaps at a moral level, perhaps at a literary or "factual" level—and hence cannot mean what it says. What we have tried to do in these pages is very modest. We have tried to let the Bible speak for itself. In the end, the bifurcation of saying and meaning is an unnecessary but heuristic principle in biblical studies—which is to say, a principle that works because it works, not because it can be justified. Origen, Philo, and perhaps some contemporary evangelicals find their justification in the belief that the essential or "real" meaning of the text is spiritual and that what it literally says is, so to speak, a veil cloaking that meaning. So long as some form of that opinion continues to influence biblical study, what the Bible means will "mean" more than what it says.

Serious scholarship, however, must learn to insist on the separation—or, at the very least, not to confuse meaning and saying. It is important to recognize that in the history of biblical religions—Judaism, Christianity, and Islam—it is *meaning* that gets canonized, not merely books. To speak of a Catholic, Protestant, or Jewish "Bible"—despite our ecumenical leanings and pluralist ambitions—is not yet an extravagance. When one so speaks, one refers to a canon of meaning—a whole freight-load of interpretation—and not to a compilation of literature. Indeed, from book to book the average reader will find differences negligible. A Catholic, a Protestant, and a Jew would feel pretty much at home with any modern translation, say, of the Book of Genesis; real divergences in translation are few and far between. What the Bible *means,* on the other hand, is the source of denominational and religious difference—in other times, of denominational and religious war.

Perhaps a book designed to explore what the Bible says is not so presumptuous after all.

R. Joseph Hoffmann

LIST OF ABBREVIATIONS

OLD TESTAMENT

Genesis	Gen.	Joshua	Josh.
Exodus	Exod.	Judges	Judg.
Leviticus	Lev.	Ruth	Ruth
Numbers	Num.	1 Samuel	1 Sam.
Deuteronomy	Deut.	2 Samuel	2 Sam.
1 Kings	1 Kings	Ezekiel	Ezek.
2 Kings	2 Kings	Daniel	Dan.
1 Chronicles	1 Chron.	Hosea	Hos.
2 Chronicles	2 Chron.	Joel	Joel
Ezra	Ezra	Amos	Amos
Nehemiah	Neh.	Obadiah	Obad.
Esther	Esther	Jonah	Jon.
Job	Job	Micah	Mic.
Psalms	Ps. (*pl.* Pss.)	Nahum	Nah.
Proverbs	Prov.	Habakkuk	Hab.
Ecclesiastes	Eccles.	Zephaniah	Zeph.
Song of Solomon	Song of Sol.	Haggai	Hag.
Isaiah	Isa.	Zechariah	Zech.
Jeremiah	Jer.	Malachi	Mal.
Lamentations	Lam.		

APOCRYPHA

1 Esdras	1 Esd.
2 Esdras	2 Esd.
Tobit	Tob.
Judith	Jth.
The Rest of Esther	Rest of Esther
The Wisdom of Solomon	Wisd. of Sol.
Sirach	Sir.
Baruch	Bar.
The Song of the Three Holy Children	Song of Three Children
Susanna	Sus.
Bel and the Dragon	Bel and Dragon
Prayer of the Manasses (*or* Manasseh)	Pr. of Man.
1 Maccabees	1 Macc.
2 Maccabees	2 Macc.

NEW TESTAMENT

Matthew	Matt.	1 Timothy	1 Tim.
Mark	Mark	2 Timothy	2 Tim.
Luke	Luke	Titus	Titus
John	John	Philemon	Philem.
Acts of the Apostles	Acts	Hebrews	Heb.
Romans	Rom.	James	James
1 Corinthians	1 Cor.	1 Peter	1 Pet.
2 Corinthians	2 Cor.	2 Peter	2 Pet.
Galatians	Gal.	1 John	1 John
Ephesians	Eph.	2 John	2 John
Philippians	Phil.	3 John	3 John
Colossians	Col.	Jude	Jude
1 Thessalonians	1 Thess.	Revelation	Rev.
2 Thessalonians	2 Thess.		

BIBLICAL CITATION INDEX

Genesis, 1:1-2:4a, **197**; 1:9-10, **34**; 1:11, **137**; 1:12, **206**; 1:14, **100**, **172**; 1:14f, **172**; 1:24, **35**, **206**; 1:26, **197**; 1:27, **217**, **219**; 1:28, **75**; 2, **197**, **221**; 2-3, **222**; 2:4b-3:24, **197**; 2:7, **35**, **172**; 2:14, **217**; 2:16, **27**; 2:18, **75**, **219**; 2:22, **172**; 2:23, **78**; 2:24, **79**, **80**, **81**, **97**, **225**; 3, **197**; 3:2, 12, **222**; 3:8-13, **222**; 3:11, **222**; 3:16, **79**, **173**, **219**, **222**; 3:18, **173**; 3:19, **35**; 3:20, **79**; 4:1, 25-5:3, **79**; 4:10, **27**; 4:19, **81**; 4:26, **80**; 5:3, **79**; 5:3, 28-29, **80**; 5:3-16, **222**; 5:24, **49n**; 6:8, **137**; 6-9, **137**; 7:21-22, **35**; 9, **100**; 9:1, 3, **25**; 9:1-7, **25**; 9:4, **25**; 9:13-20, **174**; 9:18-27, **137**; 10:20, **76**; 11:5-7, **34**; 12:2, **39**; 12:3, **39**; 12:10-20, **84**, **200**; 12:11, 14, **209**; 13, **50**; 13:10, **172**; 14:13-16, **150**; 14:14, **76**; 15, **173**; 15:18, **39**; 15:20, **134n**; 16, **198**; 16:1-4, **81**; 16:1-16, **138**; 16:2, **138**; 16:3, **81**; 16:4, **93**; 16:11, **79**; 16:15, **79**, **80**; 16:16, **138**; 17:2, 4, **39**; 17:23, 27, **76**; 18:12, **224**; 18:20-21, **34**; 19:8, **200**; 19:14, **78**; 19:17, **88**; 19:26, **216**; 19:30-38, **85**, **199**; 19:37-38, **79-80**; 20:1-18, **85**, **200**; 20:3, **79**; 21:1-21, **198**; 21:8-21, **138**; 21:10, **76**; 21:11, **138**; 21:14, **139**; 21:17, 19, **50**; 21:21, **89**; 22, **77**; 22:20-21, **88**; 22:24, **200**; 22:17, **173**; 22:18, **173**; 23:1, **88**; 23:17-20, **173**; 24, **83**, **89**; 24:7, 16, 26, **209**; 24:15, **84**; 24:34, **173**; 24:55, **88**; 24:60, **89**; 24:67, **89**; 25:1-6, **200**; 25:7, **37**; 25:19, **88**; 25:20, **81**; 26:6-11, **84**; 26:7, **209**; 26:11, **13**; 26:28-30, **89**; 27, **94**, · **174**; 27:1-45, **198**; 27:11-17, **76**; 27:46-29:30, **83**; 28:10-17, **34**; 29, **198**; 21:1-30, **80**; 29:1-30:25, **200**; 29:17, **209**; 29:19, 28, **78**; 29:20, **90**; 29:23, **91**; 29:23, 28, **89**; 29:27-28, **90**; 29:30-31, **93**; 29:31, **90**; 30:1, **81**; 30:1-2, **93**; 80:1-24, **82**; 30:3, **81**; 30:6, **81**; 30:15-30, **90**; 31:15, **90**; 31:54, **89**; 34:8, **89**; 34:12, **90**; 35:22-26, **200**; 36:1-5, **82**; 36:2, **83**; 36:21, **90**; 38, **87**, **198**; 38:11, **89**; 38:15-24, **93**; 38:24-25, **21**;